I0793559

Chinese Characters

www.royalcollins.com

GREAT CHINESE INVENTIONS

Chinese Characters

Edited by
Hua Jueming and Feng Lisheng

By Peng Yu

Translated by
Chen Wei and Chen Zhijia
(Jiangnan University)

RC

Books Beyond Boundaries

ROYAL COLLINS

Great Chinese Inventions:
Chinese Characters

Edited by Hua Jueming and Feng Lisheng
By Peng Yu
Translated by Chen Wei and Chen Zhijia (Jiangnan University)

Project Coordinator: Zhang Shaowen and Wang Xiaoyuan

First published in 2025 by Royal Collins Publishing Group Inc.
Groupe Publication Royal Collins Inc.
550-555 boul. René-Lévesque O Montréal (Québec) H2Z1B1 Canada

10 9 8 7 6 5 4 3 2 1

ISBN: 978-1-4878-1286-7

To find out more about our publications,
please visit www.royalcollins.com.

Contents

Preface

The "Four Great Inventions" of China have attracted significant attention from the Chinese people due to their profound impact on the course of modern world history. The term "Four Great Inventions" is widely known, but it originated from Western scholars. While this term holds classical significance, it carries a specific background and meaning. However, it fails to comprehensively reflect the significant inventions and technological cultural traditions of China. Throughout its five-thousand-year history of civilization, China's major inventions far exceed these four great inventions. Since the 20th century, especially in recent decades, China's science and technology have undergone rapid development, playing an increasingly important role in social and economic development. The question of what great inventions and creations exist in Chinese history has become a matter of concern not only for the academic community but also for the public. To answer this question truthfully, objectively, and scientifically, further exploration and sorting are needed based on the study of the history of science and technology in China. This involves selecting major inventions that are original, distinct in character, and have made outstanding contributions and significant impacts on both Chinese and world civilizations and discussing their background and evolutionary processes. To this end, we invited experts in the history of science and related fields to compile the book *Thirty Great Inventions of China*, which was published in May 2017. The book received praise from academia and readers, gaining widespread attention. It was awarded the 13th Wenjin Book Award and the National Excellent Popular Science Works Award by the Ministry of Science and Technology in 2018. It was also selected as one of the "Good Books of China" for 2017 and one of the "40 Most Influential Popular Science Books in China in 40 Years of Reform and Opening Up."

To further promote the research on the history of inventions in China and disseminate knowledge of Chinese science and technology culture, we have organized and compiled the Great Chinese Inventions series based on the book *Thirty Great Inventions of China*. The aim is to provide a more comprehensive and detailed exposition of the significance of major technological inventions in China, to understand their origins and developments, and to enable readers to better comprehend and appreciate the historical and modern value of important ancient Chinese technological inventions and creations. Each book in this series is relatively concise, focusing on knowledge dissemination with rich illustrations, aiming to allow readers to obtain relevant information and knowledge about each invention from the narratives of historians of science and technology in a relatively short period of time.

China boasts a profound history and culture, with the Chinese nation having made numerous great inventions and creations that not only propelled the advancement of Chinese civilization but also exerted significant influence on the progress of world civilization. Every Chinese individual should strive to understand history as accurately as possible. Chinese affairs should be clarified by the Chinese themselves, and Chinese people should have a say in matters of invention and creation. This series of books aims to embody the concept of cultural consciousness and comprehensively summarize the significant contributions of the Chinese nation to human technological civilization as much as possible. In the selection of great inventions, adjustments and expansions have been made, expanding the original thirty inventions to more than forty items, particularly adding significant inventions of modern and contemporary China. This series of books examines Chinese great inventions from both cultural tradition and a global perspective. For instance, Chinese characters and traditional Chinese cooking techniques were previously less regarded as major inventions. Still, they serve as important symbols of Chinese civilization and hold significant positions in Chinese cultural and technological traditions, qualifying as great Chinese inventions. Particularly, Chinese characters, as tools for recording information and expressing thoughts for Chinese people, remain vibrant to this day. They not only play an irreplaceable role in the formation, dissemination, and inheritance of Chinese culture but also have had a significant influence on neighboring countries and regions such as Japan, Korea, and Vietnam. Traditional Chinese cooking techniques have played a crucial role in improving the quality of people's lives and enhancing physical health. With the strengthening of China's comprehensive national strength and international influence, Chinese cooking techniques have spread to various parts of the world and are playing an increasingly important role. Traditional Chinese medicine also embodies some pioneering achievements in modern science and technology, such as the practice of variolation, which is a pioneering immunological achievement with global impact.

We also pay attention to significant inventions in modern and contemporary China. For example, Tu Youyou, representing a group of Chinese scientists, extracted artemisinin, a highly effective and low-toxicity antimalarial drug, based on the inheritance of traditional clinical experience in Chinese medicine and the application of modern scientific methods. After its clinical application, artemisinin has saved the lives of thousands of patients, making a tremendous contribution to human health. Rice is one of the world's major food crops, serving as the staple food for about half the global population. The super hybrid rice cultivation technology invented by Yuan Longping is considered a world-class original and significant invention. Hanzi laser typesetting technology, founded by Wang Xuan, is a great invention in the history of modern printing technology in China. It has played an important role in promoting the dissemination of science and culture. Cultural consciousness is a challenging process. On the one hand, we need to understand our technological and cultural traditions to enhance cultural identity and confidence. On the other hand, we need to update and transform our cultural traditions and technology, integrating traditional techniques with modern and foreign technologies and enabling modern technology to take root and develop vigorously in China.

Invention and discovery are inherent drivers of the development of human social civilization. Ancient Chinese science and technology have achieved remarkable success, with our ancestors making significant contributions to the progress of world civilization. Over the past century, China has undergone drastic social changes and cultural transformations, so it is understandable that there haven't been many great inventions and creations during this time. While cherishing and valuing our national cultural traditions and historical experiences, we should also take the initiative in cultural transformation and technological development, continuously enhancing our capacity for independent innovation and making greater contributions to the development of human technology and civilization. Looking at the long-term trend of historical development, Chinese science and technology have entered a new period of accelerated development. The innovation consciousness and capability of the Chinese people have been activated, and we can expect more and more original inventions and creations in the future. The prosperity of Chinese science and technology is something to look forward to.

The question of how many great inventions there have been in Chinese history is subjective, and opinions or disputes are inevitable. We hope that the publication of this series of books will attract more attention and participation from experts and readers, stimulating further discussion and exchanges and contributing to the improvement of related research. We also welcome corrections and feedback from colleagues in the academic community and readers on our work.

Hua Jueming and Feng Lisheng
July 28, 2021

Introduction

Characters are a milestone invention in the history of human civilization. The invention of the character and its evolution into a tool for fully recording linguistic information have played a significant role in individuals acquiring the collective experience and knowledge accumulated by society over the long course of history, thereby promoting and accelerating the progress of civilization.

The phonetic scripts used in many countries around the world evolved from cuneiform writing, an ancient invention by the Babylonians. In contrast, Chinese characters in China and some neighboring countries differ significantly from phonetic scripts. Chinese characters have a unique origin and have lasted for thousands of years. They have played an irreplaceable role in the formation, development, and heritage of Chinese culture.

CHAPTER I

General Discussion on Chinese Characters

Chinese characters are symbols used to record the Chinese language. The term "Chinese" here shouldn't be simply understood as referring to the Han ethnicity or the Han Dynasty, as the history of both of them is relatively recent compared to the much earlier emergence and use of Chinese characters.

When we talk about Chinese language and characters, it originally refers to the language and characters used by various ethnic groups, with the Huaxia people as the main body, whose main activities were within the territory of modern-day China.

For example, during the Spring and Autumn and Warring States periods (770–221 BC), with the collapse of rituals, proprieties, and ceremonies and the chaos of various states, many countries and ethnic groups had their own scripts. Qi had its own script, and Chu had its own script. Today's ancient philologists can clearly point out the differences between them. However, in the history of script development, these scripts still fall within the scope of Chinese character research.

Chinese characters are divided into ancient and modern categories.

In the field of linguistics, small seal script is generally considered the watershed between ancient and modern characters. The scripts before it are collectively referred to as ancient scripts, including oracle bone script, bronze inscriptions, Warring States script, and Qin small seal script. After the Qin Dynasty (221–206 BC), the form of Chinese characters was basically established, with the official use of seal script and the popular use of clerical script.

The transition from seal script to clerical script marked a milestone in the development of Chinese characters. Since then, the form of Chinese characters no longer changed as much in appearance as ancient scripts did. Their structure and semantic function gradually stabilized, with variations mainly in the style of writing.

There are many stories and legends about the origin of Chinese characters.

According to the records in *Mo Sou*, written by a Tang Dynasty calligrapher:

> Fuxi obtained a sign from a huge dragon, initiating the creation of a dragon script.
>
> Shennong, Yan Emperor, due to the extraordinary and beautiful growth of the eight-ear wheat in the Yangtou Mountain in Shangdang, created the eight-ear script and promulgated seasonal regulations.
>
> Cang Jie, the historian of the Yellow Emperor period, depicted the footprints of birds and animals as images, creating seal script.
>
> Because of the auspicious clouds, cloud script was also invented during the era of the Yellow Emperor.
>
> Shaohao created bird and phoenix script to record officials, articles, and

> clothing, imitating ancient texts.
>
> ...
>
> Emperor Yao created a turtle script based on Xuanyuan's divine tortoise image.
>
> Xiahou created an inscription on bells and tripods, taking the form of bells and tripods as their symbols.
>
> ...

Among them, the most enduring and renowned is the creation of writing by Cang Jie:

> *Master Lü's Spring and Autumn Annals · Ruler's Governance* states, "Xi Zhong made chariots, Cang Jie made characters, Houji made crops, Gaoyao made punishments, Kunwu made pottery, Xia Gun made cities. These six individuals made what was needed."

Starting from the Han Dynasty (202 BC–AD 220), this legend gradually took on a mysterious color:

> *Huainanzi · The Basic Principles* states, "In ancient times, Cang Jie created characters, and it rained millet from the sky, causing ghosts to cry at night."

The legend of Cang Jie creating characters was popular during the Han Dynasty and is also reflected in unearthed cultural relics. Not only are there images and inscriptions of Cang Jie on carved stones (Figure 1.1), but in recent years, Han Dynasty bamboo slips have also contained phrases like "Cang Jie created characters to teach future generations." In the Eastern Han to Three Kingdoms period, bronze mirrors even bore inscriptions like "Cang Jie created characters to teach later generations, and then the people created fire, so they could eat cooked meat and taste more flavors than when they were only restricted to raw meat" (Figure 1.2).

According to the legend, Cang Jie was a historian during the time of Huangdi and, due to the nature of his work, he would have been exposed to more writing than the average person. Based on modern scholars' research, the credibility of Cang Jie's creation of characters may not be entirely reliable. However, any major invention originates from the people and is inseparable from the contributions of outstanding individuals. Although Chinese characters may not have been created by one person, they were likely systematically organized by the authorities during a certain period.

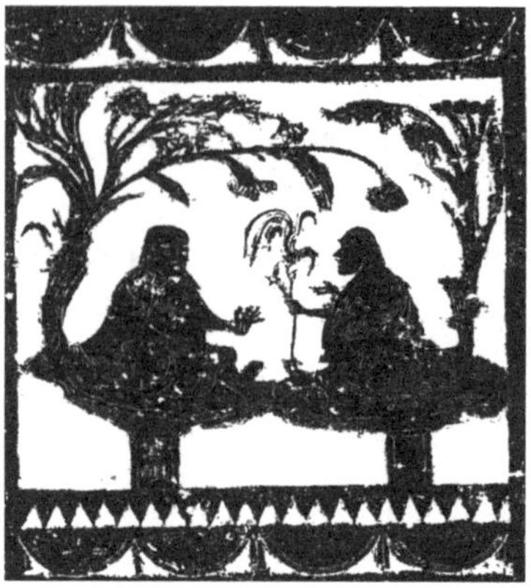

Figure 1.1 Stone carving portrait of Cang Jie at the General's Tomb in Beizhai, Yinan, Shandong

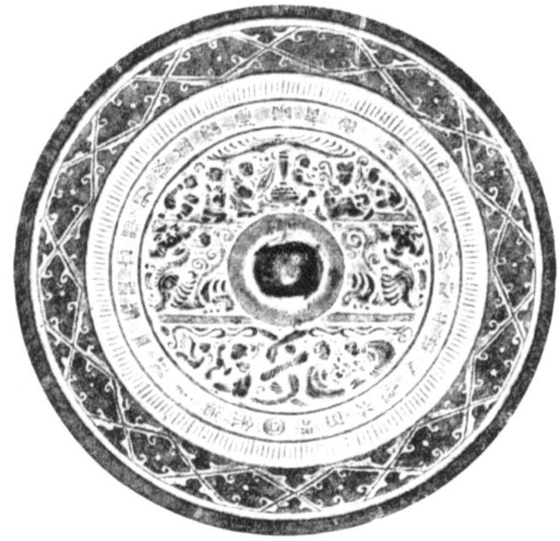

Figure 1.2 Rubbing of the Cang Jie inscription on a bronze mirror unearthed in Xi'an

Among the known systems of Chinese characters, the oracle bone script from the Yin Ruins is the earliest script unearthed through archaeology. There are a large number of characters, and the scale of usage is also substantial. However, when examining aspects such as character structure and the principles of character construction, the oracle bone script is already quite mature and is unlikely to represent the primitive stage of Chinese characters.

Archaeology undoubtedly serves as an extremely effective means of tracing the origin and early evolutionary process of Chinese characters, especially with the exploration of oracle bone inscriptions. In a series of archaeological excavations related to this, the symbols carved on turtle shells and bone artifacts unearthed from the Peiligang Culture site in Jiahu Village, Wuyang County, Henan Province, are particularly noteworthy.

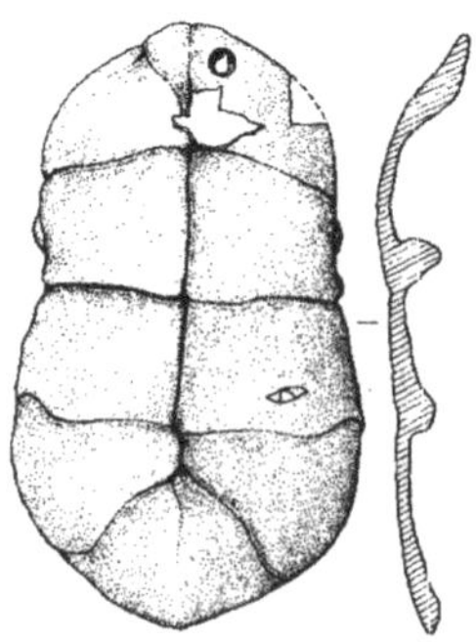

Figure 1.3 Turtle shell with carved-symbol unearthed from the Jiahu Peiligang Cultural site in Wuyang

Among them, the eye-shaped patterns on the ventral shell of the turtle are identical to the character "目" (eye) in oracle bone script (Figure 1.3), and the structure resembling a door or gateway is remarkably similar to the oracle bone script character "户" (door), suggesting that these resemblances are unlikely to be mere coincidence.

The Radiocarbon Laboratory of the Chinese Academy of Social Sciences Institute of Archaeology conducted radiocarbon dating on charcoal samples unearthed from the Jiahu Peiligang site. The dating indicates they appeared in an age range of 7,000 to 8,000 years ago. Among them, tombs with symbol-bearing turtle shells unearthed date back to earlier than 6200 BC, more than 1,000 years earlier than the eras of the legendary figures Huangdi and Cang Jie. Therefore, the collection, organization, and standardization of characters during the time of Huangdi are entirely plausible.

However, there is still controversy in the academic community regarding whether the unearthed artifacts from the Jiahu Peiligang site represent characters or symbols. To systematically study ancient characters today, scholars primarily rely on the Yin-Shang oracle bone script, dating back over 3,000 years.

The oracle bone script, also known as "Qiwen," "oracle bone inscriptions," or "turtle-shell and animal-bone script," mainly refers to a form of characters engraved on the ventral or dorsal shells of turtles or shoulder blades of cattle (occasionally using other animal bones) (see Figures 1.4 to 1.6).

The rulers of the Shang Dynasty (1600–1046 BC) were highly superstitious about spirits and ghosts. In the face of significant events, they would use turtle shells and animal bones for divination, inscribing the divination content (sometimes including the results) using characters alongside the indications of good or bad omens on the oracle bones.

Therefore, similar to modern official documents, the oracle bone script also follows a fixed format. The content largely revolves around sacrifice, hunting, weather, warfare, diseases, and other related aspects, recording and reflecting the political, economic, and military situations of the Shang Dynasty.

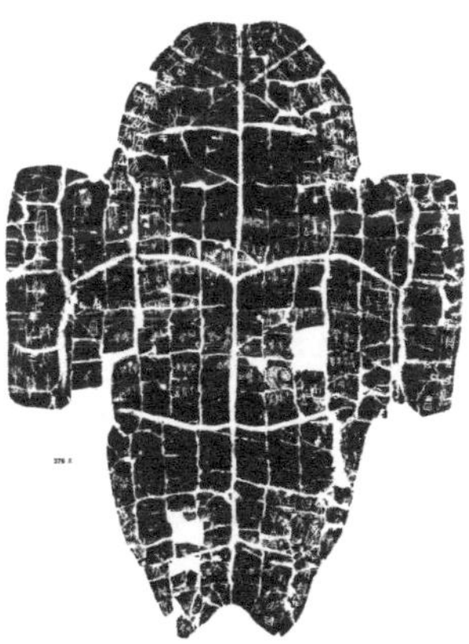

Figure 1.4 Collection of oracle bone inscriptions 376 obverse

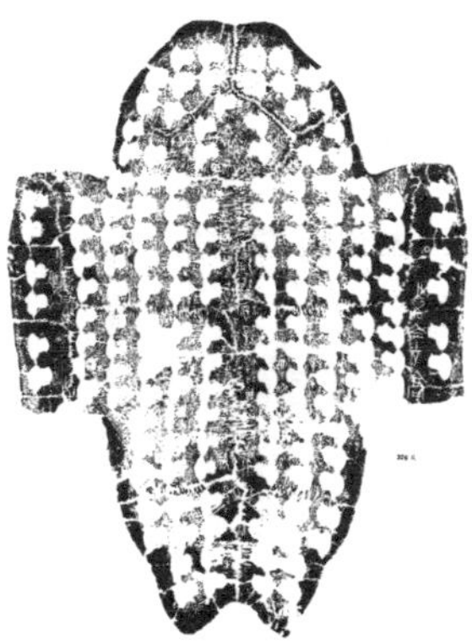

Figure 1.5 Collection of oracle bone inscriptions 376 reverse

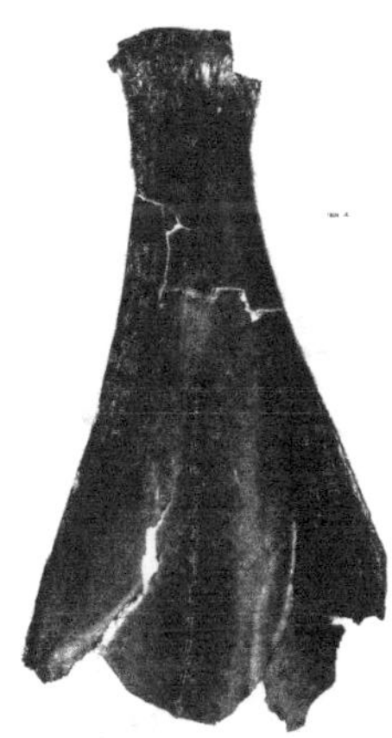

Figure 1.6 Supplement to the collection of oracle bone inscriptions 1804 obverse

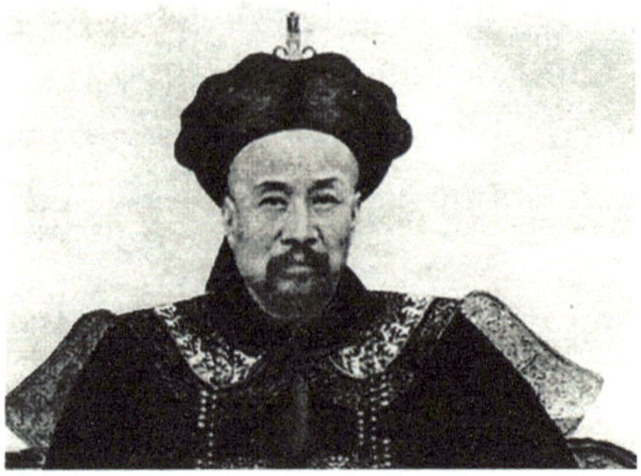

Figure 1.7 Portrait of Wang Yirong

It should be noted that for a considerable period, the oracle bones from the Yin Ruins, serving as a medium for characters, were treated as medicinal materials by later generations. To highlight their special value, they were reverently referred to as "dragon bones." It was not until the late 19th century that a Qing Dynasty official named Wang Yirong (see Figure 1.7), while taking medicine for an illness, accidentally discovered inscriptions on these bones and collected them at a high price. The oracle bone inscriptions, which had slept for thousands of years, gradually entered people's awareness.

It is said that before Wang Yirong's discovery of oracle bone inscriptions, herbalists had already noticed the inscriptions on oracle bones. However, these markings were mostly considered ominous, and the characters were often scraped off for ease of sale. In this context, it appears that the oracle bone inscriptions Wang encountered while treating his illness were like "fish that slipped through the net." Before this discovery, countless oracle bone inscriptions may have ended up being ingested by people.

Today, scientific research on oracle bone inscriptions has evolved into an independent discipline. Following Wang Yirong, individuals like Liu E, Luo Zhenyu, and others engaged in the collection and organization of oracle bones (see Figure 1.8). Scholars such as Wang Guowei, Guo Moruo, Dong Zuobin, Hu Houxuan, Yu Xingwu,

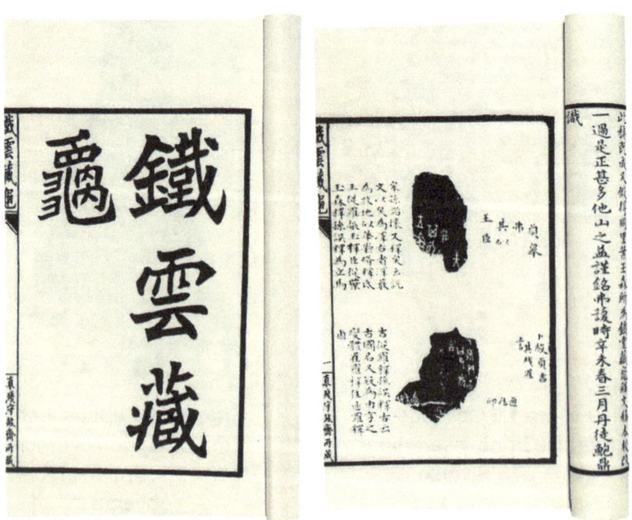

Figure 1.8 Photocopy of Liu E's *Iron Cloud Conceals Turtles*

Qiu Xigui, Huang Tianshu, Lin Yun, Liu Zhao, and others have made invaluable contributions to the deciphering of oracle bone inscriptions.

Among them, Luo Zhenyu was known as Xuetang, Wang Guowei as Guantang, Guo Moruo as Dingtang, and Dong Zuobin as Yantang. Because their names or titles all include the character "堂" (tang), in honor of their contributions to oracle bone inscription research, contemporary scholars reverently refer to them as the "Four '堂' (tang) of Oracle Bones" (see Figure 1.9). Through their research, oracle bone inscriptions are no longer an enigmatic "heavenly script," and the genealogy of the Shang kings has gradually become a historical fact.

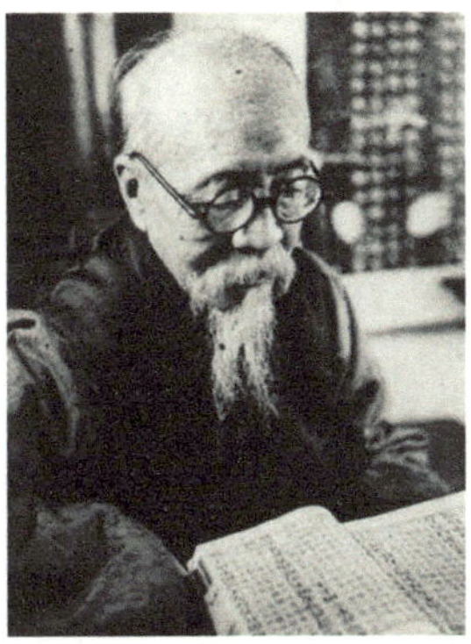

Luo Zhenyu (Xuetang)

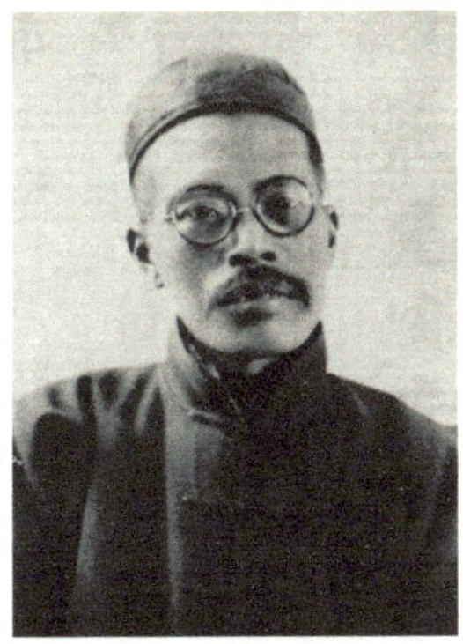

Wang Guowei (Guantang)

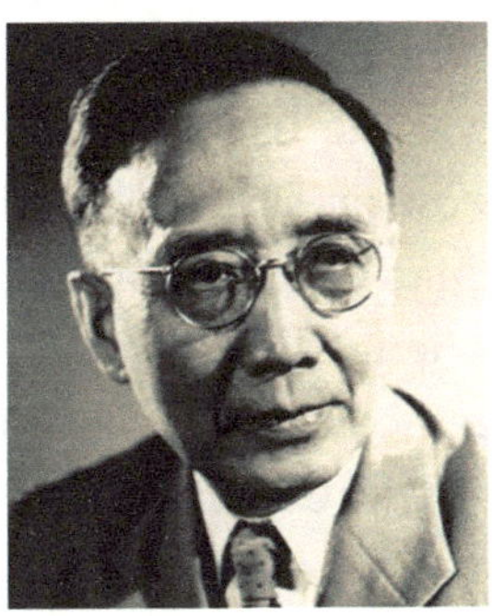

Guo Moruo (Dingtang)

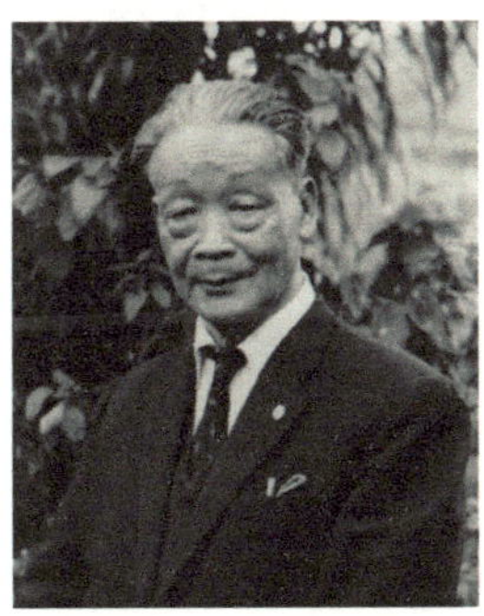

Dong Zuobin (Yantang)

Figure 1.9 Photos of the "Four '堂' (tang) of Oracle Bones"

According to incomplete statistics, over 150,000 oracle bones from the Shang Dynasty have been discovered to date, containing more than 4,000 different characters. However, less than one-third of these characters are currently recognized by scholars.

Nevertheless, the majority of those yet to be recognized pertain to personal names, place names, and ritual practices, and they do not hinder scholars from grasping the overall understanding of their content. These oracle bones are mostly from Anyang, Henan Province. Before the establishment of the People's Republic of China, due to reasons such as looting and trading, they were scattered across various countries and cities. Nowadays, many museums in different regions have exhibitions and displays of oracle bones.

The early Shang Dynasty experienced frequent capital relocations. Historical records indicate that there were a total of 13 capital relocations during the Shang Dynasty until King Pan Geng stabilized the capital, moving it from Yan in Shandong to Yin in Henan. Over the next 273 years, Yin gradually became the political, economic, and cultural center of the Shang people. Eight generations and twelve kings ruled from Yin, issuing edicts. Yin also became a symbol of a great metropolis in the eyes of the people. The Shang people proudly referred to it as "Da Yi Shang," while other ethnic groups habitually called them "Yin Shang," where "Yin" initially referred to the Shang people's capital.

In the early morning of the 11th century BC, King Wu of Zhou from the western border of the Shang Dynasty led a coalition of vassals against the formidable Shang army in Muye near the capital, known as the "Battle of Muye." The beleaguered King Zhou of Shang eventually met his defeat and self-immolation, leading to the downfall of the Shang Dynasty. (Although Wugeng, the son of King Zhou, was granted the title of feudal lord, he had already become a vassal of the Zhou people, and the Shang Dynasty was no longer a dynasty ruling the world.) The once prosperous Yin became a desolate ruin engulfed in flames, later known as the "Yin Ruins."

The Yin Ruins are located in the northwest outskirts of present-day Anyang, Henan Province, spanning both banks of the Huan River. It is a vast area with crucial geographical importance. According to Sima Qian's records in *Records of the Grand Historian*, after Chu's Hegemon Xiang Yu gained fame in the Battle of Julu, he represented the coalition forces and met with Qin General Zhang Han in the Yin Ruins south of the Huan River. There, he accepted the surrender of several hundred thousand Qin soldiers, hastening the downfall of the tyrannical Qin Dynasty.

Since the 20th century, archaeologists have unearthed rich cultural remains from the Shang Dynasty at the Yin Ruins through excavations. In addition to tens of thousands of oracle bones, numerous precious bronze artifacts (including the famous Houmuxin Square *Ding*, Fuhao Square *Ding* with Bent Feet, Fuhao Three Bronze Steamers in One, Square *Ding* with Bent Feet, Ou Fang *Yi*, and more), exquisite jade and ivory artifacts, over 50 palace sites, and various other sites such as royal tombs,

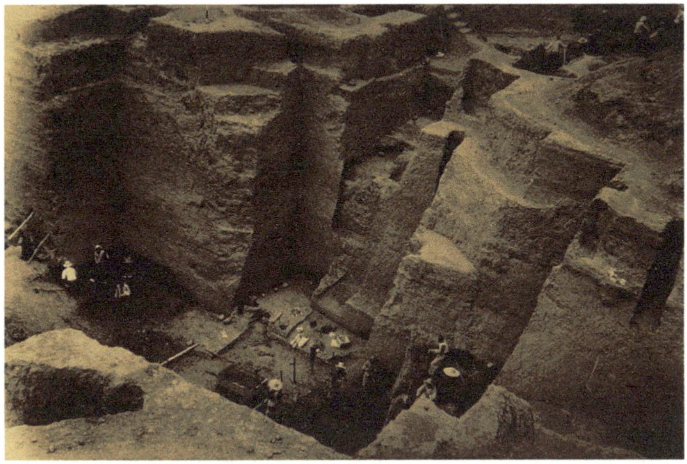

Figure 1.10 Archaeological excavation at the Yin Ruins in Anyang

commoner areas, bronze casting sites, workshops, and large sacrificial sites (see Figure 1.10).

In the past, many people used to feel intimidated when it came to oracle bone inscriptions, comparing them to heavenly scripts. However, this is entirely unnecessary. While they may seem mystical, they are not as mysterious. The interpretation of oracle bone inscriptions does differ from deciphering the sacred writings of other ancient civilizations, such as the hieroglyphs of ancient Egypt or the cuneiform script of the Sumerians. This is mainly because oracle bone inscriptions have not been lost for a long period like the ancient writings of other nations, making them more accessible and recognizable. The script from the Yin and Shang periods is the precursor to the Zhou, Qin, and Warring States scripts, with many Chinese characters exhibiting continuity in terms of sound, form, and meaning, providing a traceable lineage. The inheritance of Chinese characters has, in fact, never been interrupted, just like the development of ancient Chinese civilization.

Additionally, Chinese dynasties have placed great emphasis on the standardization and organization of characters. For example, the Qin Dynasty (221–206 BC) had the "San Cang" (three popular textbooks for teaching children to recognize characters in ancient China, Li Si's *Compilation by Cang Jie*, Zhao Gao's *Yuan Li Compilation*, and Huwu Jing's *Learned Compilation*). During the Han Dynasty (206 BC–AD 220), there was the *Shuo Wen Jie Zi* (*Analytical Dictionary of Characters*). During the Wei and Jin dynasties (AD 220–420), Li Si's *Compilation by Cang Jie*, Yang Xiong's *Xun Zuan Compilation*, and Jia Fang's Pang Xi *Compilation* were combined into a single volume (also known as the "San Cang") and widely promoted in society. The Tang

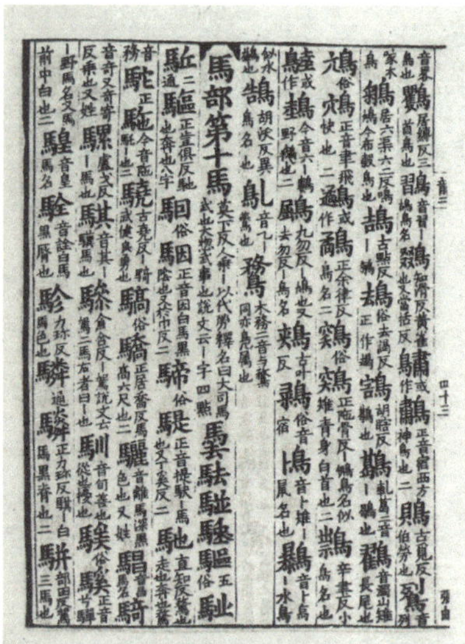

Figure 1.11 Book shadow of *Longkan Shoujing*

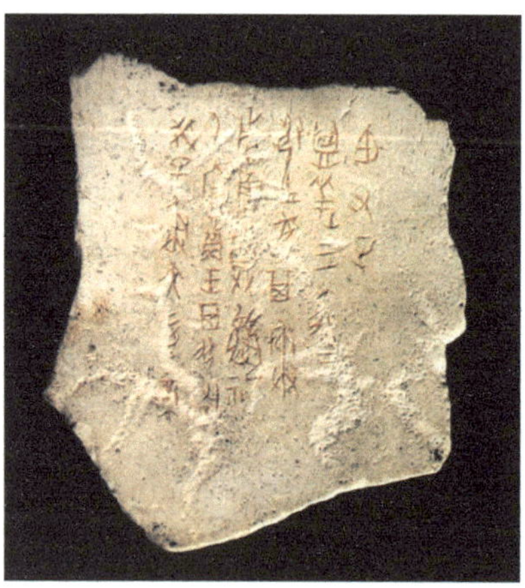

Figure 1.12 Zhouyuan oracle bones

Dynasty (AD 618–907) had the *Gan Lu Zi Shu* (a dictionary printed with standardized Chinese character forms.), the Liao and Song dynasties (907–1279) had the *Longkan Shoujing* (a dictionary compiled for the study of Buddhist scriptures) (Figure 1.11, with over 20,000 characters), the Ming Dynasty (1368–1644) had the *Zi Hui* (a dictionary arranged by radicals, with over 30,000 characters), and the Qing Dynasty (1644–1911) had the *Kangxi Dictionary* (with over 40,000 characters). In addition, there were collections of circulated "ancient peculiar characters" like the *Han Jian* and *Four Tones and Rhymes of Ancient Chinese* (two books specifically compiling and transcribing ancient texts and their script forms in the Song Dynasty), providing important exegetical foundations for interpreting oracle bone inscriptions.

In addition to the Yin people, according to archaeological discoveries, the Zhou people also used oracle bone inscriptions at that time (Figure 1.12).

In 1977, in Fengchu Village, Qishan County, Shaanxi Province, a pit inside the remains of a Western Zhou building yielded over 13,600 pieces of turtle plastron and over 300 pieces of cow scapula. Among them, 289 pieces of turtle plastron were inscribed with characters, varying in the number of characters per piece, ranging from 1 to 30.

In 1979, in Qijia Village, Fufeng County, Shaanxi Province, another collection of 22 oracle bones was gathered, including six pieces with inscriptions.

Qishan County, located at the southern foothills of Mount Qi, and Fufeng County were historically referred to as "Zhouyuan," the ancient capital before the Zhou people conquered the Shang Dynasty. The inscribed turtle shells unearthed from this area align with the records in the *Book of Songs · Da Ya · Mian*, stating, "The land in Zhouyuan is truly fertile, and the bitter vegetables are as sweet as malt sugar.

Initiating plans and discussions, then carving tortoise shells to observe and divine." Therefore, scholars call them "Zhouyuan Oracle Bones."

The creation and use of oracle bone inscriptions exemplify the wisdom of our ancestors.

Taking the pictographs as examples, the character "日" () depicts the shape of the sun. The character "月" () resembles the crescent moon. The character "龟" () imitates the side profile of a turtle. The character "牛" () portrays the frontal view of a cow. The character "马" () highlights the mane and tail of a horse. Similarly, the character "兔" () emphasizes the short tail of a rabbit. Other examples include the character "车" (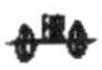), which depicts the wheels, axles, and carriage of a vehicle, and the character "火" (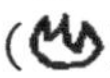), which illustrates burning flames. Although ideographic characters may appear simple, they are challenging to replicate and imitate accurately without careful observation and analysis of natural phenomena.

According to experts, the origin of pictographs may be related to early pictographic symbols. As one of the most primitive character creation methods, this form of writing is highly pictorial with weak symbolic elements. It should be considered a type of character created and disseminated during the initial stages of human civilization.

On a global scale, in addition to the oracle bone inscriptions of the Shang and Zhou dynasties in China, many ancient civilizations and ethnic groups have also created and used pictographs. Examples include the sacred script of ancient Egypt (Figure 1.13), the cuneiform script of the Sumerians (Figure 1.14), and the "Harappan" seal script of ancient India (Figure 1.15). Within China, apart from the Han ethnic group, the Dongba script used by the Naxi ethnic group in Yunnan (Figure 1.16) and the Shui script used by the Shui ethnic group (Figure 1.17) both preserve a significant number of pictographs to varying degrees.

However, pictographs themselves have limitations. Some concrete and abstract concepts cannot be easily depicted, such as big, small, many, few, thick, thin, etc. Thus, clever ancient people invented other methods to represent these characters. During the Han Dynasty, scholars categorized them into six types: indicative characters, syssemantographs, picto-phonetic characters, transformational characters, borrowed characters, and pictographs. They are collectively referred to as the "Six Scripts" or "Four Forms, Two Uses" (with transformational and borrowed characters being considered as the methods for using characters and the other four being the methods for creating characters).

Nevertheless, some of these new methods still needed to be based on pictographs, creating new characters by adding components related to form or sound. All four types of character creation were present in the discovered oracle bone inscriptions

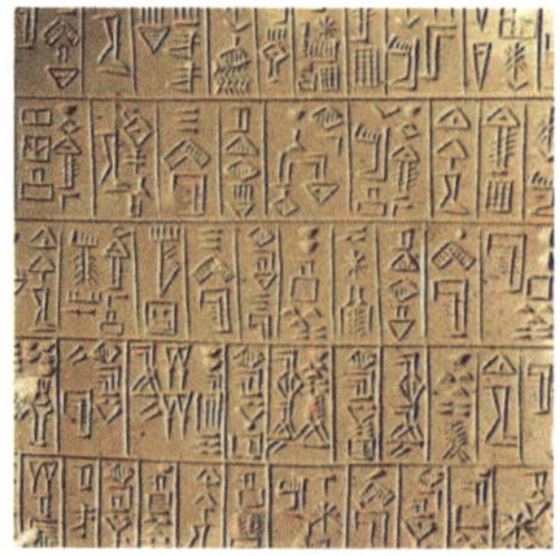

Figure 1.13 (FAR LEFT) Ancient Egypt sacred script

Figure 1.14 (LEFT) Sumerian cuneiform script

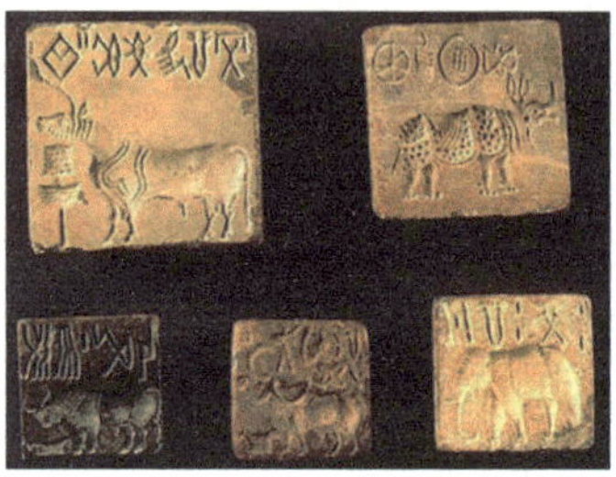

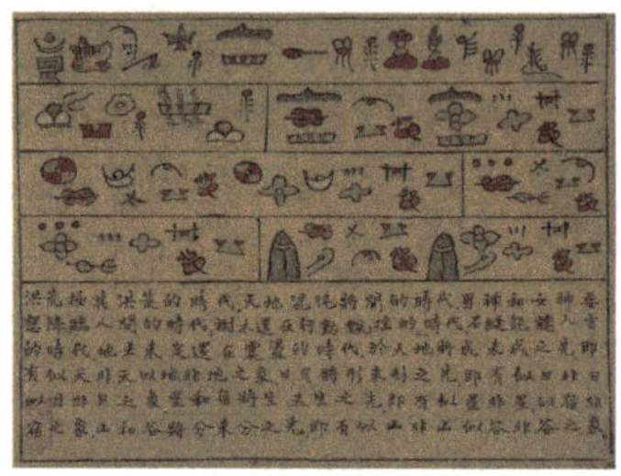

Figure 1.15 (FAR LEFT) Ancient Indian "Harappan" seal script

Figure 1.16 (LEFT) *Genesis* in Dongba script of the Naxi ethnic group

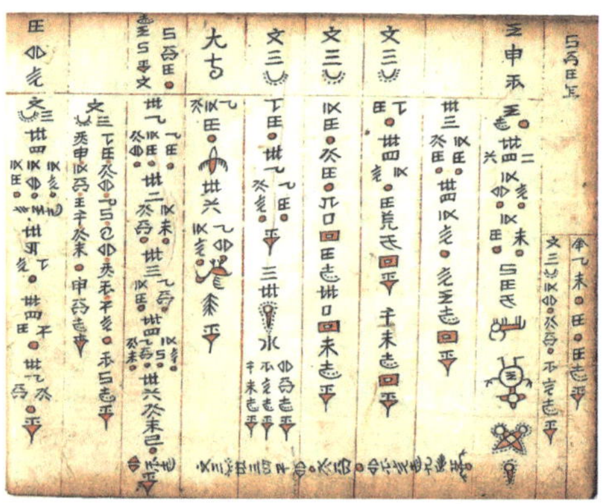

Figure 1.17 Shui script of the Shui ethnic group

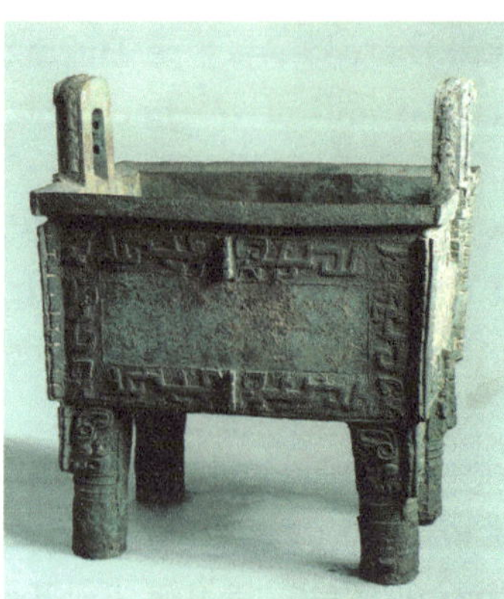

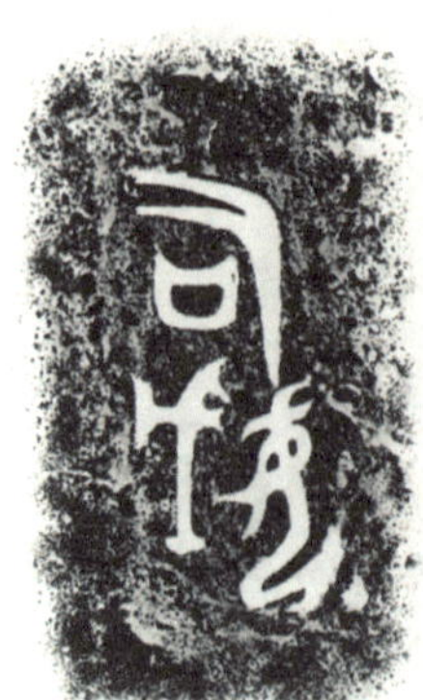

Figure 1.18 (FAR LEFT) Houmuwu *Ding*

Figure 1.19 (LEFT) Inscriptions on the Houmuwu *Ding*

from the Yin Ruins. The extensive use of picto-phonetic characters indicates that oracle bone inscriptions were already a fairly mature form of writing, and this method of character creation became the most predominant one in subsequent dynasties.

According to unearthed materials, it has been discovered that the nobility of the Yin and Shang periods not only carved inscriptions on oracle bones but also on bronze vessels (Figure 1.18, Figure 1.19).

In ancient times, sacrificial rituals were considered auspicious, as summarized in *Zuo Qiuming's Commentary on Spring and Autumn Annals*, which states, "The major affairs of the state are sacrifices and warfare." Therefore, bronze ritual vessels were also referred to as "ji jin" (auspicious metal), and the inscriptions on bronze artifacts were called "ji jin wen" or simply "jin wen" (Chinese bronze inscriptions) or "ming wen" (inscriptions). There is another viewpoint in the current academic community suggesting that the original meaning of "吉" (ji) was hardness, not auspiciousness. Thus, "ji jin" describes the durability and sturdiness of bronze objects, which is also a reasonable interpretation.

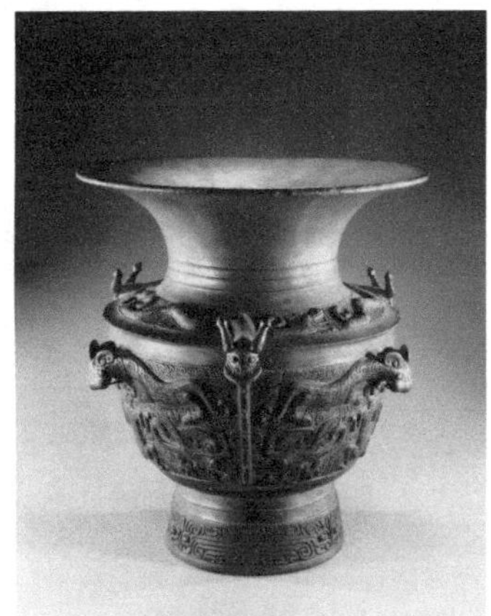

Figure 1.20 Bronze ritual vessel depicting a dragon and tiger unearthed in Fuyang, Anhui

Unlike the predominantly discovered oracle bones in the capital of the Shang Dynasty, the distribution of Shang bronze artifacts covered a much wider geographical area. They have been unearthed as far south as beyond the Yangtze River, west into Gansu, east to Shandong, and northeast to Liaoning. Besides the Yin Ruins in Anyang, Henan, significant quantities of important bronze artifacts have been found in various locations, including Fuyang in Anhui (Figure 1.20), Panlongcheng in Hubei (Figure 1.21), Ningxiang in Hunan (Figure 1.22), Dayangzhou in Jiangxi (Figure 1.23), Subutun in Shandong (Figure 1.24), and Shilou in Shanxi (Figure 1.25, Figure 1.26). These regions were either under Shang rule or had interactions with Shang people. Today, when people admire these exquisite artifacts in museum displays, they can still discern traces of ancient civilization exchanges and cultural integration.

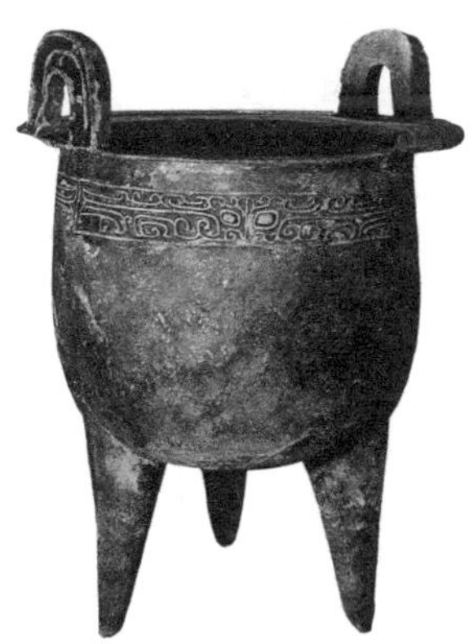

Figure 1.21 Bronze artifact unearthed in Panlongcheng, Hubei

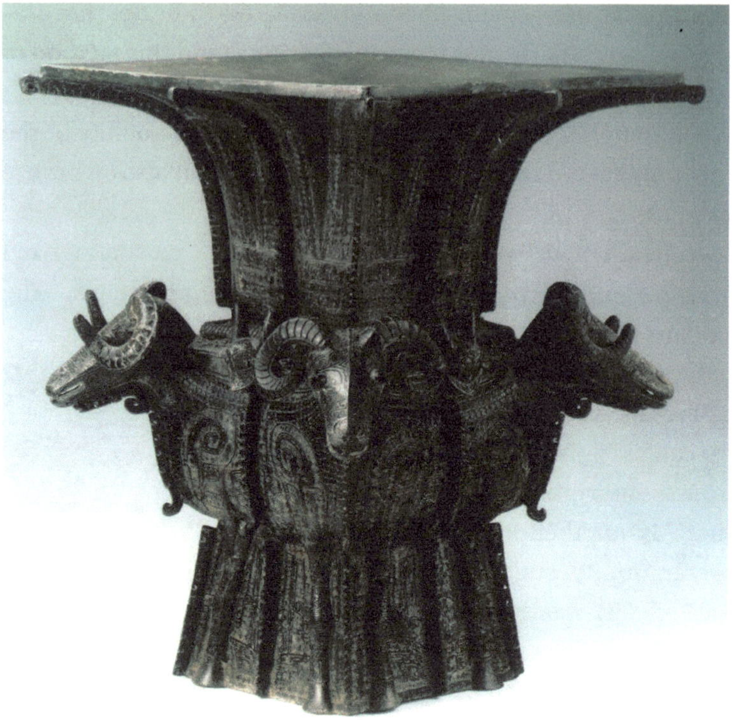

Figure 1.22 Four Rams Square *Zun* unearthed in Hunan

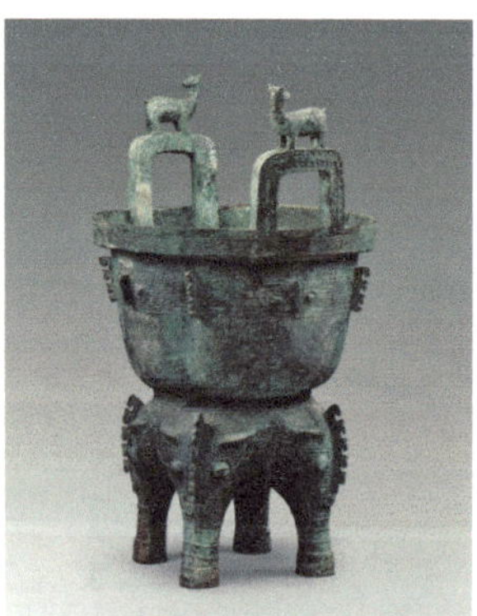

Figure 1.23 Bronze *yan* unearthed in Dayangzhou, Jiangxi

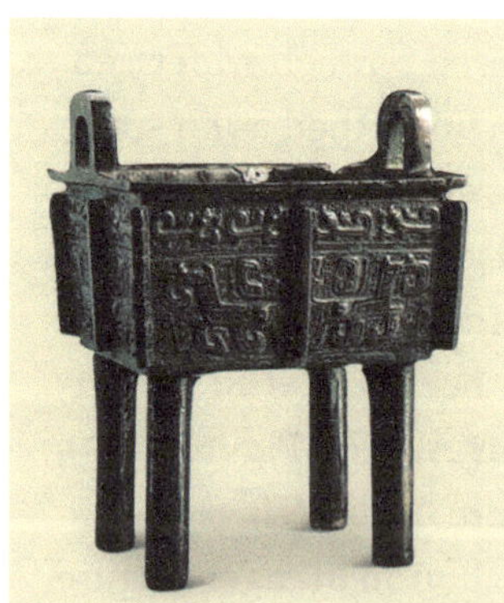

Figure 1.24 Bronze *ding* unearthed in Subutun, Shandong

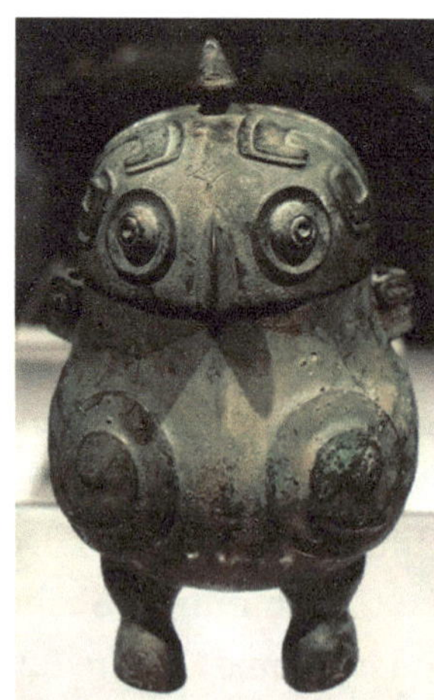

Figure 1.25 Bronze owl-shaped *you* unearthed in Shilou, Shanxi

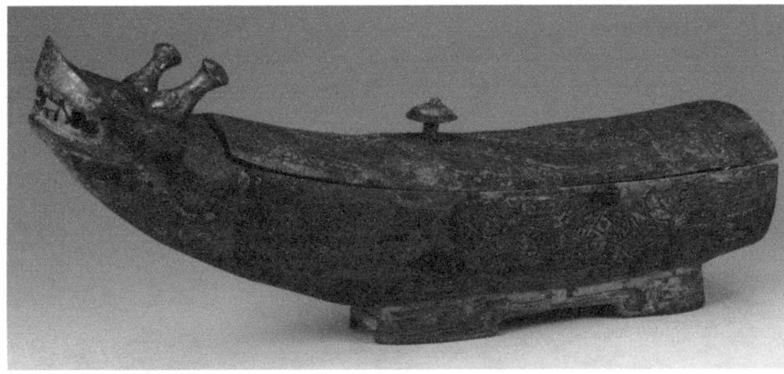

Figure 1.26 Dragon-shaped goblet unearthed in Shilou, Shanxi

Generally, it is believed that during the Yin-Shang period, when oracle bone and bronze inscriptions coexisted, the former represented a divination culture, while the latter represented a sacrificial culture. Oracle bone inscriptions can be considered vernacular characters compared with the more elegant and dignified bronze inscriptions. Some bronze inscriptions even underwent intricate embellishments and beautification at considerable cost.

As we entered the Western Zhou Dynasty (1046–771 BC), significant changes occurred in the shape and decoration of bronze vessels (such as the popular "gui" vessel with a pedestal, as shown in Figure 1.27). Moreover, lengthy inscriptions on bronze vessels gradually increased. For instance, the Duke Mao *Ding*, housed in the National Palace Museum in Taipei, features an inscription with a staggering 497 characters (Figure 1.28). In terms of content, compared with the sacrificial and self-naming functions of Yin-Shang bronze inscriptions, Western Zhou bronze inscriptions display a more diverse and rich content, emphasizing the splendor of the present world (Figures 1.29–1.31).

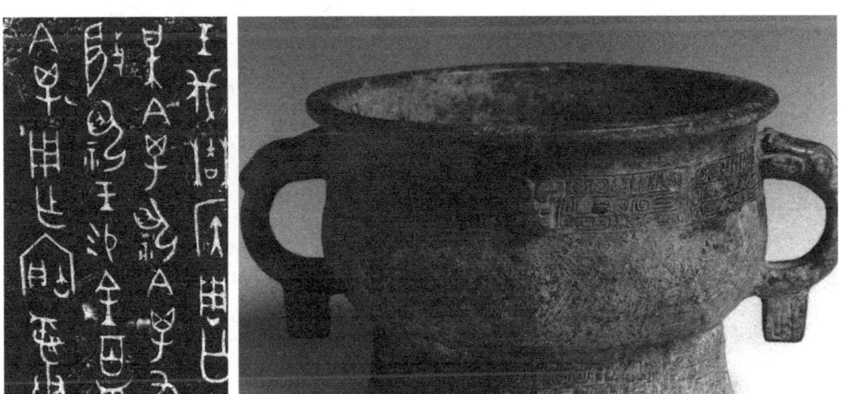

Figure 1.27 Bronze vessel with the shape of birds in the Western Zhou Dynasty

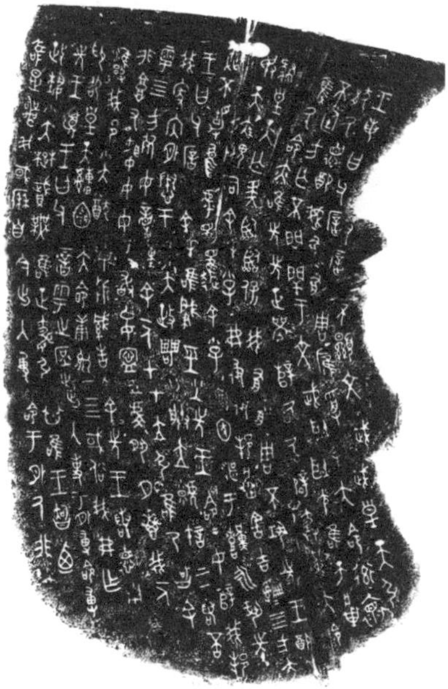

Figure 1.28 Partial rubbing of Duke Mao *Ding*

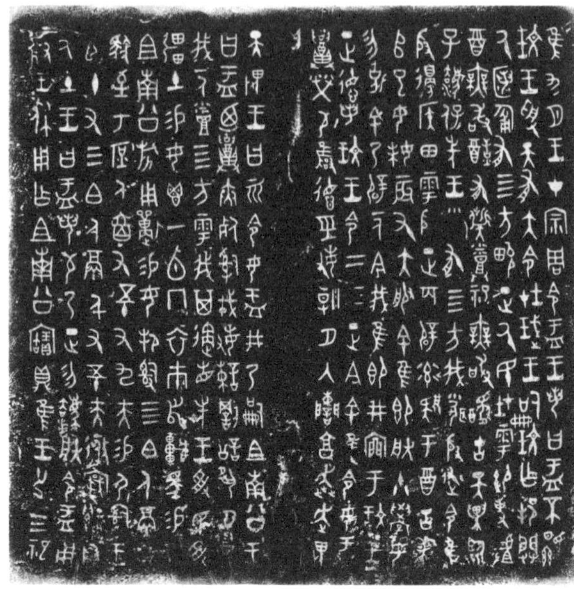

Figure 1.29 Rubbing of Da Yu *Ding* (inscriptions record King Kang of Zhou narrating the founding experiences of King Wen and King Wu in the Western Zhou Dynasty to Minister Yu)

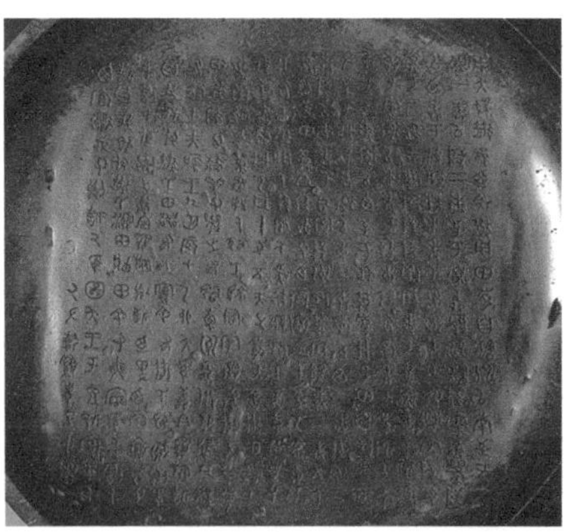

Figure 1.30 Photograph of the inscriptions on Family San's Plate

Figure 1.31 Rubbing of the inscriptions on Family San's Plate

In the past, bronze inscriptions were also commonly referred to as "Zhongding Wen." Among the prevailing bronze vessels in the Shang and Zhou dynasties, "ding" represented ritual vessels, and "zhong" represented musical instruments. Both "zhong" and "ding" had larger shapes and could carry more inscriptions, making them more representative. The academic discipline that primarily focused on the study of bronze inscriptions was also called epigraphy.

Epigraphy was initiated by scholars in the Song Dynasty and focused on the study of inscriptions on metal and stone. "Metal" primarily refers to bronze artifacts but is not limited to bronze. Any inscriptions on metal objects are collected for study.

Among bronze inscriptions in the Zhou Dynasty, there is also a unique form of writing known as "bird and insect script."

"Bird and insect script," also known as "bird and insect seal," roughly originated in the later period of the Spring and Autumn period and flourished during the Warring States period. It was mainly popular in the middle and lower reaches of the Yangtze River and had an influence in the Central Plains. This type of writing has been found on bronze artifacts in states such as Wu, Yue, Chu, Cai, Xu, and Song (Figure 1.32). Its feature is often presented in the form of inlaying gold, with a looping and twisting style based on seal script. Some integrate the characters with bird shapes or add bird shapes as decorations beside the characters, as seen in the inscription on the sword of Goujian, King of the Yue State (Figure 1.33), and the inscription on the sword of Zhou Gou, King of the Yue State. Some strokes meander and twist, with a bulging middle, pointed ends, and long hanging feet, resembling the curved bodies of insect-like creatures, such as the inscription on Prince Wu *Ding* of the Chu State in the

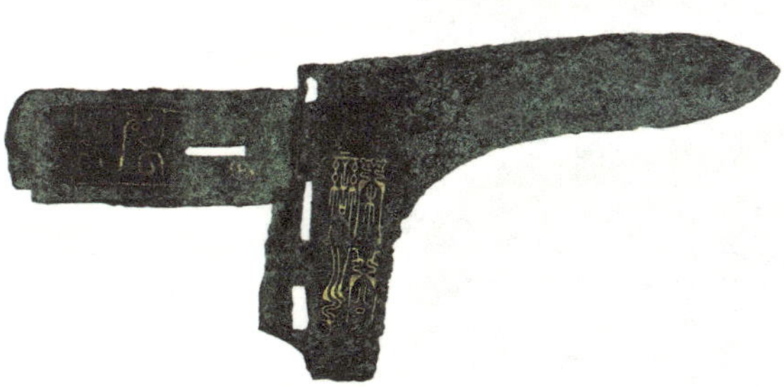

Figure 1.32 Duke Jing of Song's (the ruler of the State of Song) Gold-Inlaying Dagger-Axe

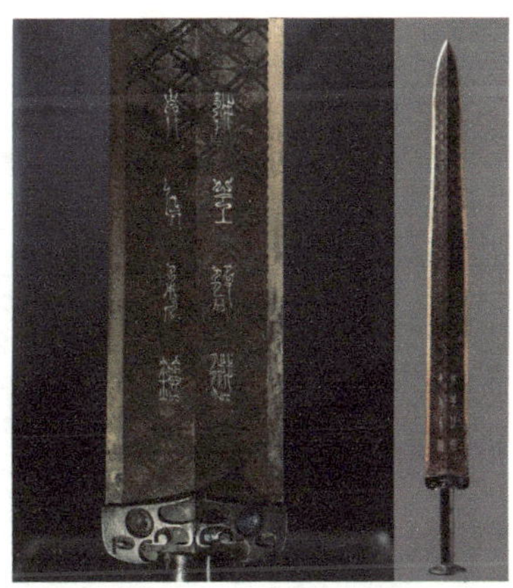

Figure 1.33 Inscription on Sword of Goujian, King of the Yue State

late Spring and Autumn period (Figure 1.34, Figure 1.35). The variations are diverse, making it quite challenging to identify.

The bird and insect script is a decorative writing style rather than a distinct writing system. Moreover, it is elaborately crafted, but its usage is extremely limited. Today, we can see it primarily in the inscriptions on bronze artifacts, especially weapons, and occasionally on containers (Figure 1.36 to Figure 1.38) and seals (Figure 1.39). After the Qin and Han dynasties, the use of it gradually declined. However, it can still occasionally be found in stone inscriptions from certain periods.

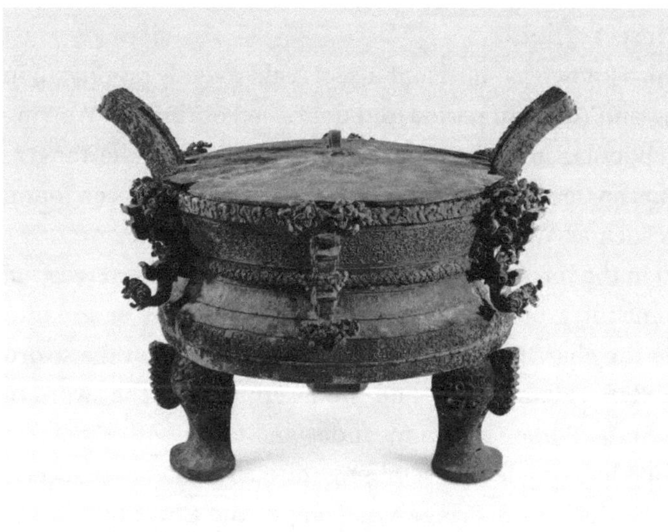

Figure 1.34 Prince Wu *Ding* of the Chu State

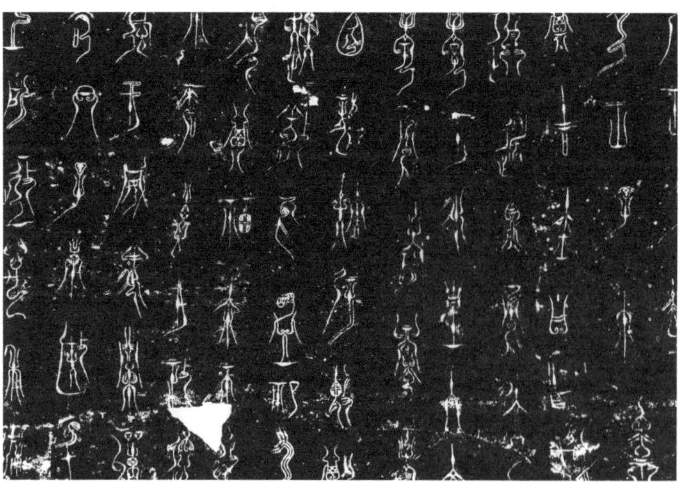

Figure 1.35 Rubbing of the inscription on the body of Prince Wu *Ding* of the Chu State

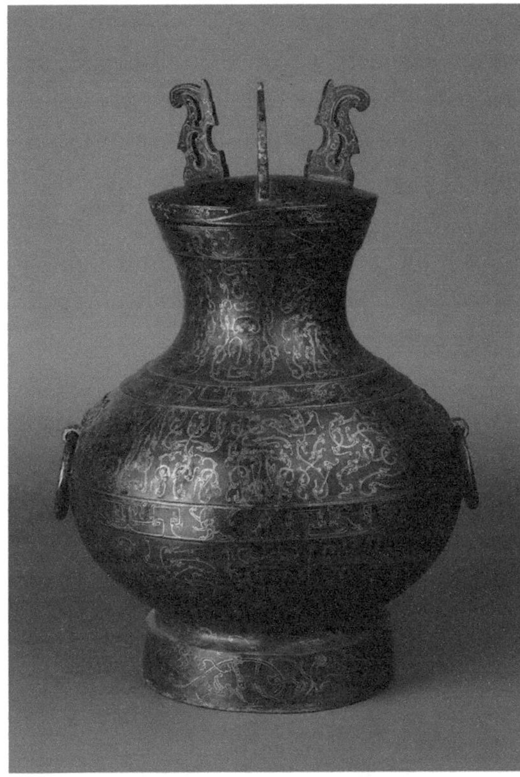

Figure 1.36 Bird and Insect Seal Bronze Pot of Western Han unearthed in Hebei

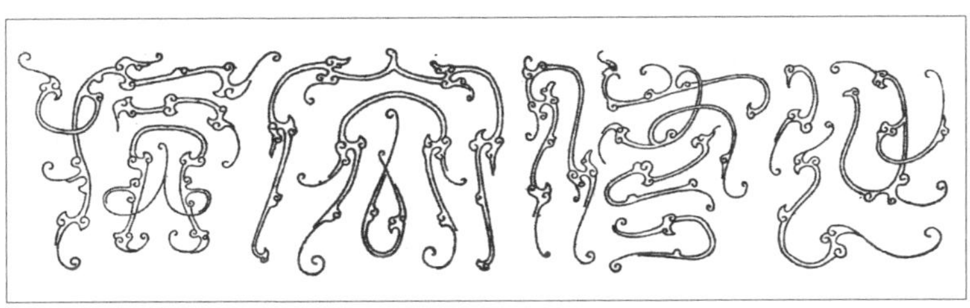

Figure 1.37 Rubbing of the inscription on the abdomen of a Western Han Bird and Insect Seal Bronze Pot (partial)

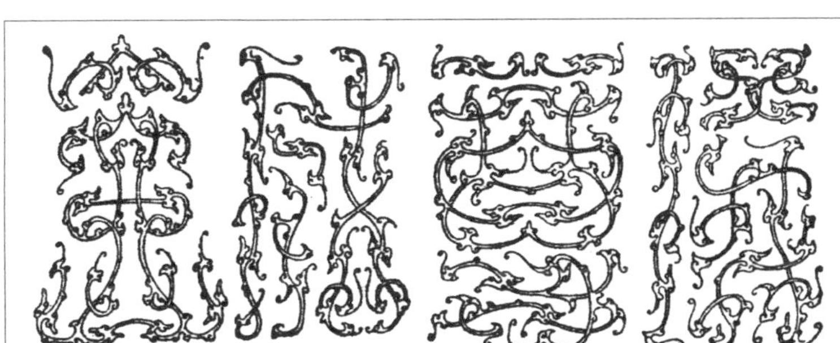

Figure 1.38 Rubbing of the inscription on the abdomen of another Western Han Bird and Insect Seal Bronze Pot (partial)

Before the Spring and Autumn period, the majority of bronze inscriptions were cast together with the objects. However, from the mid-Warring States period onwards, they were often carved with a knife after the objects were made. For example, the inscriptions on weapons from the Qin State were mostly carved with a knife (Figure 1.40). This represents another change and is also an important reference for distinguishing the authenticity of bronze artifacts.

During the Spring and Autumn and Warring States periods, texts were also found on various other mediums besides appearing on bronze artifacts. Here, a few are briefly introduced.

(1) Seal script (Figure 1.41). According to ancient records, the use of seal script began during the Spring and Autumn period at the latest. Many official and private seals from the Warring States period have been preserved. Most of these seals are made of bronze, and some are also made of silver or jade.

(2) Currency inscriptions. This primarily refers to the writing on currency. During the Eastern Zhou period, with numerous vassal states and ongoing conflicts, the forms

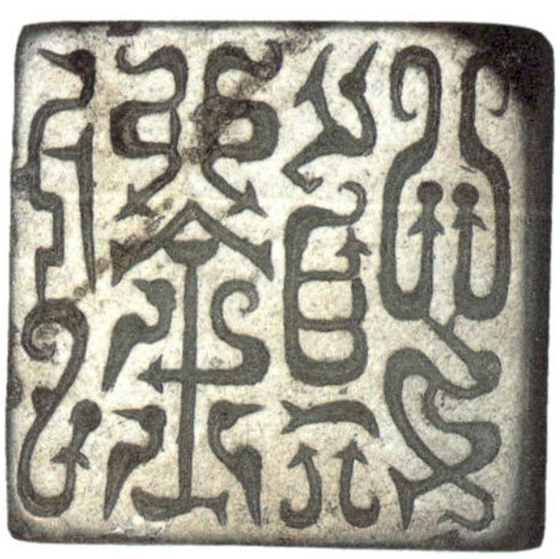

Figure 1.39 Liu Shen's bird and insect script covered Cauldron Knob Jade Seal in Western Han Dynasty (currently held in the Xuzhou Museum)

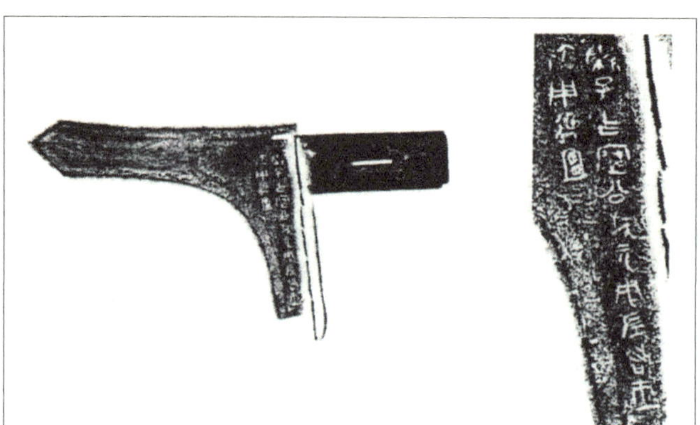

Figure 1.40 Rubbing of the inscription on Qin Zige's Dagger-Axe

Figure 1.41 Seal script

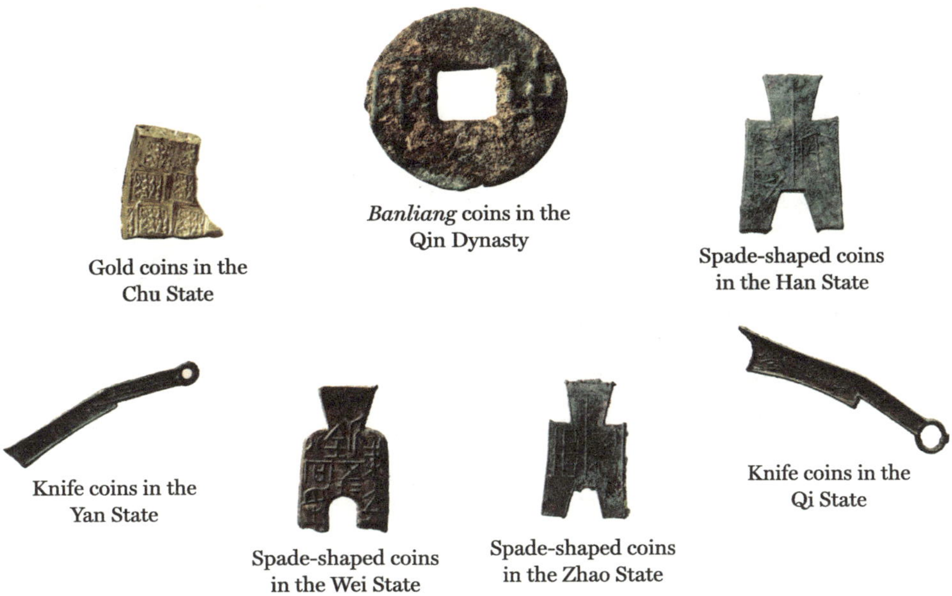

Figure 1.42 Diagram of the currencies used by various vassal states during the Warring States period

of currency were complex and diverse (Figure 1.42). Unearthed currencies mainly fall into four categories: spade-shaped coins, knife coins, round coins, and ant-nose coins (sea shell-shaped coins). Spade-shaped coins were mainly used in the regions of the Three Jin states and the Yan State; knife coins circulated mainly in states like Zhao, Yan, and Qi; round coins appeared later and seemed to be used in various states; ant-nose coins were popular mainly in the Chu State.

Most of these currencies were inscribed with the names of places, likely indicating the cities issuing the currency. Some also had inscriptions indicating weight or value (Figure 1.43). The meanings of inscriptions on certain currencies, such as those on ant-nose coins, remain unclear to this day.

(3) Pottery Inscriptions. Texts are often found on pottery from the Warring States period. The discovered pottery inscriptions are mostly stamped with a seal before firing, while a few are incised before or after firing. Among the pottery inscriptions found in the six eastern states, Qi and Yan have the highest quantity (Figure 1.44).

(4) Lacquerware inscriptions. During the Warring States period, states such as Qin and Chu often had inscriptions and engravings on lacquerware. Notably, examples include the lacquer chessboard from the Chu tomb in Zuozhong, Jingmen, Hubei (Figure 1.45) and the lacquer box with the twenty-eight constellations from the tomb

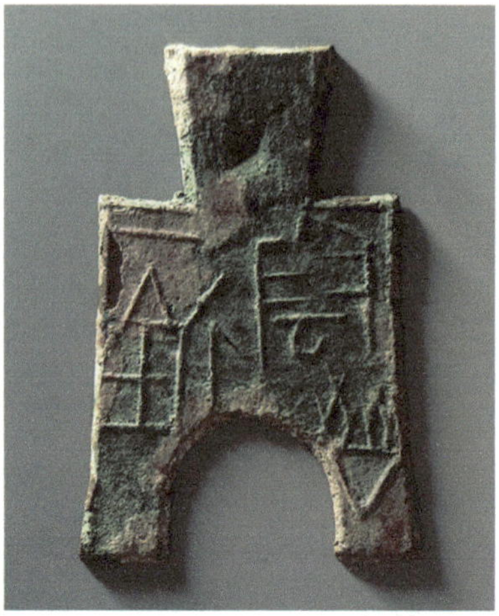

Figure 1.43 Spade-shaped coins in Yinjin from the Warring States

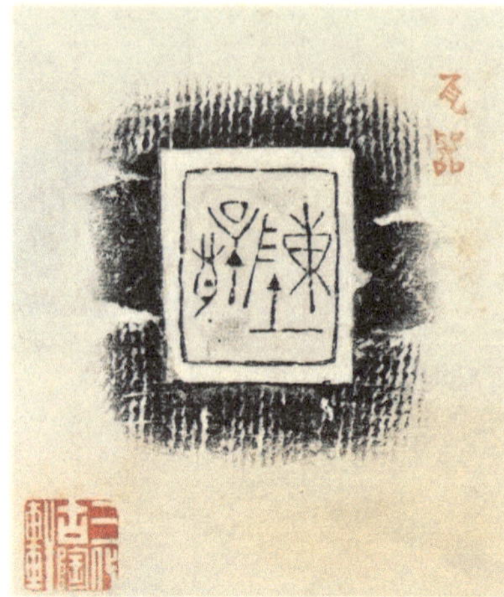

Figure 1.44 Pottery inscriptions from the collection of Chen Jieqi in the Warring States

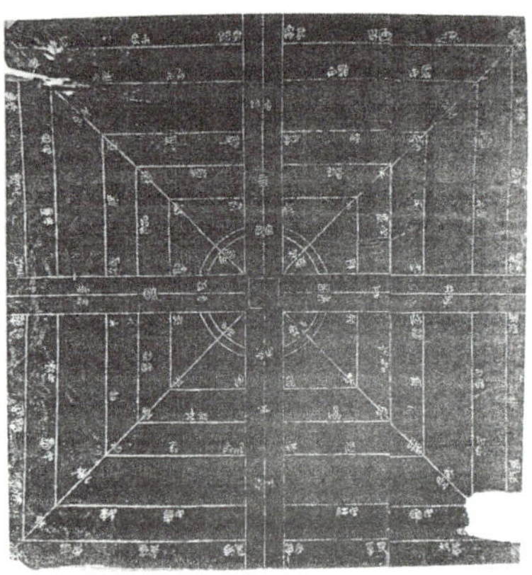

Figure 1.45 Lacquer chessboard from the Chu tomb in Zuozhong, Jingmen, Hubei

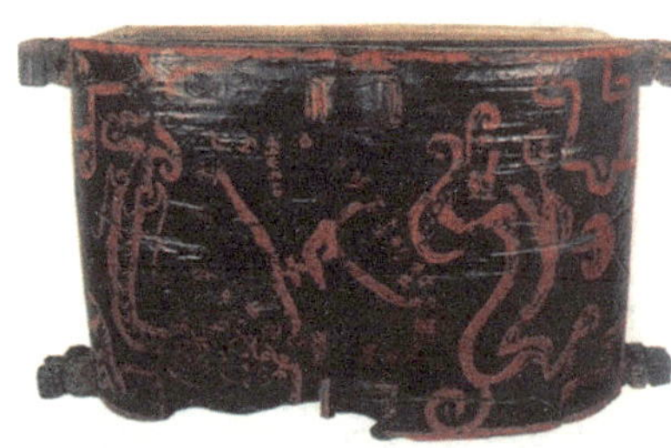

Figure 1.46 Lacquer box with the twenty-eight constellations from the Tomb of Marquis Yi of Zeng

of Marquis Yi of Zeng (Figure 1.46). Lacquerware from the early Western Han period also frequently featured inscriptions, typically in seal script.

(5) Jade and stone inscriptions. Writing or carving on jade and stone was also practiced during the Spring and Autumn and Warring States periods. An example is the alliance letter excavated from Houma in Shanxi in 1965, dating back to the Spring and Autumn period (Figure 1.47). This inscription, written with a brush on a jade tablet, records an alliance oath in both vermilion and ink scripts (in separate

sections). The brush strokes are elegant, and the overall presentation is exquisite. This artifact bears witness to the brutal internal struggles within the State of Jin, evolving from contention among six ministers to the establishment of four powerful ministers, ultimately leading to the division of Jin into three states. This marked the beginning of the Warring States period.

Later, in Xizhangji Village, Wen County, Henan, a large number of ink-written alliance letters were discovered, dating to a period similar to the *Houma Alliance Letter*. Scholars refer to these as the *Wen County Alliance Letter* (Figure 1.48).

In the early 1940s, a similar type of jade book was unearthed in this region, referred to as the "Qinyang Jade Inscriptions." Additionally, other notable inscriptions on jade and stone include the Qin stone drum inscription (Figure 1.49), the curse on Chu inscription, and the Qin jade tablet for praying against illness (Figure 1.50, Figure 1.51).

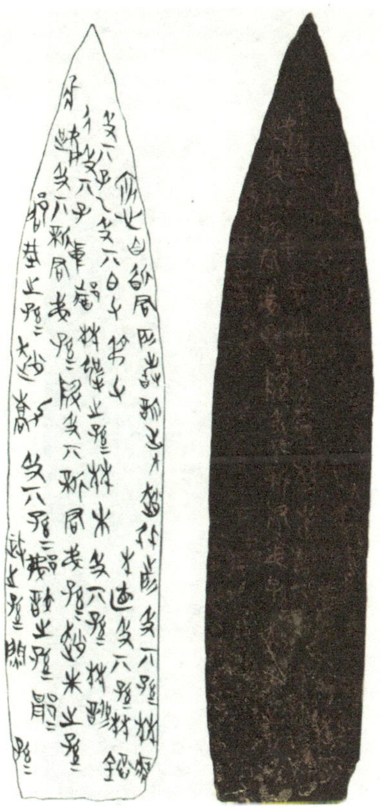

Figure 1.47 *Houma Alliance Letter* and its rubbing

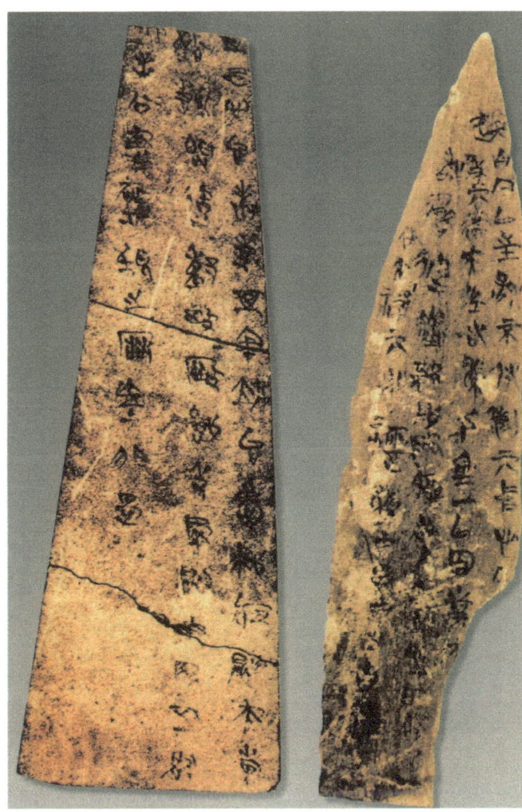

Figure 1.48 *Wen County Alliance Letter*

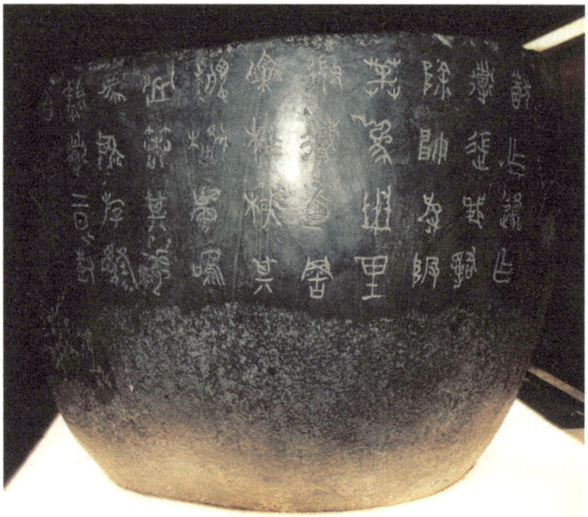

Figure 1.49 Stone drum inscription

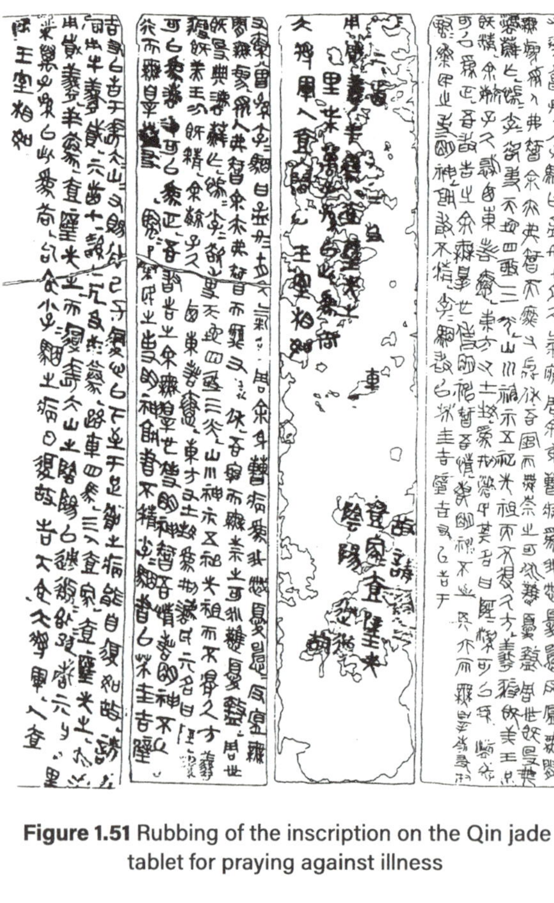

Figure 1.51 Rubbing of the inscription on the Qin jade tablet for praying against illness

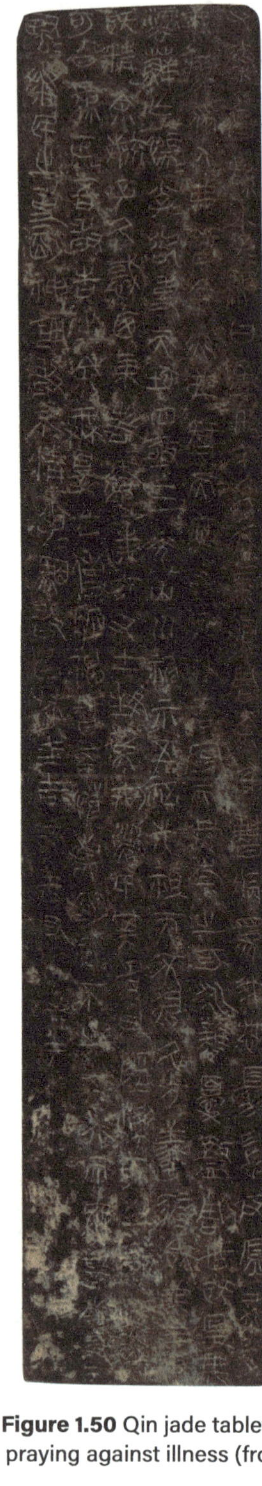

Figure 1.50 Qin jade tablet for praying against illness (front)

(6) Bamboo and silk inscriptions. Before the widespread use of plant fiber paper, bamboo and silk were the most commonly used writing materials. Scholars suggest that bamboo slips were already in use at the beginning of the Shang Dynasty, while the use of silk as a writing material might have come a bit later. Due to the easy damage and decay of bamboo and silk, early inscriptions on these materials are hard to preserve. Only sporadic records exist in literature, and the earliest discovered bamboo and silk inscription is Chu bamboo, dating back to the Warring States period (Figure 1.52).

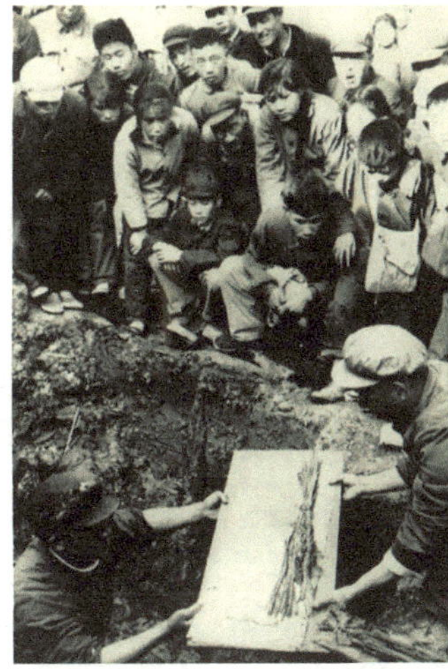

Figure 1.52 Photos of excavating bamboo and silk inscriptions

The discovered Chu bamboo slips were all written with a brush dipped in ink. The content is mostly related to records of burial objects or the presentation of funeral vehicles. Additionally, there are records of divination, legal documents, and texts related to ancient books, whether extant or lost, such as the *Book of Documents*, *Chapters Outside the Book of Zhou*, *Book of Songs*, *Book of Changes*, and *Classic of the Way and Virtue* (Figure 1.53 to Figure 1.56).

Figure 1.53 (LEFT) Excerpt of *Laozi* from Chu bamboo slips in Guodian

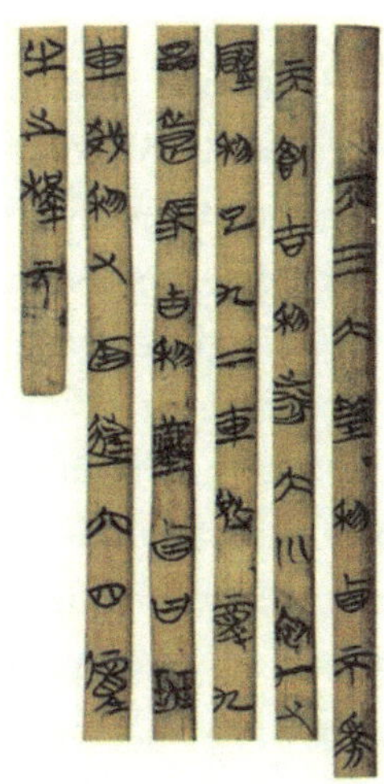

Figure 1.54 (RIGHT) Selected excerpt from the Warring States Chu bamboo slips of the *Book of Changes* at the Shanghai Museum

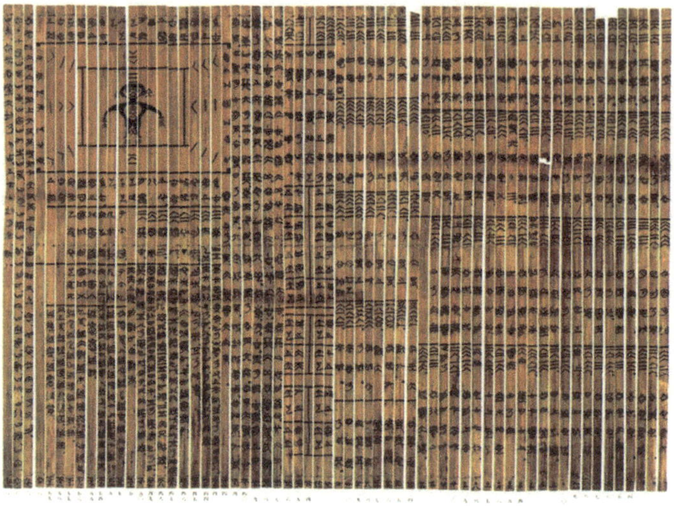

Figure 1.55 Warring States Chu bamboo slips of *Shifa* in the collection of Tsinghua University

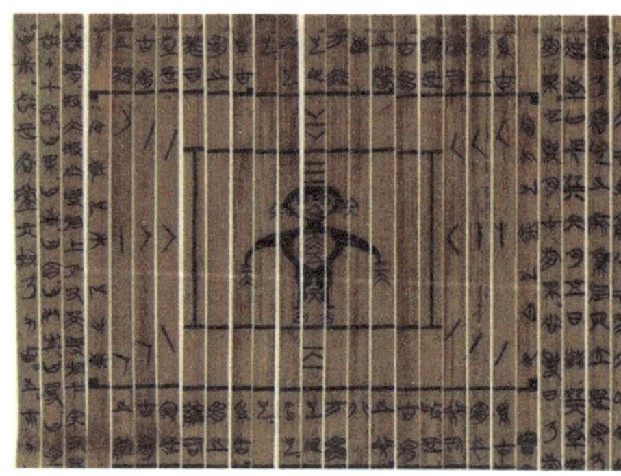

Figure 1.56 Partial view of Warring States Chu bamboo slips of *Shifa* in the collection of Tsinghua University

Only one piece of silk texts with complete texts from Warring States has been discovered to date. Legend has it that it was illegally excavated from a Chu tomb from Warring States in Zidanku in the eastern suburbs of Changsha City, Hunan Province. Therefore, it is also known as the "Chu Silk Book" or "Chu Zeng Book."

Unfortunately, this silk book had entered the United States before the 1950s and is currently housed at the Sackler Gallery in Washington. There are over 900 discernible characters written in ink on it, surrounded by 12 peculiar divine images. Scholars speculate that these divine images represent the twelve gods in the Chu people's concept, which aligns perfectly with the records in the *Er Ya*. The four corners of the silk depict tree images in green, red, white, and black colors, illustrating myths and taboos passed down in Chu about celestial phenomena, disasters, the rotation of the four seasons, and lunar calendar prohibitions (Figure 1.57).

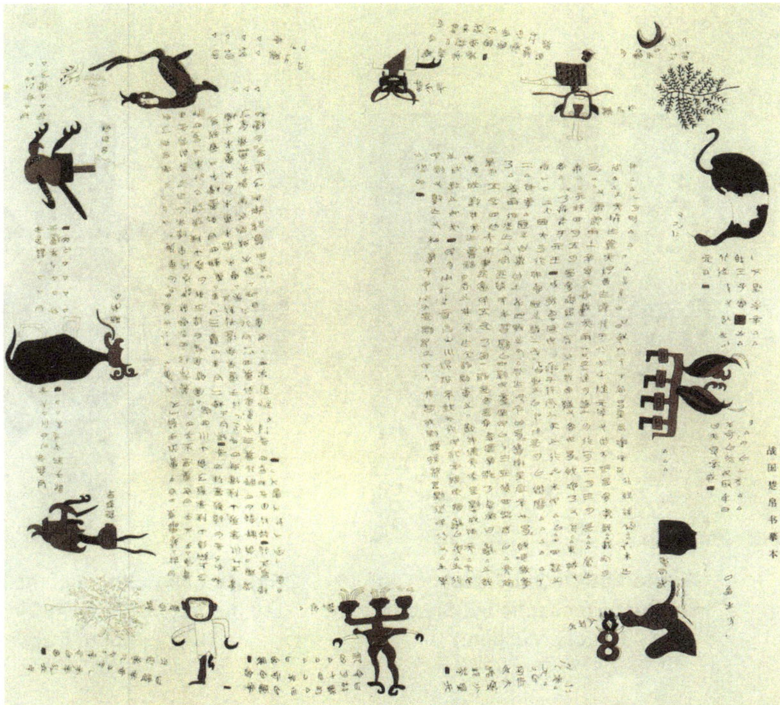

Figure 1.57 Chu silk book from the Warring States period unearthed from Zidanku in Changsha

After the unification by the Qin Dynasty, the small seal script was implemented nationwide, and inscriptions were carved on weights and measures (Figure 1.58 to Figure 1.60). Qin Shi Huang (the first emperor of Qin) traveled across the country and inscribed achievements on stones in places like Mount Yi, Mount Tai, Langya Terrace, Jieshi, and Kuaiji. During the reign of the second emperor, additional inscriptions were added to decree tablets to explain that the inscriptions on these stones were made by Qin Shi Huang. These inscribed stones and decree tablets provide valuable material for studying the small seal script. Still, unfortunately, most of the original artifacts have been destroyed, with only some fragments remaining, along with some rubbings passed down (Figure 1.61).

The *Analytical Dictionary of Characters* collects over 9,000 small seal characters, making it the richest and most systematic source of Qin-era written characters (Figure 1.62). However, the compilation took place in the mid-Eastern Han Dynasty, and by that time, there were already some errors in the small seal characters written by people. In addition, scholars, including Xu Shen, were limited by the social environment of that time, leading to some incorrect understanding of the structural aspects of small seal characters, resulting in erroneous modifications in the book.

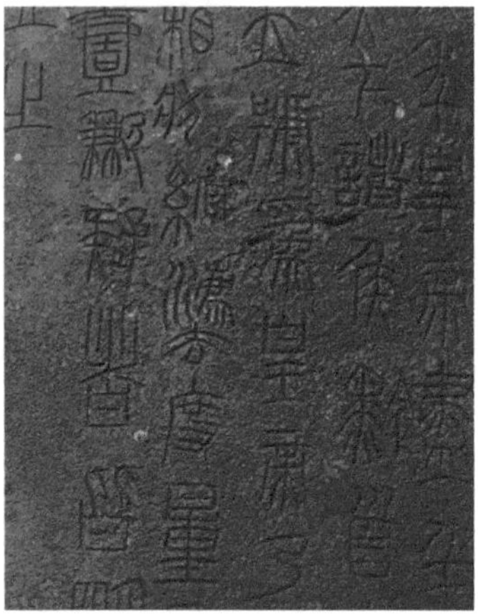

Figure 1.58 Decree tablet of Qin Shi Huang (collection of Shaanxi History Museum)

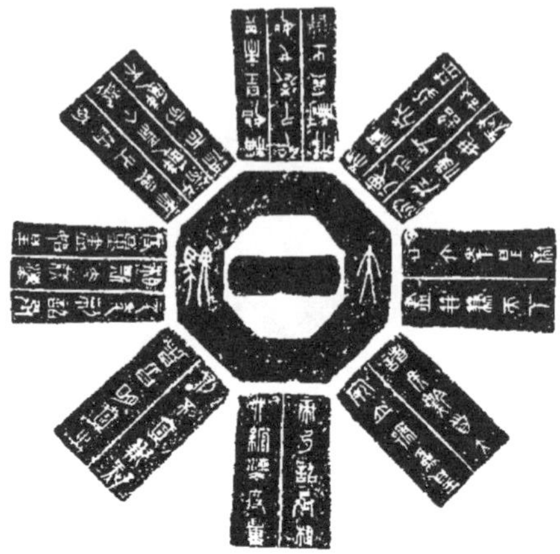

Figure 1.59 Rubbing of the inscription on the bronze weight from Qin Shi Huang at Mount Dagui

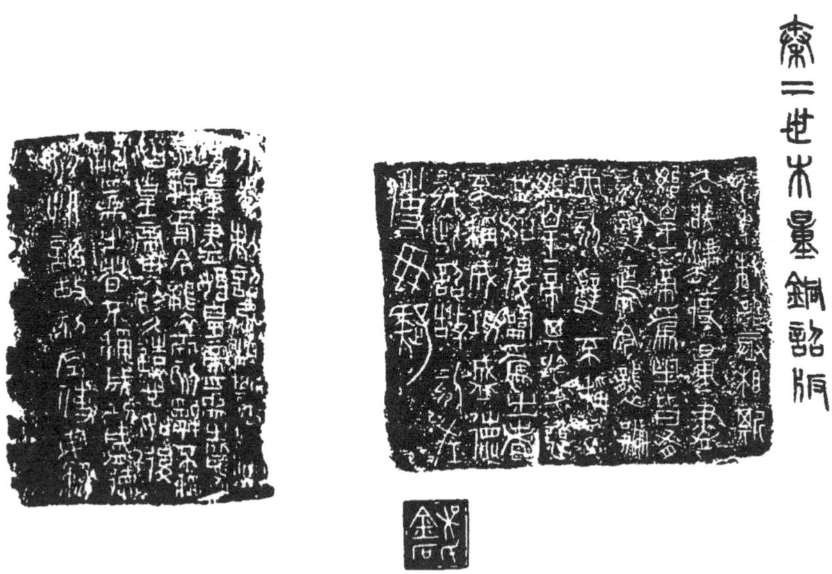

Figure 1.60 Bronze decree tablet of the Second Emperor of the Qin Dynasty

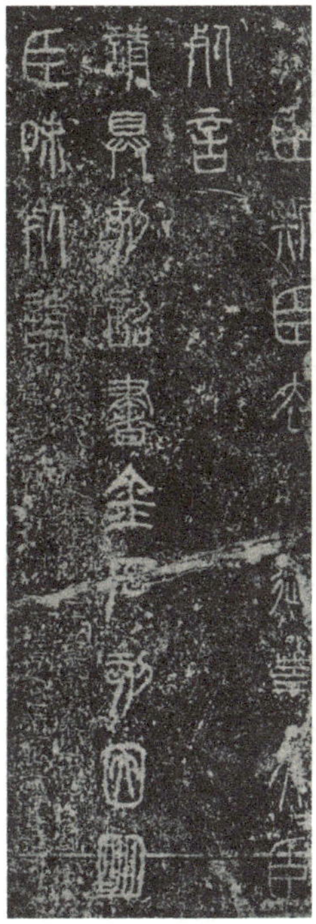

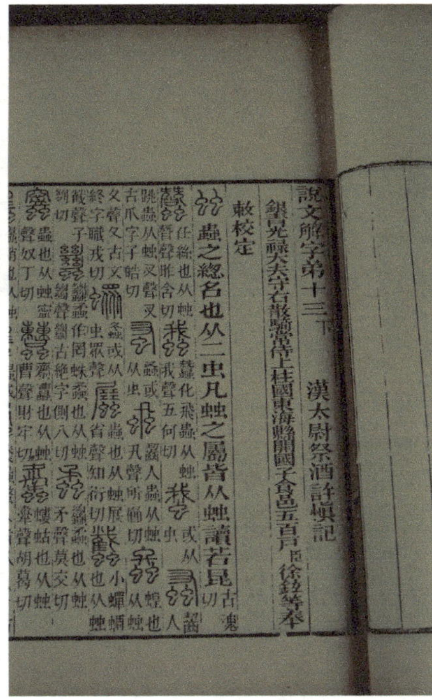

說文解字弟十三下　漢太尉祭酒許慎記

銀青光祿大夫守右散騎常侍上柱國東海縣開國子食邑五百戶臣徐鉉等奉

敕校定

蟲之總名也从二虫凡䖵之屬皆从䖵讀若昆

Figure 1.61 (RIGHT) Rubbing of the inscription on the stone at Mount Tai

Figure 1.62 (FAR RIGHT) Shadow of *Analytical Dictionary of Characters*

After the compilation of the *Analytical Dictionary of Characters*, it underwent numerous copies, engravings, and corrections by scribes, engravers, and some less skilled collators throughout the ages, causing further errors. Therefore, some small seal characters in it are unreliable and need correction using that on Qin and Han artifacts, such as inscriptions on gold and stone.

After the 1970s, a large number of Qin slips, mainly written on silk and bamboo, were unearthed, providing important material for the study of Qin-era characters. Notably, bamboo slips of the Qin Dynasty at Shuihudi, discovered in 1975 in Yunmeng, Hubei, consisted of over 1,100 bamboo slips containing Qin laws, *Ri Shu* (*Daily Records*), and major events (Figure 1.63). Subsequently, in 1979,

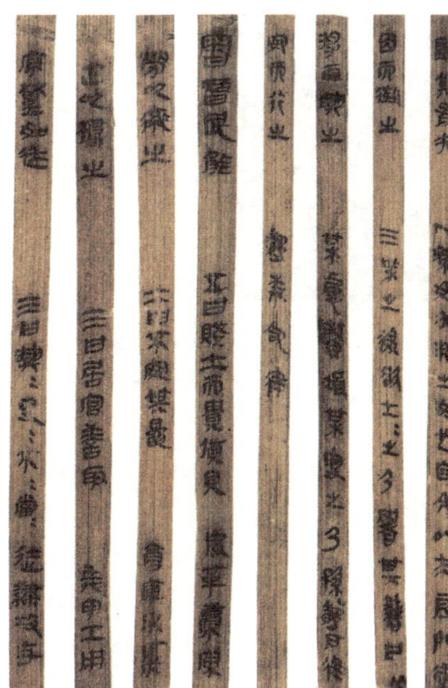

Figure 1.63 Qin bamboo slips from Shuihudi

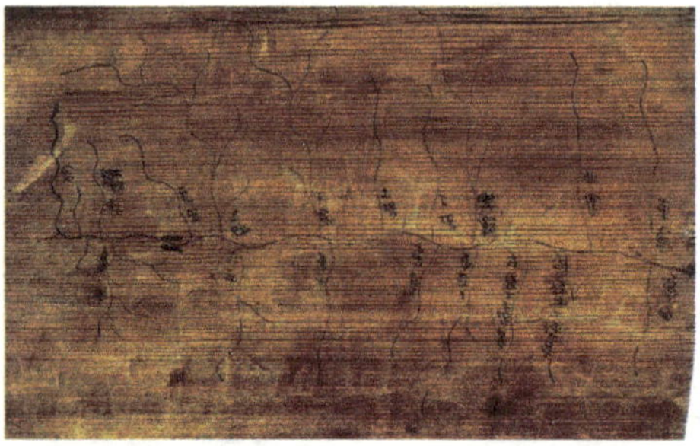

Figure 1.64 Map unearthed from the Qin tomb in Fangmatan, Tianshui, Gansu

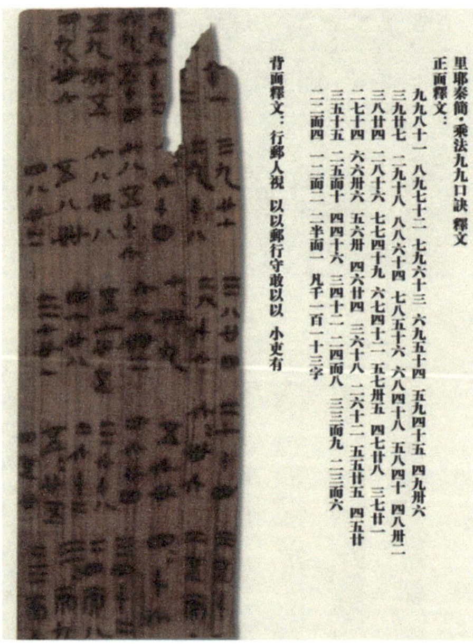

Figure 1.65 Partial view of the Qin bamboo slips from Liye Ancient City

wooden documents with legal content from the Qin era were excavated in Qingchuan County, Sichuan. In 1986, more than 460 bamboo slips were unearthed in a Qin tomb from the late Warring States period in Fangmatan, Tianshui, Gansu, along with four wooden boards bearing inscriptions forming a map (Figure 1.64).

In 2002, over 38,000 Qin bamboo slips were unearthed from the Liye Ancient City site in Hunan Province (Figure 1.65). Among them, approximately 18,000 bamboo slips had inscriptions, significantly surpassing the cumulative total unearthed in previous years. Subsequently, both Yue Lu Academy of Hunan University and Peking University acquired batches of Qin bamboo slips, and the contents of these slips were also highly significant.

According to scholars' research, during the Spring and Autumn and Warring States periods, Qin characters gradually evolved into small seal scripts, and there was no clear boundary between the two kinds of characters. The terms "large seal script," "Qin seal script," and "small seal script" were only used from the Han Dynasty onwards, and during the Qin Dynasty, there was probably only the general term "篆" (seal script) for this style of script.

"篆" (zhuan) and "瑑" (zhuan) have the same pronunciation, with the latter meaning carving or engraving. In *Master Lü's Spring and Autumn Annals · Cautionary Strategies*, it is mentioned, "Achievements are recorded on pans and bowls, and inscriptions are made on vessels and mirrors." During that time, the clerical script was not considered an elegant script, and only the seal script was qualified to be engraved on metal and stone. Thus, it was deemed worthy and left a lasting legacy.

In the early Spring and Autumn period, the Qin characters already exhibited significant stylistic differences from the characters of other states. As the Warring States period progressed, the variations in characters among different regions intensified, highlighting the differences with Qin characters. The phenomenon of diverse scripts greatly affected economic and cultural exchanges among regions and was not conducive to the Qin Dynasty's rule beyond its homeland. Therefore, after unification, Qin rapidly implemented the "standardization of Chinese writing system policy," using Qin characters as the standard to unify the written language throughout China. In reality, Qin had already begun this work gradually in newly conquered areas, as evidenced by unearthed textual materials from various regions.

However, people's writing habits are formed through long-term practice. Thus, it can be imagined that changing the writing habits of the conquered populations was not an easy task for the Qin Dynasty.

Today, based on unearthed textual materials, scholars have discovered that although the Qin Dynasty rapidly achieved the unification of characters through strict laws and penalties, the influence of the characters of the six states did not completely disappear. Traces of Chu characters were still abundant on bamboo slips from the early Western Han period. Nevertheless, the Qin Dynasty's approach essentially eliminated the situation of diverse scripts in society at that time, holding a crucial position in the development history of Chinese characters.

After the Qin Dynasty, within the territory of China, both official and civilian usage gradually shifted towards a unified kind of characters as a tool for recording and social communication, playing a significant role in strengthening interactions among different ethnic groups and enhancing the Han ethnic identity.

By the Han Dynasty, clerical script replaced small seal script as the primary script, marking the transition from ancient script to clerical and regular script. *Book of Han · Literature Records* states that clerical script originated in the Qin Dynasty and was created as a simplified script to handle busy official and legal matters.

However, archaeological findings of Qin-era textual materials suggest that clerical script emerged in the late Warring States period.

During this time, people in the Qin State had already been continuously modifying the formal shapes of characters for convenience in daily writing, creating colloquial forms of Qin characters. In the colloquial forms of Qin characters, the use of square and angular strokes to alter the round turns of regular seal script became popular, imparting a distinct clerical script flavor.

In inscriptions from the time of Duke Xiao of Qin, we can observe the coexistence of regular and colloquial forms, and a closer examination of the Qin bamboo slips from Shuihudi reveals that during the period of copying these bamboo slips, clerical script had already taken shape. Although the clerical script represented by the Qin bamboo slips had not yet fully matured and was still an emerging auxiliary script, it was evidently more convenient to write than the small seal script. Therefore, it quickly underwent rapid development.

It is generally believed that the era of Emperor Wu of the Western Han Dynasty was the stage when clerical script transformed from an immature stage to maturity. As a result, the clerical script from the Qin Dynasty and the early Western Han Dynasty is referred to as the early clerical script. It is an immature form of clerical script, with many characters showing a clear resemblance to seal script (Figure 1.66 to Figure 1.70). After the late period of Emperor Wu, this phenomenon gradually diminished.

Clerical script is also known as "bafen," and this term probably appeared around the Han and Wei dynasties.

At that time, approximately starting from the mid-Eastern Han Dynasty, a more convenient colloquial form evolved from the daily usage of clerical script. This colloquial form had a distinct difference from the formal clerical script, so it became necessary to assign a separate name for the previously formal clerical script, leading

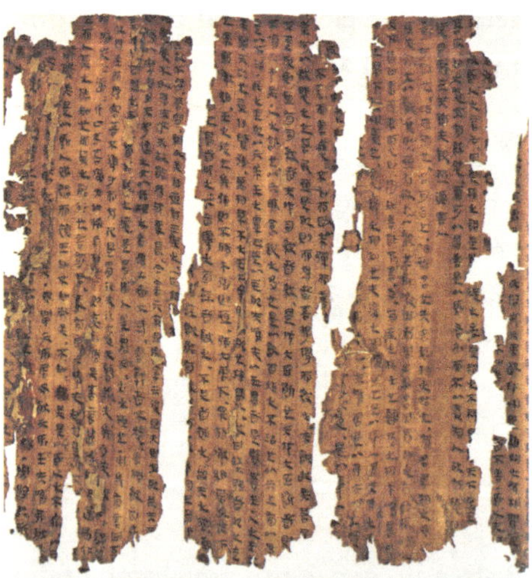

Figure 1.66 Partial view of the silk book *Laozi* from the Han Dynasty tombs at Mawangdui

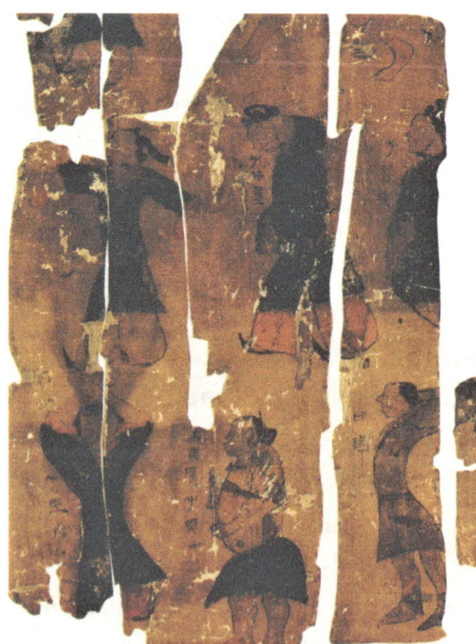

Figure 1.67 Partial view of the silk book *Physical and Breathing Exercises Picture* from the Han Dynasty tombs at Mawangdui

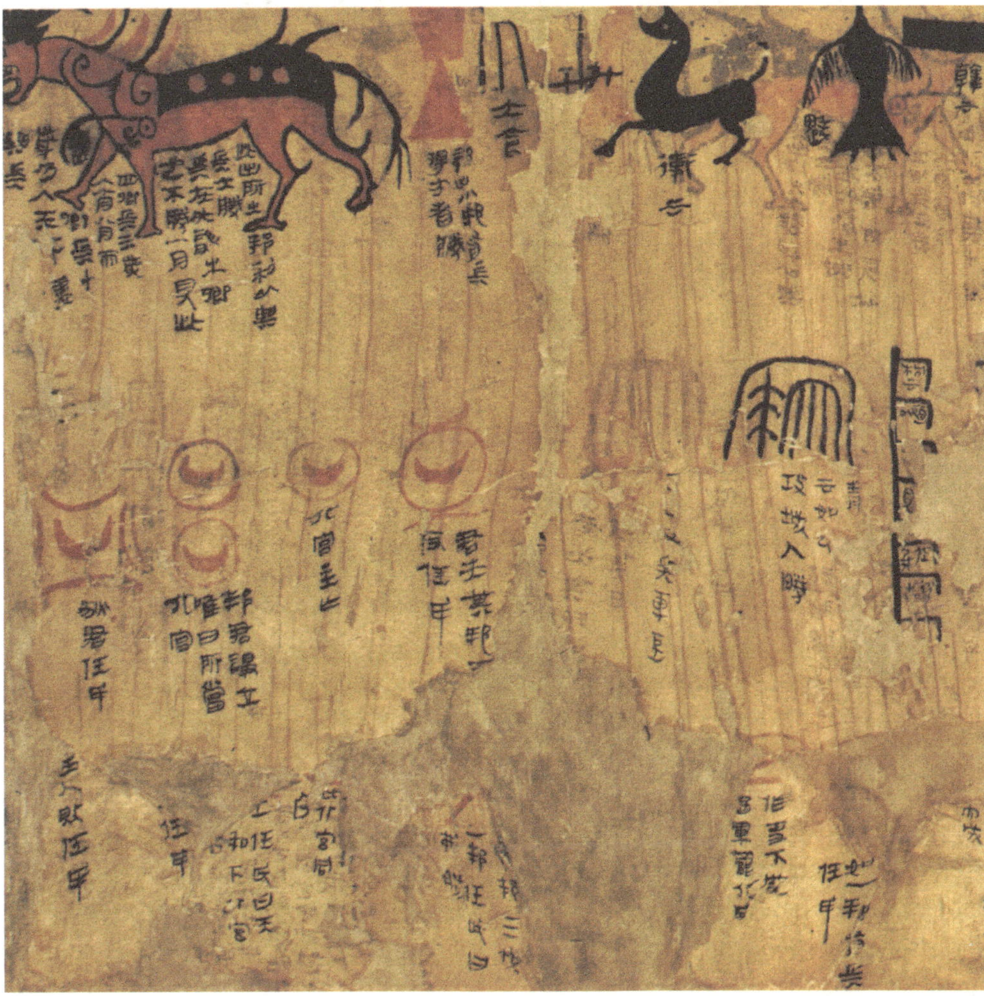

Figure 1.68 Partial view of the silk book *Divination by Astrological and Meteorological Phenomena* from the Han Dynasty tombs at Mawangdui

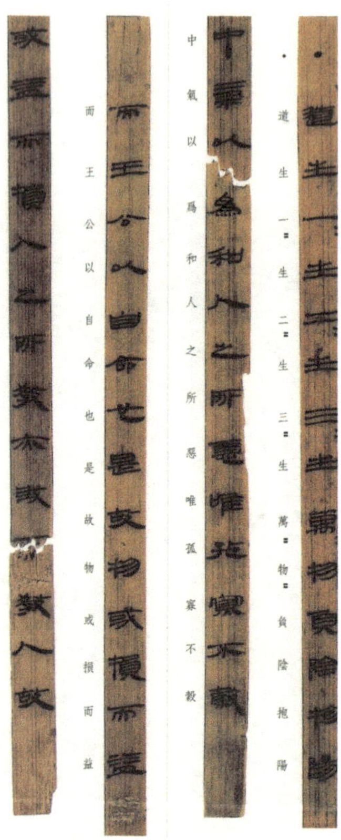

Figure 1.69 Partial view of the bamboo slips from the Han Dynasty of *Laozi* from Peking University

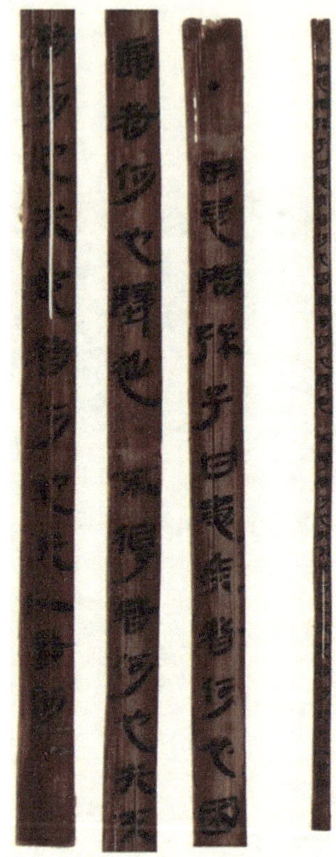

Figure 1.70 Partial view of the bamboo slips from the Han Dynasty of *Sun Bin's Art of War* from Yinqueshan

to the emergence of the term "bafen." Until the Tang Dynasty, people generally still referred to the prevalent script of that time (i.e., regular script) as clerical script while calling Han clerical script "bafen." In the history of character development, Han clerical script is also referred to as "fenshu" and "fenli," both of which originated from the name "bafen."

In the evolution of character forms, the transition from seal script to clerical script was the most significant reform. This transformation brought about a tremendous change in the appearance of Chinese characters and had a profound impact on their structure. It involved dissolving seal script, changing curves to straight lines, and extensively simplifying and omitting strokes of seal script (Figure 1.71).

During the Han Dynasty, in addition to clerical script, there was also cursive script (Figure 1.72 to Figure 1.74).

Cursive script can be broadly categorized and narrowly defined.

Broadly speaking, any hastily written characters, regardless of the period, can be considered as the cursive script. In a narrow sense, cursive script refers specifically to the type of writing that emerged during the Han Dynasty.

Approximately starting from the Eastern Jin Dynasty, in order to differentiate it from the contemporary new style of cursive script, the cursive script from the Han Dynasty was referred to as "zhangcao," while the new style was called "jincao."

The term "zhang" in "zhangcao" implies order and organization, and "zhangcao" was probably named because its calligraphy was more regulated compared with "jincao."

The formation of the cursive script came a bit later than "bafen." However, the casual colloquial form of clerical script, which served as the foundation for the cursive script, had existed early on. It is generally believed that "zhangcao" and "bafen"

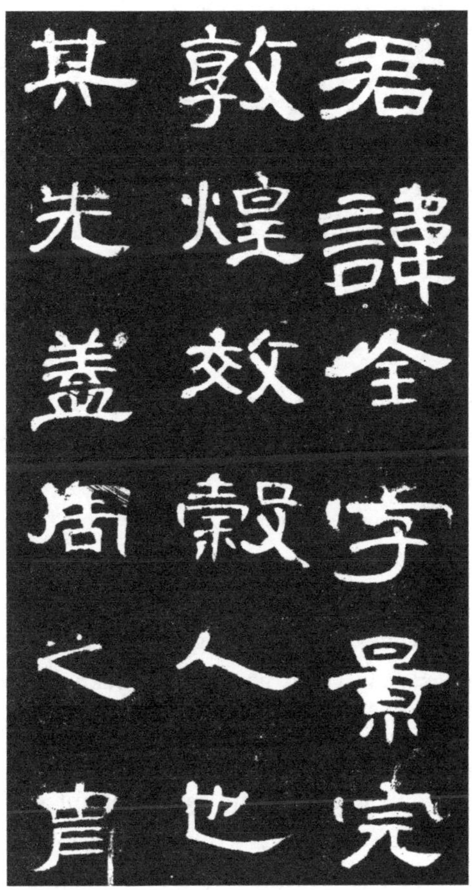

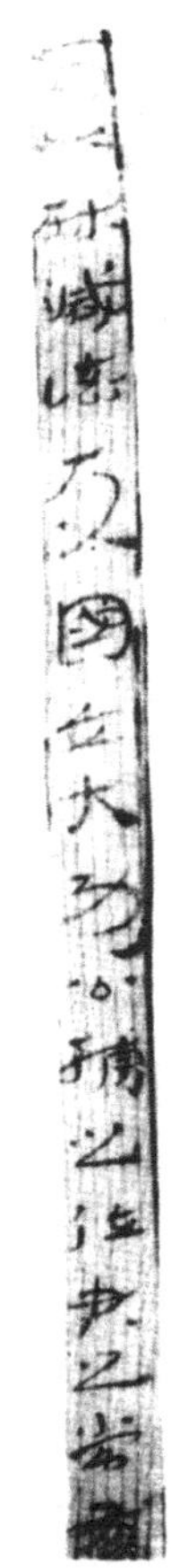

Figure 1.71 (RIGHT) Partial view of the Cao Quan Stele

Figure 1.72 (FAR RIGHT) Dunhuang Han bamboo slips

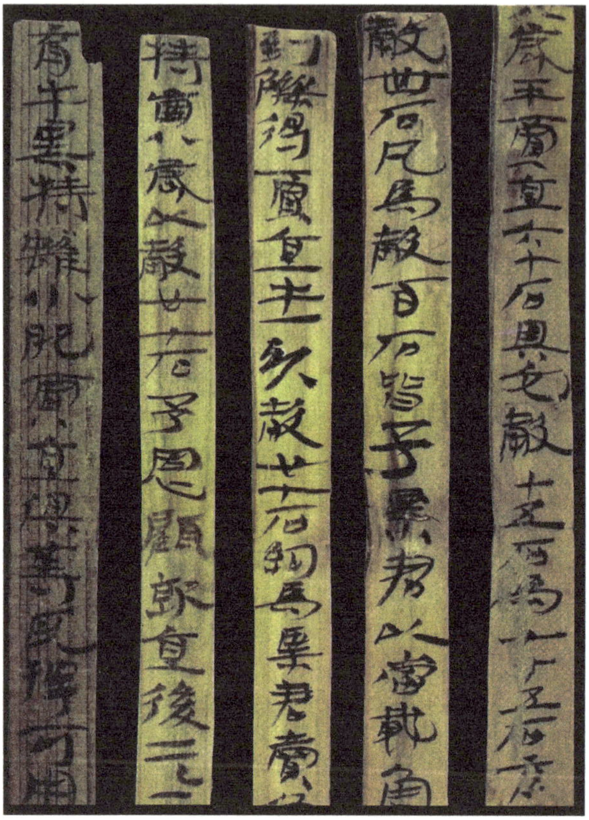

Figure 1.73 Partial view of Juyan Han bamboo slips

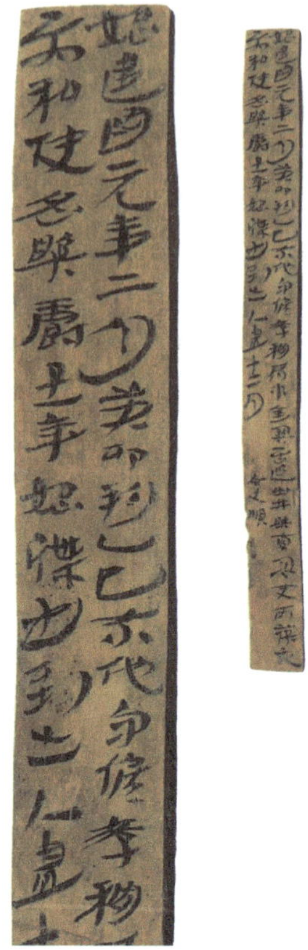

Figure 1.74 Partial view of Jianshuijinguan Han bamboo slips

originated from the colloquial form and formal form of clerical script, respectively, similar to how the formal form of Qin characters evolved into small seal script, and the colloquial form developed into clerical script during the Warring States period.

As a simplified script serving as an auxiliary to clerical script, cursive script was mainly used for drafting manuscripts and letters. It was also highly favored by calligraphers. It is said that several calligraphers of that time used "zhangcao" to write *Jijiu Pian* (the book used for teaching children to recognize characters during the Western Han Dynasty), but only copies have been passed down to the present day.

Today, people are fortunate enough to see examples of cursive script written by people of that time on the unearthed bamboo slips of the Han Dynasty. However, due to the overly simple nature of the cursive script and its proneness to confusion, it couldn't replace the clerical script as the main script.

In the late Eastern Han period, a new script called "semi-cursive script" emerged.

The semi-cursive script familiar to us today is a script that falls between regular script and "jincao." According to experts, the semi-cursive script may have been named because of its faster writing speed (Figure 1.75).

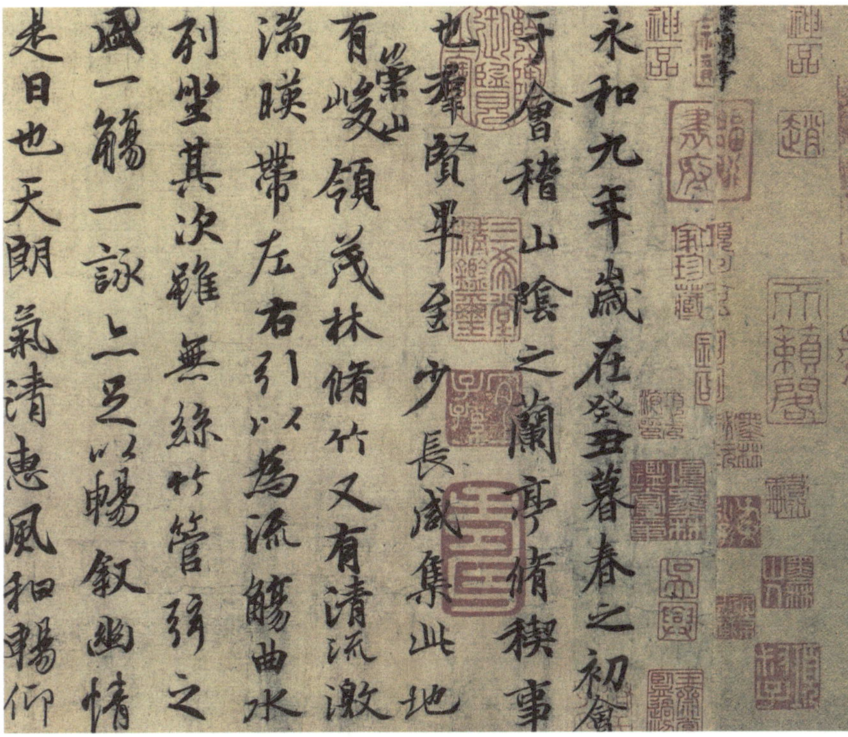

Figure 1.75 Partial view of *The Preface to the Collection of Poetry at Lan Pavilion*

After entering the period of the Southern and Northern Dynasties, the regular script finally became the main script (Figure 1.76).

"Regular script" is called "kai shu" in Chinese. The term "kai" means a model, so the original meaning of "kai shu" is likely to refer to characters that can serve as models rather than the name of a specific script.

After entering the regular script stage, the simplification of character forms continued. Due to different writing habits, a large number of colloquial and variant characters emerged, but the script itself did not undergo significant changes. Many later dictionaries, such as the *Yupian* and *Longkan Shoujing*, included a considerable number of colloquial characters alongside the formal ones.

The above is the main process of the formation and standardization of Chinese characters from their inception.

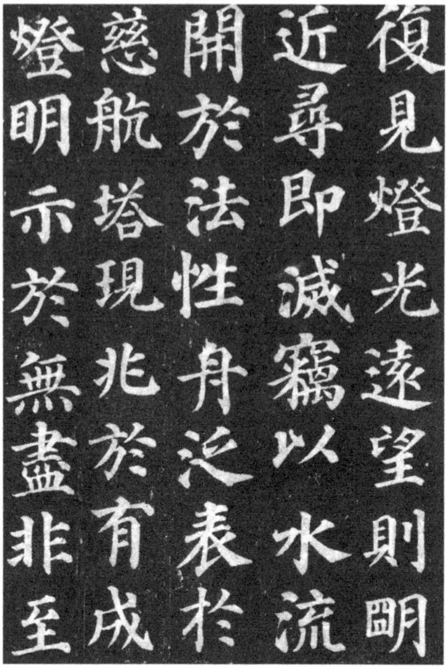

Figure 1.76 Partial view of a rubbing of Yan Zhenqing's inscription at Duobao Pagoda

In this lengthy process, it is easy to observe the developmental patterns of Chinese characters: the form gradually shifts from pictorial representations to strokes, from complexity to simplicity; the principles of character creation change from predominantly pictographic and semantic to predominantly phonetic-semantic; and the total number of characters increases, but commonly used characters remain around three to four thousand.

It's worth mentioning that after the New Culture Movement (1915–1923), there were opinions circulating in society suggesting that Chinese characters were outdated and should be eliminated.

For example, Mr. Lao She once said, "Chinese characters are difficult to recognize and even more challenging to write. If we don't try to change them, education will never progress easily."

Even in recent years, some people still believe that pinyin writing is superior to Chinese characters. They argue that many Chinese characters have too many strokes, making them inconvenient to write, and the multiple meanings of many characters are not conducive to learning Chinese characters and the Chinese language.

However, these views may not be entirely appropriate.

On the one hand, using Chinese characters to record the Chinese language has linguistic reasons.

Chinese is unlike other languages. In pinyin writing, a written unit can represent a word. However, in Chinese characters, a character may represent multiple words. The prevalence of monosyllabic morphemes and the abundance of homophones in Chinese make the use of Chinese characters particularly suitable. The combination of sound, form, and meaning in Chinese characters is advantageous for users to guess the meaning of the words and quickly distinguish between homophones.

This is particularly evident in picto-phonetic characters, such as "盉" (he) and "龢" (he). Although they have the same pronunciation, people can quickly differentiate between them based on their semantic components: "盉" is associated with utensils, while "龢" is associated with musical instruments.

On the other hand, each writing system has its own long-term practical process and must align with people's language habits and ways of thinking.

Throughout thousands of years of development and change, Chinese characters and the Chinese language have mutually influenced and permeated each other. Just as language shapes thought, Chinese characters also play a role in shaping people's thinking. When creating characters, individuals often incorporate their life experiences and various thoughts. Later generations, when learning and using these characters, are not only using them as a means of communication but also learning and inheriting their predecessors' life experiences and various thoughts.

For instance, the character "协" (xie), which means cooperation, used to be written as "協," composed of "心" and "劦." The component "劦" also represents sound. The character expresses the deep meaning of working together towards a common goal.

Due to the subtle influence of Chinese characters in shaping thought, people unknowingly accept the civilization and culture that Chinese characters represent when learning and using them. This enhances cultural identity and psychological identification. Therefore, the "standardization of Chinese writing system policy" has significant implications for strengthening national identity and promoting national integration, playing a crucial role in the formation and cohesion of the Chinese nation.

Furthermore, Chinese characters possess practicality and innovation.

Taking the *Kangxi Dictionary* as an example (Figure 1.77), although it includes more than 47,000 Chinese characters, upon closer inspection, many of them were used in history but are no longer in use today.

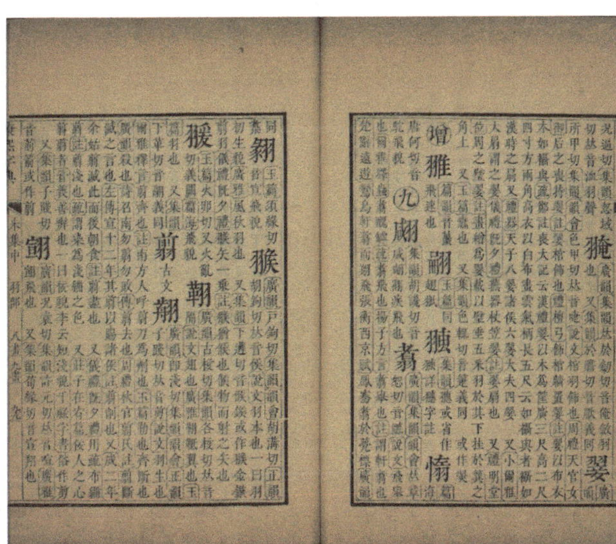

Figure 1.77 Shadow of the *Kangxi Dictionary*

This indicates that Chinese characters keep pace with the times and self-elimination during their usage. This is a significant reason why the scripts of many other ancient civilizations gradually declined while Chinese characters still stood out. Chinese characters' inherent innovativeness and practicality enable them to meet the diverse needs of different social classes in every dynasty.

In simple terms, over the course of thousands of years, although Chinese characters have undergone changes, the total number of commonly used characters has remained relatively fixed at around 3,000 for each era. As society develops and the amount of information people need to record using writing is increasing, Chinese characters must have the strength to evolve with the times. They continuously differentiate new characters, assimilate and integrate old characters, and eliminate unfamiliar and easily confused characters, thereby updating and developing the entire language system.

Even more fascinatingly, while characters were originally intended as a tool to record language, the development of Chinese characters and the Chinese language has not always been entirely synonymous. Besides accurately recording spoken Chinese, Chinese characters have the ability to give birth to new written systems. Examples include the talismanic script used in the Song Dynasty and the nüshu script (women's script) in the Qing Dynasty. They are both related to Chinese characters but have their own form, sound, and meaning systems. Although their usage is limited, they can fulfill the needs of specific groups. This is also a demonstration of the strong vitality of Chinese characters.

As research deepens, linguists discover that the functions of Chinese characters are more powerful than people could imagine.

With the development of society and economy, typewriters gradually became popular in China. Due to technological limitations, only English input was feasible, and Chinese character input was excluded from the new trend. However, with technological innovation in recent years, people suddenly realized that Chinese characters could be input into computers for typesetting and printing, and modern Chinese character input is also much faster than English input when recording language.

Furthermore, due to the relatively fixed number of commonly used characters (around 2,500), which is the fewest among various languages, Chinese characters, in the era of big data, are expected to unleash even more powerful vitality through cloud computing and associative memory methods.

However, with the advent of the information age, more and more Chinese people use computers for daily writing, and the opportunities for handwriting have decreased significantly. While some of the drawbacks of Chinese characters, such as difficulty in writing and numerous strokes, have been alleviated, concerns about the future of Chinese characters have emerged. People worry about whether future Chinese children will have a unique feeling for Chinese characters. In the information age, with closer interactions between countries worldwide, a large number of foreign words, neologisms, and internet terms have entered the Chinese character system. There is concern about whether the purity of Chinese characters can be maintained.

In fact, looking back at the history of the development of Chinese characters, historical Chinese characters were never entirely pure. The greatest advantage of Chinese characters lies in their ability to be inclusive and evolve with the times. The Chinese characters and language used today have derived from many other countries and ethnic groups in history. If Chinese characters cannot absorb and record the latest language, they will inevitably lose their functional advantages and eventually be abandoned.

From the characteristics of Chinese characters themselves, this does not seem to be a major concern.

Taking classical Chinese and vernacular Chinese as examples, there has been a significant change in people's language expression habits, but the Chinese characters used have not undergone massive changes. This indicates that Chinese characters have tremendous potential to record the Chinese language and can cope with significant language changes. Although some internet words like "囧" (jiong) and "槑" (mei) have taken on new meanings, their usage is limited, and it is challenging for them to enter the system of commonly used Chinese characters, let alone influence the system of Chinese characters. This is another powerful aspect of Chinese characters themselves.

Tracing the origin is a common human interest. In the field of Chinese character research, the exploration of character origins and the investigation of text structures are equally fascinating. As one of the world's oldest writing systems, Chinese characters are a crucial means of knowledge transmission and have given rise to a unique art form—Chinese calligraphy (Figure 1.78). Over the millennia, people have tirelessly delved into this subject, producing numerous renowned experts. This phenomenon is truly worth exploring in the realm of culture.

Additionally, Chinese is one of the six official languages stipulated in *The Charter of the United Nations*, and the role of simplified Chinese characters in international affairs naturally attracts attention. Chinese characters have also received acclaim for their concise expression, and it is said that the thinnest official document among the six UN languages is undoubtedly written in Chinese characters.

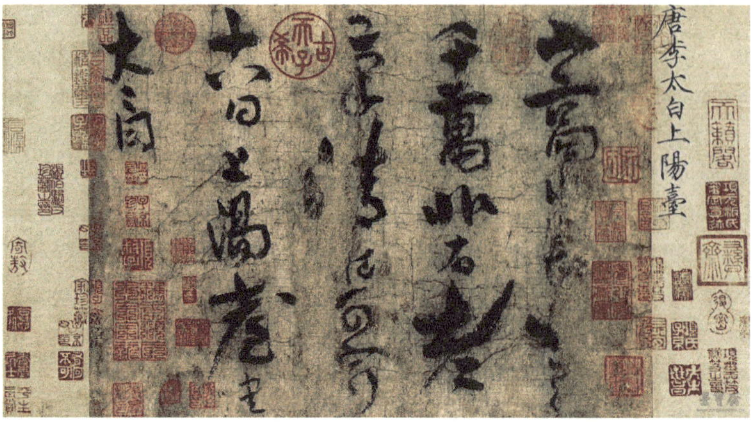

Figure 1.78 Li Bai's *Shangyangtai Tie*

Although having evolved through the ages, Chinese characters remain vibrant. They are not only a magnificent creation of the Chinese nation but also a symbol of Chinese civilization. With its powerful cultural influence, unique structural system, and unparalleled aesthetic essence in calligraphy, Chinese characters embody the fundamental characteristics of Chinese culture. They stand as a well-deserved cultural treasure in the world's heritage and are rightfully recognized as one of China's most significant inventions within the global community of nations.

CHAPTER II

Structure of Chinese Characters

1. Pictographs

Pictography is a commonly used method for creating characters in early writing systems. Its characteristic is that the character's shape resembles the external form of the object it represents, as described in the *Analytical Dictionary of Characters* as "drawing the object, following its form closely." Characters created using this method are referred to as "pictographs."

The oldest surviving pictographs in the world is the sacred script of ancient Egypt, dating back approximately 5,000 years. This type of writing was slow and challenging to decipher, and over time, even the Egyptians themselves lost the ability to interpret it.

Early Chinese characters, such as oracle bone scripts and bronze inscriptions from the Shang and Zhou periods, also contain numerous pictographs. For example:

日	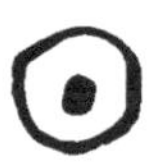	Resembles the shape of the sun.
月	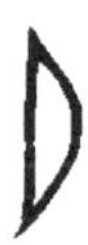	Resembles the crescent shape of the moon.
山	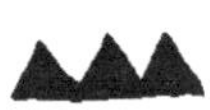	Resembles the shape of a group of mountains.
田	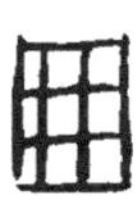	Resembles the plowed field, with decorative pathways.
木	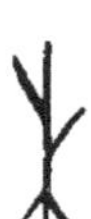	Resembles the shape of a tree, with branches above and roots below.
水	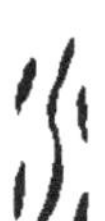	Resembles the flow of a river, with a prominent water droplet.
目	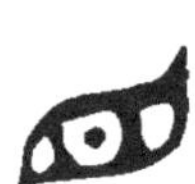	Resembles the shape of an eye.

角 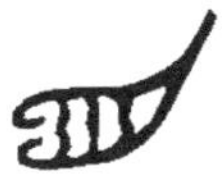 Resembles the shape of animal horns.

鹿 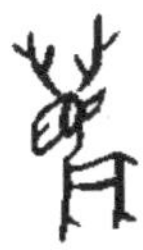 Resembles the shape of a deer, emphasizing the deer's antlers.

象 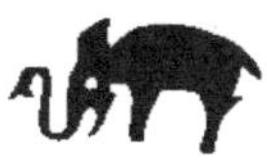 Resembles the shape of an elephant, with a prominent trunk.

册 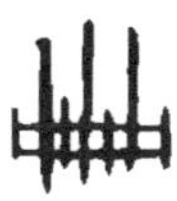 Resembles a bound book made of intertwined silk threads.

These pictographs are distinctive in that their written forms bear a resemblance to the physical shapes of the objects they represent. Therefore, simply by observing the character's shape, one can understand its meaning.

At times, pictographs also represent the whole object by depicting certain parts of its form. For example:

牛 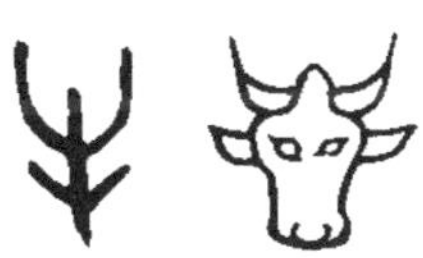 Depicts the head of a cow, symbolizing the entire animal.

竹 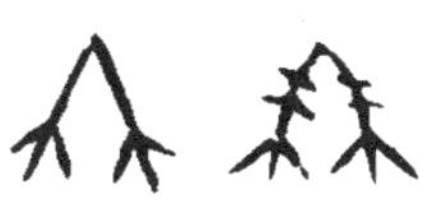 Depicts the shape of bamboo leaves, symbolizing bamboo.

Sometimes, pictographs, in order to make the represented objects more vivid, will deliberately add the images of related objects, for example:

眉 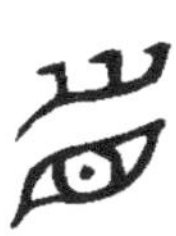 The character takes the form of an eyebrow, with the addition of the shape of an eye to indicate its position.

冒 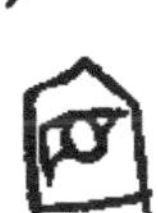 The character takes the form of a hat, adding the shape of an eye to convey the meaning that the hat is worn on the head. Later, it was written as "帽" (hat).

足 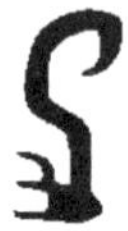 The character takes the form of a foot, adding the shape of the lower leg to indicate its position.

面 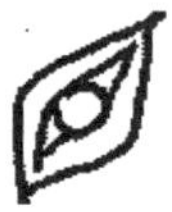 The character takes the form of the contour of a human face, with the addition of the shape of eyes to represent a person's face.

血 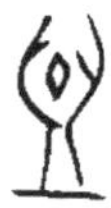 The character takes the form of a blood drop. Due to blood being stored in a vessel, the shape of a vessel is added.

州 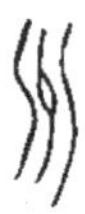 Originally referred to a small piece of land in the water. In order to emphasize, the river water is depicted together.

Sometimes, the concept of a group can be represented by the cumulative addition of pictographic components, for example:

林 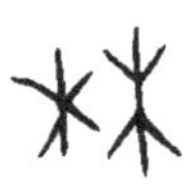 The character takes the form of a cluster of trees, and two trees are used to represent a forest.

艸 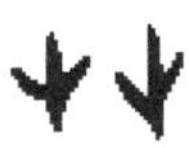 The character takes the form of a clump of grass, and two strokes of grass are used to represent a patch of grass.

茻 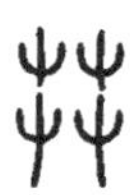 The character takes the form of a dense growth of grass, and four strokes of grass represent a large grass expanse.

Today, many Chinese characters have undergone significant changes, making it difficult to discern their original forms. However, do you know that they were truly pictographic characters originally? For example:

衣 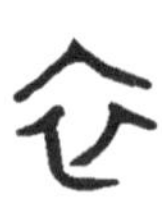 Resembles the shape of upper garments with a collar.

带 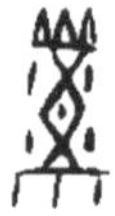 Resembles the shape of a belt with upper and lower cloth interwoven.

帚 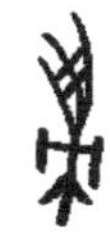 Resembles the shape of an inverted placed broom.

页 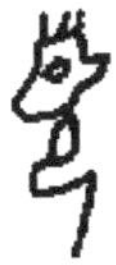 Resembles the shape of a human head.

须 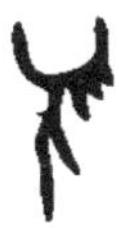 Resembles the shape of facial hair on the chin.

而 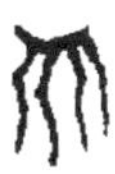 Resembles the shape of facial hair under the chin, later evolved into "耏."

文 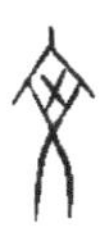 Resembles the shape of tattoos on the chest.

我 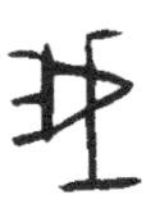 Resembles the shape of a toothed weapon.

There are also some pictographs, which have already been simplified in the oracle bone script. Without comparison, it's difficult to immediately discern the relationship between them and the objects they depict, such as:

刀 (knife): The full form is 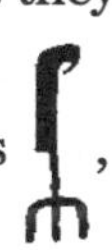, and the simplified form is 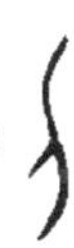.

Fortunately, these examples are relatively rare, and most pictographs are still relatively easy to recognize.

It should be noted that as a method of character creation, pictograph, despite its apparent simplicity, is not arbitrary. For example, in the natural world, both the sun and the moon are round. Why is the character "日" (sun) represented as a circle, while the character "月" (moon) is represented as a semicircle?

This is because the moon goes through phases, with the crescent moon being the most common state in a month, while a full moon is relatively rare. In contrast, the sun is always in a circular state. Therefore, when creating characters, ancient people chose the most common and distinctive features to represent them.

So, without meticulous observation and summarization, creating characters is not an easy task, even for pictographs.

2. *Indicative Characters*

Indicative characters are written symbols that convey meaning by adding indicative symbols to pictorial symbols and a few abstract symbols. Among them, some characters are equivalent to the "indicative" characters in the traditional six categories of Chinese characters.

Regarding the term "indicative," the definition in the *Preface to Analytical Dictionary of Characters* is "recognizable at a glance, observable upon inspection." In other words, it is a method of character creation. The forms of characters created by this method are easy to distinguish, and their meanings are also easily observed.

However, in the *Analytical Dictionary of Characters*, except for explicitly stating that the characters "上" (up) and "下" (down) are indicative characters, for the rest, even those recognized as indicative characters in later generations, Xu Shen explained them as pictographs and syssemantographs. Additionally, his definition of indicative characters is concise and vague, leading to considerable differences in understanding among scholars throughout history.

According to the research of Mr. Zhan Yinxin, traditional indicative characters can be roughly divided into two categories based on the emphasis on different perspectives: one focuses on "indicating" and thus can be called "indicative characters," and the other focuses on "things" and can be called "pictorial characters depicting events."

In the entire Chinese character family, indicative characters are not numerous and constitute a relatively small proportion. Common indicative characters include:

上  Positioned above an object with an indicative symbol added to signify its upper position.

下  Positioned below an object with an indicative symbol added to signify its lower position.

中 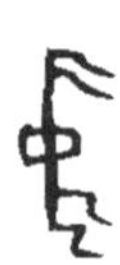 An indicative symbol added in the middle of a flagpole to indicate the middle position.

本 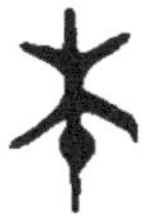 An indicative symbol added at the main root position of "木" (wood) to signify the main root of a tree.

末 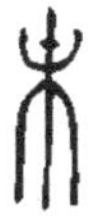 An indicative symbol added at the tip of "木" (wood) to signify the tip of a tree.

亦 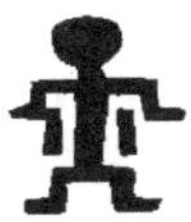 Add a directional indicator below the person's armpit to represent the meaning of the armpit. Later, add the "flesh" radical beside it, forming the character "腋" for "armpit."

厷 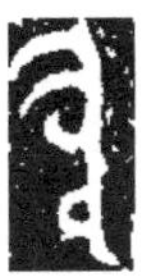 An indicative symbol added at the arm position of a person to signify the area from the wrist to the elbow. Later, with the addition of the "flesh" radical, it became the character "肱" for "forearm."

臀 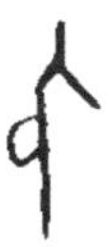 An indicative symbol added at the buttocks position of a person to signify the back or buttocks.

股 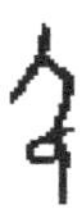 An indicative symbol added at the thigh position of a person to signify the thigh.

膝 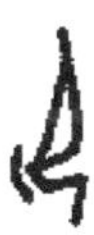 An indicative symbol added at the knee position of a person to signify the knee.

腓 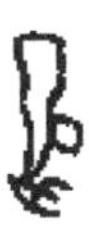 An indicative symbol added at the calf position of a person to signify the shin and calf.

甘 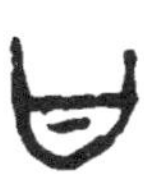 An indicative symbol added at the location of the mouth and tongue to signify sweetness and tastiness.

曰  An indicative symbol added outside the mouth to signify speech.

兀 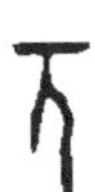 An indicative symbol added above a person's head to signify loftiness or being alone.

弦 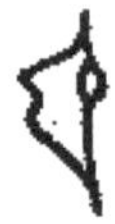 An indicative symbol added at the position of a bowstring to signify the bowstring.

刃 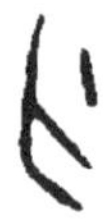 An indicative symbol added at a knife's blade position to signify the sharp edge.

亡 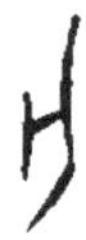 An indicative symbol added at the blade position of a knife to signify the sharp edge and later transformed into "芒."

尤 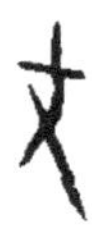 An indicative symbol added at the position of fingers to signify warts and later transformed into "疣."

3. Pictorial Characters Depicting Events

In ancient writing, there are certain individual characters that visually resemble pictographs. However, in terms of meaning, they do not represent tangible objects but rather intangible concepts. Mr. Qiu Xigui referred to them as "pictorial-type characters depicting events," while Mr. Zhan Yinxin directly termed them "pictorial characters depicting events."

Pictorial characters depicting events are a type of writing that falls between pictographs and syssemantographs. Common examples of pictorial characters depicting events include:

一 Represented by a single horizontal stroke to indicate the quantity one.

二 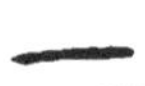 Represented by two horizontal strokes to indicate the quantity two.

三  Represented by three horizontal strokes to indicate the quantity three.

四  Represented by four horizontal strokes to indicate the quantity four.

五	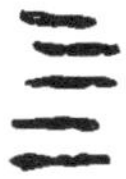	Represented by five horizontal strokes to indicate the quantity five.
方	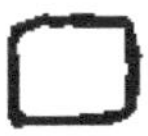	Represented by a square to signify a square shape.
圆	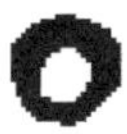	Represented by a circle to signify a circular shape.
小	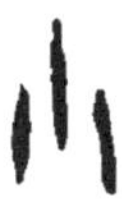	Represented by the image of a water droplet or grain of sand to indicate smallness.
大	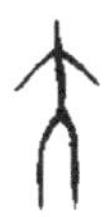	Represented by the standing figure of an adult to indicate largeness.
夨	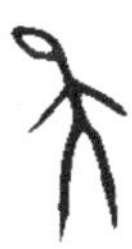	Represented by the side view of an adult figure to indicate tilt or inclination.
屰	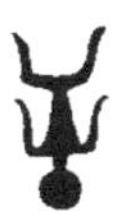	Represented by the inverted figure of an adult to indicate inversion.
走	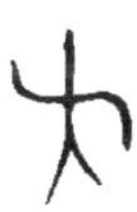	Represented by the image of a person swinging both hands to indicate running.
身	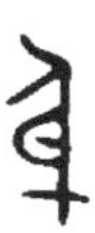	Represented by the image of a protruding belly to indicate Pregnancy.
永	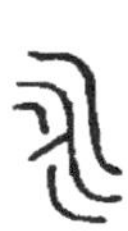	Represented by the flowing water to indicate Perpetuity.
卜	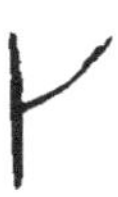	Represented by the image of cracks on a tortoise shell during burning to indicate divination.
才	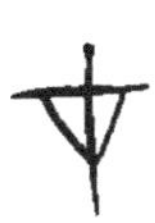	Represented by the image of young grass breaking through the soil to indicate beginnings or birth.

回 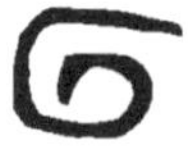 Represented by the coiling or rotating image to indicate Revolving.

黹 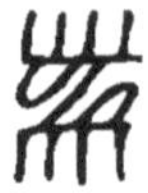 Represented by the image of a cloth sewn from top to bottom to indicate sewing.

勿 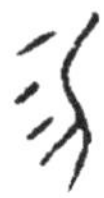 A dot added near the character “刀” (knife) to indicate cutting. Later replaced by the character “刎” to convey the same meaning.

彭 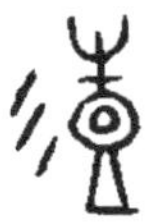 Dots added next to the drum image to indicate the sound of beating a drum.

眔 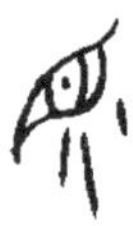 A dot added near the eye image to indicate the range of vision.

尨 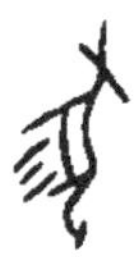 Multiple lines added next to the character “犬” (dog) to indicate a furry dog.

冬 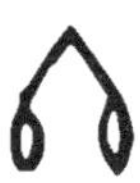 Indicative symbols added at both ends of a silk rope to indicate the end. Later replaced by the character “终” to convey the same meaning.

爪 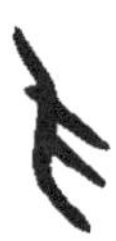 Represented by the hand shape grabbing downward to indicate a grasping action.

交 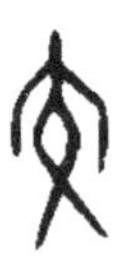 Represented by the image of two crossed lower legs to indicate crossing.

并 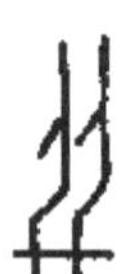 Represented by the image of tying the lower legs of two people together to indicate merging.

力 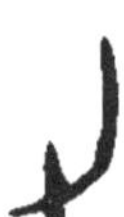 Represented by the image of a farming tool plow to indicate strength.

4. Syssemantographs

If a composite character combines two or more structural symbols to represent a meaning different from the individual meanings of these symbols, it is termed a "syssemantograph."

In terms of the ideographic method of structural symbols, syssemantographs can be divided into two categories. One is based on the form. That is to say, the meaning is conveyed through the visual representation of the structural symbols. For example:

陷	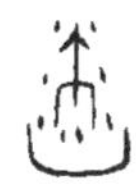	Resembles the form of a cow falling into a trap, with small dots indicating the fallen soil particles, symbolizing the concept of falling into a trap.
出	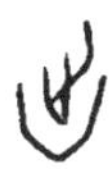	Depicts the shape of a person's feet walking out of a pit, representing the idea of departure.
即	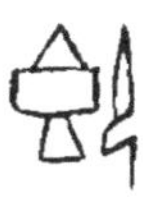	Depicts a person kneeling beside a food container, facing the container, symbolizing the meal is ready.
既	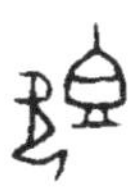	Depicts a person kneeling beside a food container with the mouth and body turned away from the container, indicating the completion of eating.
吹	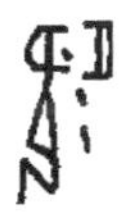	Resembles a person blowing air into a vessel with an open mouth, symbolizing the act of blowing.
执	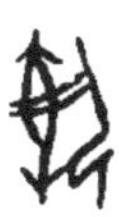	Resembles a person kneeling with hands trapped by restraining devices, signifying the concept of apprehension.
易	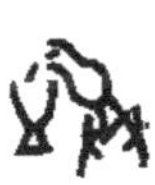	Depicts the pouring of liquid from one vessel to another using hands, symbolizing the idea of change.
铸	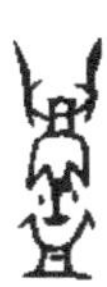	Resembles the pouring of molten metal from a crucible into a mold using hands, representing the concept of casting.
争	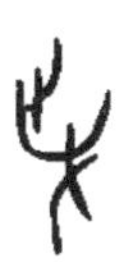	Depicts two people using hands to contend for an object, symbolizing the idea of competition.

斗 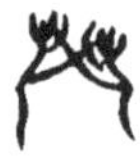 Resembles two people pulling each other's hair in a struggle, symbolizing the concept of fighting.

折 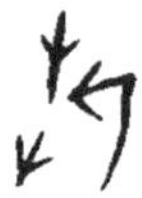 Depicts the act of cutting wood with an axe, symbolizing breaking.

辇 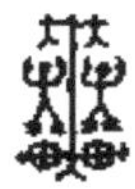 Resembles two people pulling a carriage side by side, signifying the act of drawing a carriage.

涉 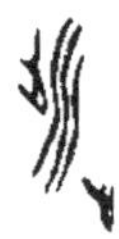 Depicts two feet stepping across a river, symbolizing the act of wading through water.

戒 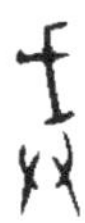 Resembles two hands holding a spear, symbolizing vigilance.

弄 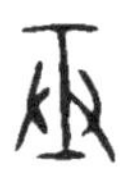 Resembles two hands holding a jade, symbolizing the act of playing and appreciating.

承 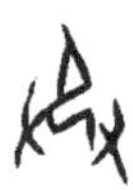 Resembles two hands lifting a human figure, symbolizing the act of flattering.

降 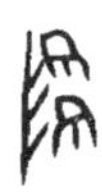 Resembles two feet descending stairs, symbolizing the act of descending.

为 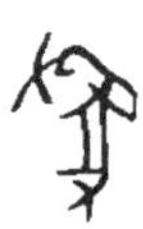 Resembles hands pulling an elephant, symbolizing labor.

及 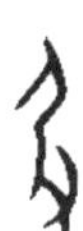 Resembles a hand catching a person in front, symbolizing catching up or seizing.

牧 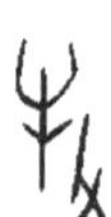 Resembles hands holding a whip guiding cattle, symbolizing the act of herding.

相 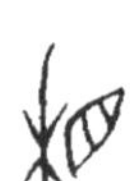 Resembles eyes examining trees, symbolizing the act of observing.

冓	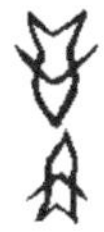	Resembles two fish meeting, symbolizing the concept of encountering.
利	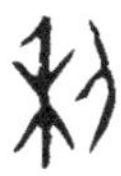	Resembles a knife cutting through the grain, symbolizing sharpness.
初	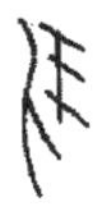	Resembles a knife carving marks, symbolizing the act of carving.
耦	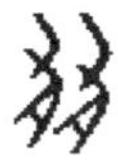	Resembles hands holding two plows for labor, symbolizing plowing together.
杳	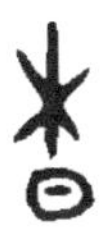	Resembles the sun setting below a tree, symbolizing darkness.
舂	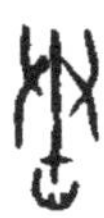	Resembles hands holding a pestle, pounding a mortar, symbolizing the act of pounding grain.
航	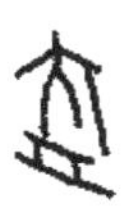	Resembles a person holding a pole steering a boat, symbolizing the act of navigating.
化	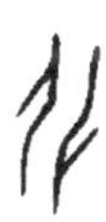	Depicts one upright and one inverted person, symbolizing the concept of change.

In terms of the ideographic method of structural symbols, syssemantographs can be divided into two categories. One is based on the form. That is to say, the meaning is conveyed through the visual representation of the structural symbols. For example:

The other type is semantic-based, which means the meaning is conveyed through the independent meanings of the structural symbols as standalone characters. This category of characters is less common among syssemantographs, and some common examples include:

尖: Combining "小" (small) above and "大" (large) below, symbolizing sharpness.
歪: Combining "不" (no) and "正" (straight), not following the correct or straight path, representing skewness.
嵩: Combining "高" (high) and "山" (mountain), symbolizing a lofty mountain.

掰: Combining two “手” (hands) and “分” (separation), symbolizing using both hands to separate an object.

嬲: Depicting two “男” (men) flanking a “女” (woman), symbolizing entanglement or teasing.

While analyzing characters’ structure, mistaking form-based compounds for semantic-based compounds can lead to misunderstandings. For example, the character “美” (beautiful) in oracle bone script is written as , combining “羊” (sheep) and “大” (big), resembling a person with horns on their head or decorations shaped like horns. This is a form-based character, expressing the concept of beauty or attractiveness. However, interpreting it as “big sheep are beautiful” would be incorrect.

So, how can one distinguish whether a character is a form-based or semantic-based compound? Two effective methods are:

(1) Based on the era of the character’s origin. Form-based compounds are more likely to have originated before the Spring and Autumn period. In contrast, semantic-based compounds are more common after the Warring States period and the Qin and Han dynasties. This trend aligns with the evolution of Chinese characters from pictographs to symbols. Generally, the earlier the era, the greater the likelihood of the character being a form-based compound.

(2) Reverse deducing based on the meaning of characters. The meanings of form-based compounds often relate to the original images of their component characters. For example, the original meaning of “删” (delete) was to use a knife to trim characters from bamboo slips. Thus, it combines “册” and “刀,” and “册” is the pictograph of bamboo slips. On the other hand, the meanings of semantic-based compounds often relate to the independent meanings of their component characters. For instance, the original meaning of “葬” (burial) was to bury, combining “茻” (plants) and “死” (death). In this case, “死” is used to represent a deceased person, but the image of a dead person is not visually evident in the character.

5. Syssemantographic and Picto-Phonetic Characters

In syssemantographs, if one of the ideograms conveys meaning and represents the pronunciation, it becomes a “syssemantographic and picto-phonetic character.” For example:

噎 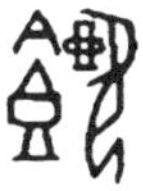 Resembles a person choking on food, symbolizing the concept of choking. The component "亚" () simultaneously represents the pronunciation.

龋 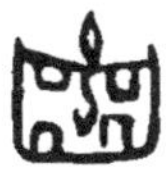 Resembles a tooth with decay caused by worms, symbolizing tooth decay or cavities. The component "禹" () simultaneously represents the pronunciation.

何 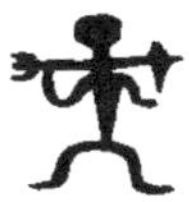 Resembles a person carrying a spear, symbolizing bearing a burden. The component "戈" (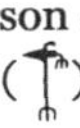) simultaneously represents the pronunciation.

冠 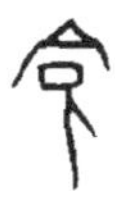 Resembles a person with a crown on their head, symbolizing the act of wearing a hat. The component "元" () simultaneously represents the pronunciation.

败 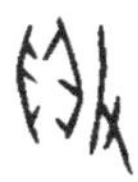 Resembles the act of striking a shell with a stick, symbolizing the concept of destruction. The component "贝" () simultaneously represents the pronunciation.

受 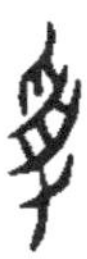 Resembles the act of exchanging objects with hands, symbolizing the concept of giving and receiving. The component "舟" (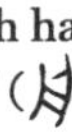) simultaneously represents the pronunciation.

Some syssemantographs originally lacked a phonetic function, but through the transformation of semantic components, they later evolved into syssemantographic and picto-phonetic characters. Examples include:

昃 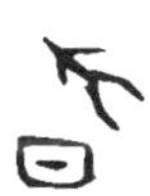 The oracle bone script of the character "昃" in the Shang Dynasty. It is composed of the components "日" and "大," using a slanted humanoid figure to indicate the meaning of tilting.

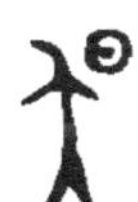 The bronze inscription of the character "昃" in the Western Zhou Dynasty underwent a modification, replacing "大" with "夨." The component "夨" simultaneously represents the pronunciation.

朝 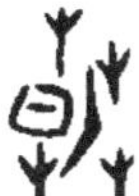 The oracle bone script of the character "朝" in the Shang Dynasty. It is composed of the components "日," "月," and "茻." It signifies the sun rising from the woods while the moon has not set, symbolizing the concept of early morning.

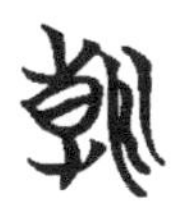 In the Warring States period of the Chu State, the character "月" was modified to "舟" in bamboo slips. The component "舟" simultaneously represents the pronunciation.

It should be noted that although the character "昗" changed its semantic component, the element "夨," which represents the tilted head, continues to serve a semantic function in this character, just as the original tilted "大" did. If semantic components in syssemantographs lose their original semantic function when acquiring phonetic function, the character would transform into a picto-phonetic character rather than remaining a syssemantographic and picto-phonetic character.

6. Picto-Phonetic Characters

Components of characters that reflect the category attribute or range of Chinese characters are called "semantic components," while those indicating the pronunciation of characters during the time of character creation are referred to as "phonetic components." Characters that possess both semantic and phonetic components are termed "picto-phonetic characters."

Xu Shen, in his work *Preface to Analytical Dictionary of Characters*, defined picto-phonetic characters as follows, "A picto-phonetic character includes a semantic part representing the category to which the character belongs and a phonetic part which is selected with a similar or identical pronunciation in colloquial language of the newly created character. This definition not only clarifies their concept but also highlights their advantages. They allow one to infer the attributes of things represented by the characters. For instance, characters with the "鸟" (bird) component are mostly related to birds, or they have evolved from the concept of birds. Similarly, characters with the "宀" (roof) component are generally associated with buildings or architecture.

The advantages of picto-phonetic characters extend beyond these examples. With one semantic component serving as a radical for multiple characters and one phonetic component providing sound information for various characters, a minimal number of semantic and phonetic components can be used to record a large number of characters.

In other words, the character-forming ability and capacity of picto-phonetic characters far exceed those of pictographs, indicative characters, and other character-forming methods. This is especially effective when recording abstract concepts without specific shapes, such as emotions like "苦" (bitterness), "怒" (anger), "怕" (fear), and "忧" (worry).

Furthermore, picto-phonetic characters overcome the limitations of pictographs, indicative characters, and other methods, which often prioritize form and meaning but face challenges in accurately representing pronunciation. Picto-phonetic characters seamlessly integrate the functions of conveying meaning and pronunciation, making the language recording more scientific and precise. This is particularly crucial in ancient times with diverse dialects and significant phonetic variations.

Moreover, the selected semantic and phonetic components in Chinese characters are generally simple and practical, making it easy for users to memorize and facilitating quick comprehension of meanings and pronunciation.

Therefore, today's Chinese children, after completing nine years of compulsory education, are well-equipped to meet their reading needs. With the help of dictionaries and reference books, they can engage in more advanced reading. The contribution of picto-phonetic characters to this ability is invaluable.

According to scholars' research, the use of picto-phonetic characters began as early as oracle bone script in the Shang Dynasty, such as:

祀 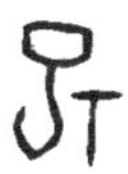 Originally meant sacrificial offering. It includes the semantic component “示” and the phonetic component “巳.”

问 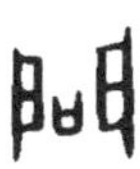 Originally meant inquiring. It includes the semantic component “口” and the phonetic component “门.”

物 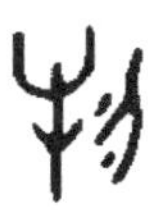 Originally meant a variegated ox. It includes the semantic component “牛” (ox) and the phonetic component “勿.”

违 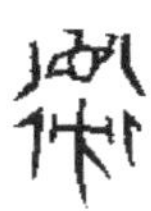 Originally meant to depart or deviate. It includes the semantic components “行” (movement) and “方” (direction), along with the phonetic component “眉.”

远 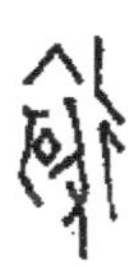 Originally meant a great distance. It includes the semantic component “彳” (footsteps) and the phonetic component “袁.”

近 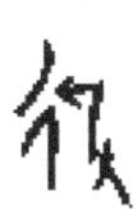 Originally meant a short distance. It includes the semantic component “彳” (footsteps) and the phonetic component “斤.”

辽 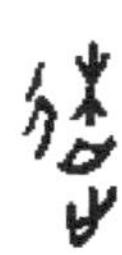 Originally meant distant or remote. It includes the semantic component “辵” (walk) and the phonetic component “尞.”

吝 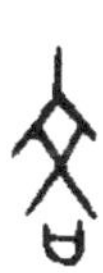 Originally meant to be stingy. It includes the semantic component “口” (mouth) and the phonetic component “文.”

渔 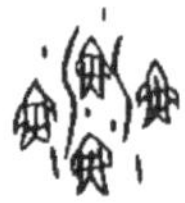 Originally meant fishing. It includes the semantic component “水” (water) and the phonetic component “鱼.”

刚 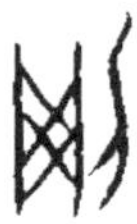 Originally meant hard or strong. It includes the semantic component “刀” (knife) and the phonetic component “网.”

Some picto-phonetic characters in oracle bone script still retain pictographic features, for example:

竽 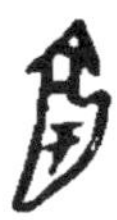 Originally meant a wind instrument. The character’s shape resembles the musical instrument and includes the phonetic component “于” (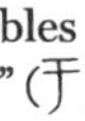), which also represents the reed and the shape of the musical instrument.

觞 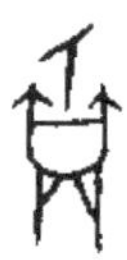 Originally meant a vessel filled with wine. The character’s shape resembles a wine vessel, including the phonetic component “丂” (), which also represents the shape of the wine-filled vessel.

麋 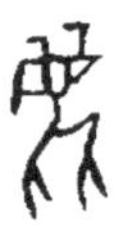 Originally meant a kind of deer. The character’s shape resembles the form of a deer, and it includes the phonetic component “眉” (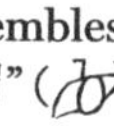), which also represents the head and eyes of the deer.

焉 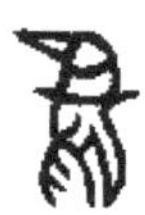 Originally meant a bird name. The character’s shape resembles a bird, and it includes the phonetic component “一” (———), which also represents the bird’s feathers.

However, in the oracle bone inscriptions of the Shang Dynasty, the proportion of picto-phonetic characters is relatively low. The number of them increased with the passage of time, especially after the Western Zhou period. Many pictographs, indicative characters, syssemantographs, and other types of characters gradually joined the ranks of picto-phonetic characters through changes in the principles of character formation (see the “Reconstruction Based on Principles” section of this book).

By the time of the Han Dynasty, picto-phonetic characters had become mainstream Chinese characters. Xu Shen of the Eastern Han period compiled more than 9,000 characters found in contemporary literature in the *Analytical Dictionary of Characters*. According to statistics, picto-phonetic characters accounted for more than 80% of them. Zheng Qiao in the Southern Song period conducted a statistical analysis of over 23,000 characters (including many colloquial characters). The results showed that picto-phonetic characters accounted for over 90%. Even today, commonly used Chinese characters are still predominantly picto-phonetic characters, and their proportion is higher for more obscure characters.

So, how many form components and sound components are there in Chinese characters?

This is a difficult question to answer. On the one hand, there are too many Chinese characters to conduct exhaustive statistics. On the other hand, many characters have complex structures, making classification challenging. Moreover, there are still many characters whose pronunciations and meanings remain unclear to people today, let alone classifying them.

However, attempts to classify Chinese characters have persisted from ancient to modern times.

Analytical Dictionary of Characters, compiled during the Eastern Han period, categorized Chinese characters into 540 radicals. The Tang Dynasty's *Kaiyuan Wenzi Yinyi* simplified this to 320 radicals, while the *Wujing Wenzi* divided characters into 160 radicals. The *Jiujing Ziyang* from the same period consisted of only 76 radicals. Later works such as the Liao Dynasty's *Longkan Shoujing* (242 radicals), the Ming Dynasty's *Leizuan Guwenzi Kao* (314 radicals), and *Zihui* (214 radicals) each made different attempts.

Today, experts have divided the Chinese characters used by people into around 200 radicals according to the needs of character retrieval. For instance, *Sea of Words* has 201 radicals, *Sources of Words* has 214 radicals, *Grand Dictionary of Chinese Characters* has 200 radicals, *Grand Chinese Dictionary* has 200 radicals, *Contemporary Chinese Dictionary* has 201 radicals, and *Xinhua Chinese Character Dictionary* has 189 radicals.

The establishment of these reference books' radicals has their respective academic basis and historical background. While these radicals are not exactly equivalent to form components, they generally reflect the form components' characteristics of Chinese characters.

As for sound components, there are more than 1,000. These form components and sound components complement each other, forming the modern system of picto-phonetic characters.

7. Characters with Two Pronunciations

Within picto-phonetic characters, there are instances where more than one sound component is present, or the form component also indicates the pronunciation. These are referred to as "characters with multiple pronunciations."

Among characters with multiple pronunciations, the most common are those with two pronunciations. Examples include:

扬 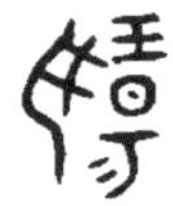 The original meaning is to raise or lift. Both "王" ( ) and "昜" ( ) serve as sound indicators.

旁 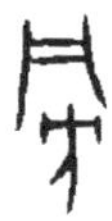 The original meaning is in all directions. Both "凡" ( ) and "方" ( ) serve as sound indicators.

宝 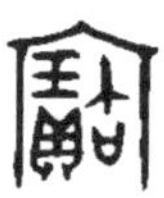 The original meaning is precious treasures. Both "缶" ( ) and "贝" ( ) serve as sound indicators.

竽 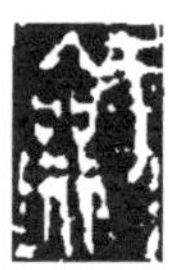 The original meaning is the name of a musical instrument. Both "龠" ( ) and "于" ( ) serve as sound indicators.

虖 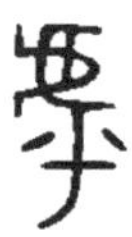 "乎" has an alternative form. Both "虍" ( ) and "乎" ( ) serve as sound indicators.

围 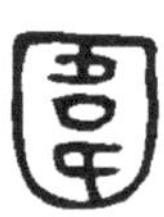 The original meaning is to surround. Both "口" ( ) and "韦" ( ) serve as sound indicators.

福 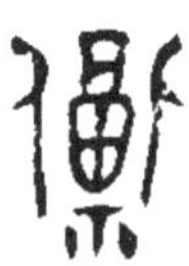 The original meaning is blessings. Both "畐" ( ) and "北" ( ) serve as sound indicators.

逋 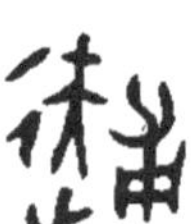 The original meaning is to escape. Both "夫" ( ) and "甫" ( ) serve as sound indicators.

Some characters did not originally have two pronunciations, such as the character "围," which was originally written as "口." It initially represented the shape of a city wall and conveyed the meaning of enclosure. In ancient writing, it was often used as a structural component, but later, the character "韦" was added to indicate its pronunciation, and it became an independent character.

Some characters appear to be characters with two pronunciations, but in fact, they are not. Misunderstandings often occurred during the evolution of Chinese characters.

For example, the character "望" was originally a syssemantograph. In the oracle bone script, it depicted a person standing on a mound of earth, emphasizing the eyes of the person and the standing earth mound, symbolizing the act of looking far into the distance.

During the Western Zhou period, the term "朔望" emerged, and by borrowing its pronunciation, a new character "朢" was created, using "月" as a semantic element. The *Analytical Dictionary of Characters* classified "望" and "朢" as two separate characters, but in modern simplified Chinese characters, they have been merged back into one character.

At first glance, "望" may seem like a character with two pronunciations, with "亡" and "王" representing its pronunciation. However, the bottom part of the character "望" is actually derived from "王" (𡈼, tǐng), indicating the concept of a person standing upright, rather than the character "王" representing a king.

Table 2.1 Evolution of the character "望"

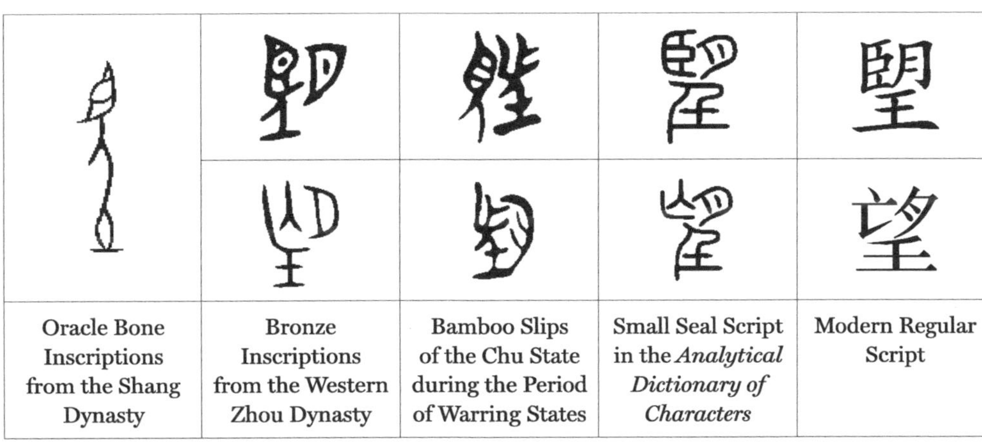

Oracle Bone Inscriptions from the Shang Dynasty	Bronze Inscriptions from the Western Zhou Dynasty	Bamboo Slips of the Chu State during the Period of Warring States	Small Seal Script in the *Analytical Dictionary of Characters*	Modern Regular Script

In the development of Chinese characters, the phenomenon of dual pronunciations is a special linguistic phenomenon that reflects the ancient emphasis on phonetics. Sometimes, based on the different sound components, it is possible to understand the phonetic changes of that time, providing important reference values in phonetics.

8. Variant Characters

The concept of "variant characters" was first proposed by Mr. Qiu Xigui. Later, Mr. Zhan Yinxin expanded their scope to mainly refer to the phenomenon of creating new characters by changing part of the sound, form, or meaning of an existing character. Common variant characters include:

(1) Pronunciation-variant characters

A pronunciation-variant character has a pronunciation similar to the original character but with a new meaning, such as:

"乒乓" (pīng pāng): These two characters were derived from the character "兵" (bīng). They have similar pronunciations but are used as onomatopoeic words unrelated to the meaning of "兵."

"毋" (wú): This character was derived from "母" (mǔ). Originally used as a negation adverb in oracle bone script, it was later modified to "毋" to distinguish it from "母," but its pronunciation remains similar to "母."

(2) Form-variant characters

A form-variant character's form is related to the original character's form, as shown in Table 2.2.

Table 2.2 Relationship between form-variant characters and their original ones

Original Character	Variant	Small Seal Script	Pronunciation	Character Meaning	Explanation
子 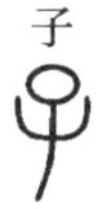	孑	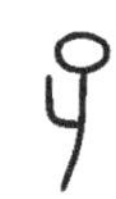	jié	*Analytical Dictionary of Characters*: "Lacking the right arm."	Both "孑" and "孓" signify a lack of one arm, and consequently, they carry the meaning of solitude or being alone. For example, expressions like "茕茕孑立" and "孑然一身" convey a sense of being alone or isolated.
	孓	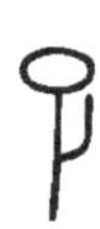	jué	*Analytical Dictionary of Characters*: "Lacking the left arm."	
	了	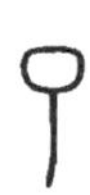	liǎo	*Analytical Dictionary of Characters*: "Derived from 子 (zǐ), lacking arms."	Having lost both arms gives rise to a sense of completion or conclusion.

行 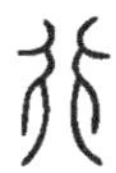	彳	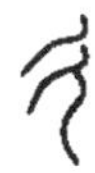	chì	*Zhengzitong*: "The left part is '彳,' the right part is '亍.' Components '彳' and '亍' form the character '行.'"	"彳" and "亍" each take half of the form of "行," hence, "彳 亍" carries the meaning of walking slowly.
	亍	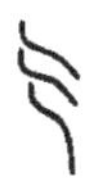	chù		

(3) Meaning-variant characters

A meaning-variant character has a connection to the meaning of the original character. For example:

"叵" originally means "not," as in "居心叵测" (having inscrutable intentions). In terms of character form, in the Bamboo Slips of the Chu State from the Warring States period, "叵" and "可" share the same form (). In the *Analytical Dictionary of Characters* small seal script, the character "可" (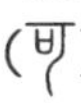) is inverted to create the variant character "叵" (). In terms of pronunciation, the pronunciation of the character "叵" is also similar to the pronunciation when reading "不可" (not permissible).

9. Reconstruction Based on Principles

At the inception of Chinese characters, most of them had a certain intention behind their construction, meaning they had specific rules and principles of character formation. These rules and principles are referred to as "principles of character construction." With the development and changes in the social environment, the principles of character construction in Chinese characters also undergo transformations.

For instance, some characters originally were pictographs but later evolved into picto-phonetic characters with the addition of sound or form components, as shown in Table 2.3.

Table 2.3 Examples of pictographs evolved into picto-phonetic characters

凤 Phoenix	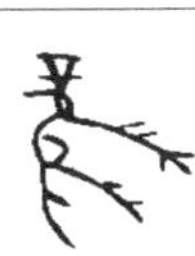	Shaped like the phoenix as imagined by ancient people	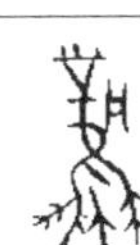	Added the sound component "凡" to indicate pronunciation
鸡 Chicken	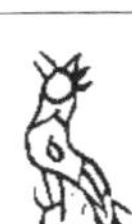	Shaped like a rooster	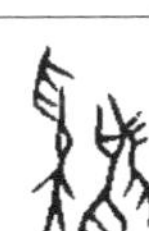	Added the sound component "奚" to indicate pronunciation

网 Net	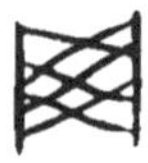	Shaped like a hunting and fishing net	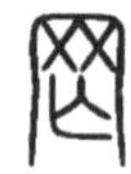	Added the sound component "亡" to indicate pronunciation
齿 Teeth	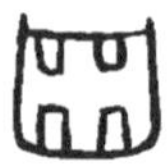	Shaped like teeth	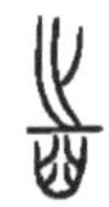	Added the sound component "止" to indicate pronunciation
鼻 Nose	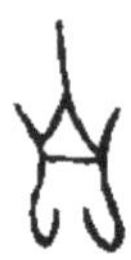	Shaped like a nose	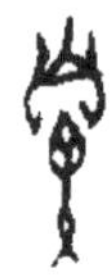	Added the sound component "畀" to indicate pronunciation
虿 scorpion	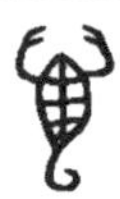	Shaped like a scorpion	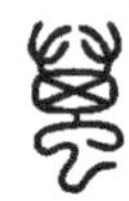	Added the "虫" radical to indicate its category
床 bed	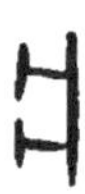	Shaped like a wooden bed	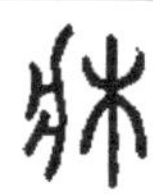	Added the "木" radical to indicate its category

Some characters were originally indicative characters, later evolving into picto-phonetic characters with the addition of sound or shape components, as shown in Table 2.4.

Table 2.4 Examples of indicative characters evolved into picto-phonetic characters

吻 kiss	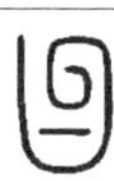	Represents the position of the mouth	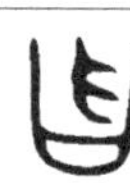	Added the sound component "勿" to indicate pronunciation
腋 armpit	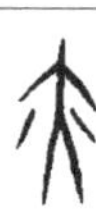	Represents the position under the armpit	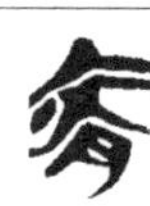	Added the "肉" radical to indicate its category
肱 upper arm	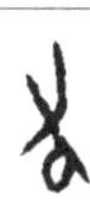	Represents the position of the upper arm	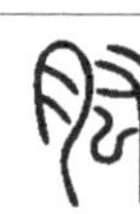	Added the "肉" radical to indicate its category
疣 wart	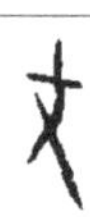	Represents the position of a wart on the hand	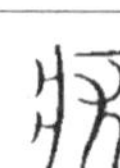	Added the "疒" radical to indicate its category

Some characters were originally pictographs, later evolving into picto-phonetic characters with the addition of sound or shape components, as shown in Table 2.5.

Table 2.5 Examples of pictographs evolved into picto-phonetic characters

戴	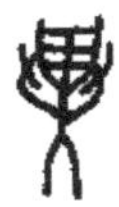	Shaped like raising both hands to put on a mask	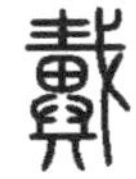	Added the "𢦏" sound component to indicate pronunciation
敬	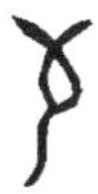	Shaped like captives from foreign tribes	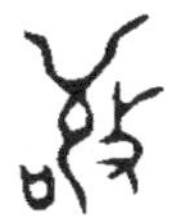	Added the "攴" sound component to indicate pronunciation
终	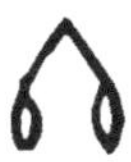	Shaped like a knot tied with silk threads	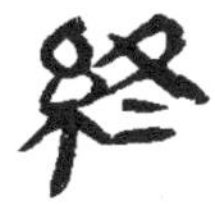	Added the "糸" radical to indicate its category

Some characters were originally syssemantographs, later evolving into picto-phonetic characters with the addition of sound or shape components or with the transformation of the semantic component into a phonetic component, as shown in Table 2.6.

Table 2.6 Examples of syssemantographs evolved into picto-phonetic characters

斗	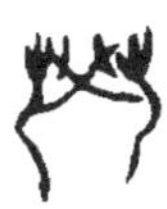	Shaped like two people fighting, indicating the concept of combat	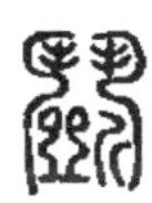	Added the "斲" sound component to indicate pronunciation. Alternatively written as "鬭," derived from the sound of "豆" (dòu)
夤	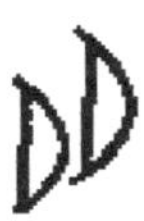	Shaped like two "夕" (sunset) characters, indicating the concept of deep into the night		Added the "寅" sound component to indicate pronunciation, while retaining one "夕" as a form component
奔	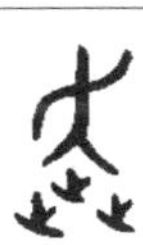	Shaped like a person swinging both arms and legs, indicating the concept of running	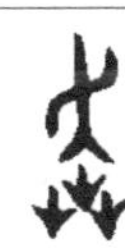	Changed the component "歮" to "卉" (bēn) to indicate pronunciation
居	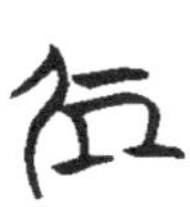	Shaped like a person sitting and leaning on a table, indicating the concept of sitting	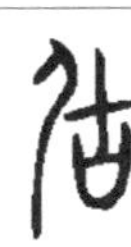	Changed the component "几" to "古" to indicate pronunciation
释	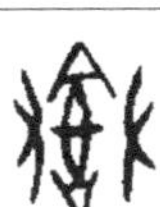	Shaped like hands bound together with handcuffs, indicating the concept of releasing	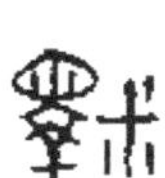	Changed to the component "采" with "睪" to indicate pronunciation

扶	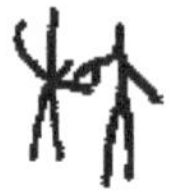	Shaped like holding hands, indicating the concept of supporting	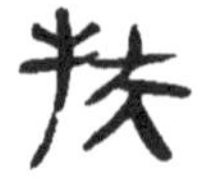	Changed to the component “手” with “夫” to indicate pronunciation
遘	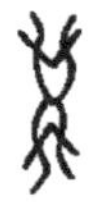	Shaped like two fish meeting, indicating the concept of encountering	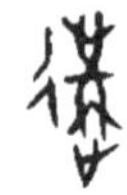	Added the “辵” radical to indicate action
搜	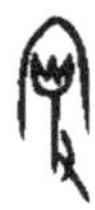	Shaped like someone holding a torch indoors, indicating the concept of searching	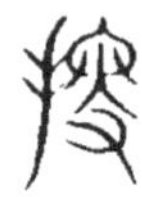	Added the “手” radical to indicate action
嗅	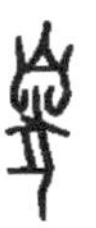	Dogs have a keen sense of smell, hence the character is formed with “犬” and “自,” indicating the concept of smelling	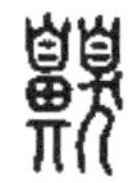	Added the “鼻” radical to indicate category

Some characters were picto-phonetic characters, later evolving into new picto-phonetic characters with the addition of sound components or modification of sound or form components, as shown in Table 2.7.

Table 2.7 Examples of picto-phonetic characters evolved into new ones

竽	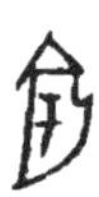	Shaped like the musical instrument “竽.” The component “于” indicates the sound	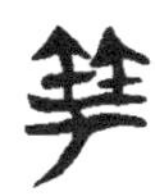	Changed the shape of “竽” to the “竹” radical, indicating the category of material
罪	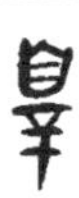	Originally from “辛.” The component “自” indicates the sound	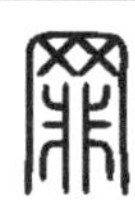	Changed to the “网” radical with “非” indicating the sound
觞	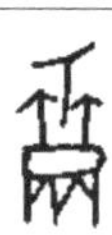	Shaped like a drinking vessel, originally from “斝.” The component “丂” indicates the sound	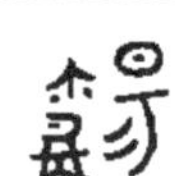	Changed to the “爵” radical with “易” indicating the sound
疗	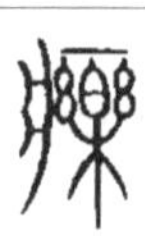	Originally from “疒.” The component “乐” indicates the sound	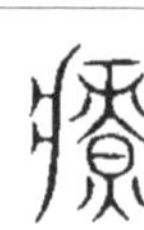	Changed to the “疒” radical with “尞” indicating the sound

It is not difficult to observe cases where the original structure of Chinese characters has been altered. These modifications generally follow two principles:

(1) To make the functions of expressing sound and meaning in Chinese characters more accurate. This is a major reason for the increasing prevalence of picto-phonetic

characters in the development of Chinese characters. Pronunciations can vary across different times and regions, so even in picto-phonetic characters, there may be instances of changing sound components.

(2) To make the writing of Chinese characters more simplified. This involves transforming the pictorial nature of characters into symbolic attributes. The character "竽" mentioned earlier is a typical example of this transformation.

It is precisely based on these principles that Chinese characters have been able to evolve with the times and continue to be in use today.

CHAPTER III

Evolution of Chinese Characters

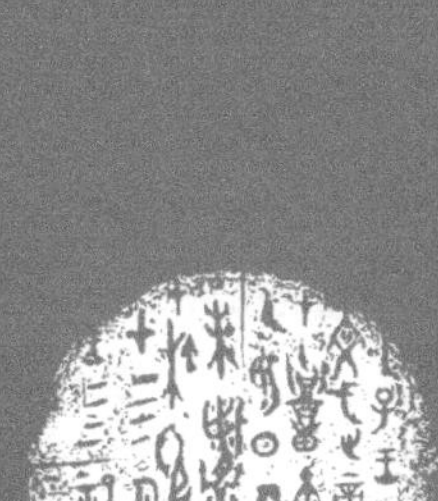

1. Cognate Graphs

Character forms represent the external appearance of Chinese characters, while in reality, they record meanings.

From the source perspective, if there is a relationship of common origin or derivation between any two words, they can be referred to as cognate words. Characters that record cognate words are called cognate characters.

In Chinese characters, cognate characters often have similar or identical pronunciations or are interchangeable in pronunciations and have a certain connection in semantics. Cognate characters can often be categorized into larger groups. For example, there are cognate characters related to the concept of "covering."

Table 3.1 Partial list of cognate characters related to the concept of "covering"

<table>
<tr><th>Cognate Characters</th><th>Pronunciation</th><th>Definition</th><th>Common Meaning</th></tr>
<tr><td>冡</td><td>méng</td><td>Originally meant "to cover," later often written as "蒙"</td><td rowspan="5">These characters all have meanings related to covering or concealing.</td></tr>
<tr><td>蒙</td><td>méng</td><td>Originally meant a type of plant, later used broadly to mean "cover"</td></tr>
<tr><td>朦</td><td>méng</td><td>Originally meant the moonlight being obscured by clouds and appearing hazy</td></tr>
<tr><td>矇</td><td>méng</td><td>Originally meant the sunlight being obscured by clouds and appearing hazy</td></tr>
<tr><td>幪</td><td>méng</td><td>Originally meant a cloth used for covering</td></tr>
</table>

Similarly, there are cognate characters related to the concept of "encountering."

Table 3.2 Partial List of cognate characters related to the concept of "encountering"

<table>
<tr><th>Cognate Characters</th><th>Pronunciation</th><th>Definition</th><th>Common Meaning</th></tr>
<tr><td>遘</td><td>gòu</td><td>Originally meant to meet or encounter</td><td rowspan="4">These characters all have meanings related to meeting or encountering.</td></tr>
<tr><td>媾</td><td>gòu</td><td>Originally meant the union of a man and a woman</td></tr>
<tr><td>覯</td><td>gòu</td><td>Originally meant to meet or encounter</td></tr>
<tr><td>篝</td><td>gōu</td><td>Originally meant a bamboo basket woven with overlapping bamboo strips</td></tr>
</table>

In the above two examples, cognate characters have the same sound components, and their meanings are also related. The ancient Chinese noticed this kind of correlation between sound and meaning early on. In fact, they even developed theories, such as the "Youwen Shuo" (using the sound element of a character to understand its meaning) from the Song Dynasty, led by prominent figures like the renowned poet and statesman Wang Anshi.

Additionally, there are some cognate characters with different sound components. In modern Mandarin, their pronunciations differ significantly, and there are also clear differences in their written forms. However, when examining the etymology of their meanings, they still belong to cognate characters.

For instance, in the case of characters related to the concept of "moon waning."

Table 3.3 Partial list of cognate characters related to the concept of "moon waning"

Cognate Characters	Pronunciation	Definition	Common Meaning
缺	quē	Originally meant a broken vessel, later extended to mean deficiency	These characters all carry meanings related to being incomplete or lacking.
阙	què	Originally meant the architectural structures on both sides of the ancient palace gate, with an empty space in the middle, thus meaning emptiness or vacancy	
决	jué	Originally meant a broken dam	
玦	jué	Originally meant a notched jade ring	
垝	guǐ	Originally meant a damaged wall or rampart	
刖	yuè	Originally meant the punishment of cutting off a foot	
髡	kūn	Originally meant the punishment of shaving off hair	
瞎	xiā	Originally meant blindness in one eye	
蘖	niè	Originally meant the regrowth of branches from a cut or fallen tree	
劓	yì	Originally meant the punishment of cutting off the nose	
刵	èr	Originally meant the punishment of cutting off the ears	
割	gē	Originally meant to cut off	

Furthermore, despite having opposite meanings, some characters may still belong to cognate characters and may even represent the differentiation of the same character. For example, "受" and "授," in the oracle bone script, both are written as 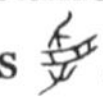. The hand (person) above represents giving, while the hand (person) below represents receiving. Although the meanings are completely opposite, they complement each other.

2. *Borrowed Characters*

In the documentation of language, if the meaning recorded by a character represents its original, fundamental, or extended sense, then the character is considered the "native character" of the recorded word. On the contrary, the character is referred to as a "borrowed character."

Scholars typically categorize borrowed characters into two types: those without inherent characters and those with inherent characters.

Borrowed characters without inherent characters refer to a word in Chinese that originally did not have a corresponding character. In such cases, characters with similar or phonetically related sounds are borrowed for recording.

Table 3.4 Partial list of borrowed characters without inherent characters

Loan Characters	Character Form	Explanation
六	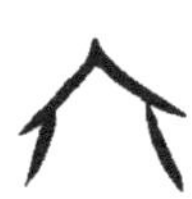	Resembles the simple structure of a thatched hut, the initial character for "庐" (hut or cottage), and borrowed for the meaning of the numeral "six"
七	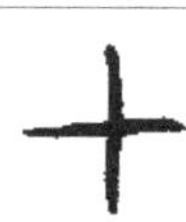	Resembles the action of cutting an object, the initial character for "切" (cut), and borrowed for the meaning of the numeral "seven"
九	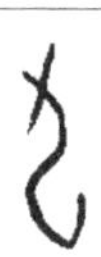	Resembles the shape of an elbow, the initial character for "肘" (elbow), and borrowed for the meaning of the numeral "nine"
我	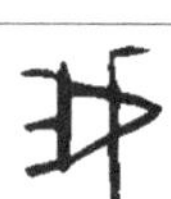	Resembles the shape of a weapon, originally with the basic meaning of a type of weapon, and borrowed for the first-person pronoun "I" or "me"

戚	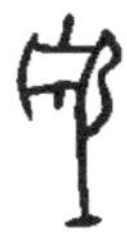	Resembles the shape of a weapon, originally with the basic meaning of a type of weapon, and borrowed for "戚" (relatives)
丑	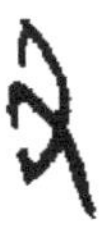	Resembles the shape of hands and claws and borrowed for the Earthly Branch name
巴	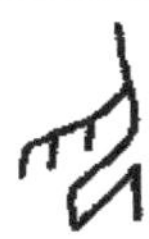	Resembles the action of a person using hands to pat the legs, the initial character for "拍" (pat), and borrowed for the term "巴" in "巴掌" (a slap)
庶	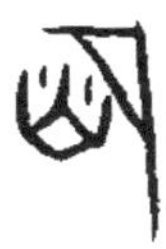	Resembles the process of cooking with stones on fire, the initial character for "煮" (cook), and borrowed for the term "庶" in "庶民" (common people)
东		Resembles the act of containing things in a bag, with ropes tied at both ends; the initial character for "橐" (a bag) and borrowed for the directional term "东" (east)

Borrowed characters with inherent characters refer to a situation in the Chinese language where a word already has a corresponding character, yet another character with similar or identical pronunciation is borrowed for recording. In the field of linguistics, this phenomenon is commonly referred to as "characters with shared pronunciations" (detailed in the next section).

In reality, if we classify based on whether there is an existing character, there is a special case. Some borrowed characters originally belonged to the category of those without an inherent character, but later, people specifically created a character to represent the borrowed meaning. For the word, it then possesses a "native character." Since this "native character" is a later addition, it can be referred to as a borrowed character with a subsequently created native character.

Table 3.5 Partial list of borrowed characters with subsequently created native characters

Borrowed Character	Character Form	Subsequently Created Character	Explanation
莫	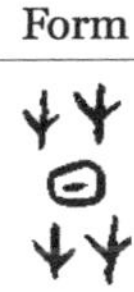	暮	Resembles the sun setting among the grass, originally meaning dusk

戚	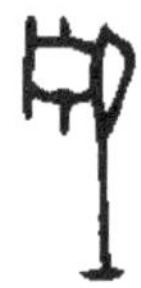	慼	Resembles the shape of a weapon, initially meaning a type of weapon, and borrowed as "悲慼 (戚)" with the addition of the "心" (heart) radical, indicating sorrow
北	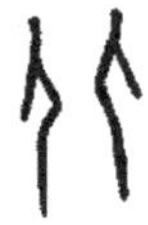	背	Resembles two people standing back to back, symbolizing departure; the initial character for "背"
然	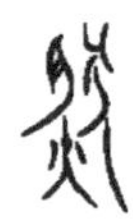	燃	A picto-phonetic character, originally meaning burning
或	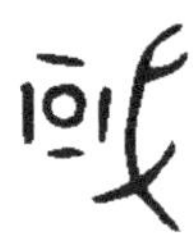	域	A syssemantograph, originally meaning an area or region

In the development process of Chinese characters, many instances of "borrowed characters without inherent characters" gradually evolved into "borrowed characters with subsequently created characters." This transformation has made the recording and usage of many meanings more explicit, allowing people to avoid numerous obstacles when reading ancient texts. This indirectly indicates that Chinese characters have been a highly adaptable writing system throughout history.

3. Characters with Shared Pronunciations

Characters with shared pronunciation, also known as homophonic borrowing characters or borrowed characters with inherent characters, is a phenomenon where ancient people substituted a character with a similar or identical sound for the intended character when recording meanings of words, even though the intended character already existed.

Why did the phenomenon emerge?

There are various reasons.

Fundamentally, it was for the sake of convenience in recording.

The principle of characters with shared pronunciation is based on borrowing sound to represent meaning. In the process of using Chinese characters to record language, as long as conventions were established and there were no communication barriers between recorders and readers, using homophones to represent words posed no significant problems. Therefore, some characters with shared pronunciation were widely used in a particular era and accepted as commonplace by the people of that time.

There were few characters but many words especially before the Qin and Han dynasties. In the absence of strict regulations for standardized character usage, people's daily use of characters was not as rigid as in later periods.

Additionally, the characters gradually became more symbolic after the evolution of Chinese characters into clerical script. Some characters became difficult to remember due to their complex forms, and with many characters having similar or identical sounds, people were prone to writing different characters hastily. Some of these alternative characters persisted and became characters with shared pronunciation after they were accepted by people.

The phenomena in ancient texts are extremely complex. Various relationships between characters with shared pronunciation and their original characters can be observed from different perspectives.

For example, phonetically, characters with shared pronunciation and their original characters often share similar or identical sounds, such as "畔 (pàn)—叛 (pàn)" and "亡 (wáng)—无 (wú)." In terms of character forms, if both of them are picto-phonetic characters, they may sometimes share the same sound component, as seen in "财 (cái)—材 (cái)," "涂 (tú)—途 (tú)," "说 (shuō)—悦 (yuè)," "刑 (xíng)—形 (xíng)," and so on.

From the perspective of borrowing relationships, there are distinctions between single borrowing and mutual borrowing.

Single borrowing means that A can be borrowed as B, but B cannot be borrowed as A, as seen in the example of "突然" (tūrán) where "突" (tū) can be borrowed as "涂," (tú) but "涂" (tú) cannot be borrowed as "突" (tū).

On the other hand, mutual borrowing means that A can be borrowed as B, and B can also be borrowed as A, as seen in examples like "已 (yǐ)" and "以" (yǐ), where both characters can be mutually borrowed.

Regarding the correspondence relationship, characters with shared pronunciation and their original characters generally have a one-to-one relationship. However, there are many characters that can be borrowed by two or more characters, forming a one-to-many relationship. For instance, the character "辩" (biàn) can be borrowed by several characters such as "办" (bàn), "变" (biàn), and "遍" (biàn).

With so many characters with shared pronunciation in ancient times, how can one distinguish them from the original characters when reading?

In general, when reading ancient texts, if a character cannot be interpreted using its original or extended meaning, one should consider whether it is a character with shared pronunciation.

Additionally, it is helpful to memorize some commonly used characters with shared pronunciation. Many ancient texts that people encounter today usually have explanations for phenomena like those in annotations. Reference books such as *Sources of Words* and *Sea of Words* also provide numerous relevant examples. These resources assist readers in overcoming obstacles related to this issue when reading ancient texts.

4. Ancient and Modern Characters

During the developmental process of Chinese characters, if a word is recorded with different characters in different eras, the earliest one is referred to as the "ancient character," and the later one is called the "modern character," collectively known as "ancient and modern characters."

Of course, "ancient" and "modern" are relative terms and do not specifically refer to ancient times and the present day. For contemporary individuals, the Qin, Han, Tang, and Song dynasties are considered "ancient." Still, for people in the Han Dynasty, the Shang Dynasty and the Spring and Autumn period are "ancient," while the Han Dynasty is considered "modern." Moreover, according to experts, the majority of ancient and modern characters were formed during the Qin, Han, Wei, and Jin periods. Therefore, the so-called "modern characters" actually have a long history.

Why does the phenomenon of ancient and modern characters occur?

This is because the primary function of Chinese characters is to record the Chinese language. However, the content of the Chinese language is vast, rich, and constantly evolving. This requires Chinese characters not only to represent the original meaning but sometimes also to represent extended and borrowed meanings. Especially in the earlier stages when there were few characters but many words, to fully record the language, a single character had to record several words.

However, if one character records too many meanings, and these words are frequently used, it is easy to cause confusion and affect reading comprehension. To clarify the meanings recorded by characters, sometimes it becomes necessary to find ways to reform certain characters to disperse their word-recording functions. The most common method is to create a new character. In this case, for the newly created character, the original character becomes the "ancient character," and for the original character, the newly created character becomes the "modern character."

For example, in the oracle bone script of the Shang Dynasty, the pictograph "自" was initially used to represent the nose. Later, "自" extended to meanings like "self" and "since," and the meaning of the nose was represented by the picto-phonetic character "鼻." When representing the meaning of the nose, "自" compared with "鼻" is considered an ancient character.

For example, in the oracle bone script of the Shang Dynasty, the character "禽" was written as , depicting a net used for capturing birds. Its original meaning was to capture or seize. In the bronze inscriptions of the Western Zhou period, it was written as , with the addition of the character "今" to indicate pronunciation. Later, it extended its meaning to captured bird species and further expanded to various flying birds. This usage persisted until the Han Dynasty, when the term continued to represent the act of capturing. For instance, in the *Records of the Grand Historian · Biography of Huaiyin Hou*, it states, "陛下不能将兵, 而善将将, 此乃信之所以为陛下禽也 (The fact that Your Majesty cannot lead troops but is skilled at commanding generals is the reason why I have been captured by Your Majesty)." Subsequently, a new character, "擒," was created, incorporating the hand radical. When expressing the meaning of capturing, "擒" became the modern character for "禽."

Sometimes, several modern characters can be differentiated from a single ancient character.

For instance, the character "厭 (厌)" not only represents its original meaning of oppression but can also signify satisfaction, aversion, nightmares, and other meanings. Later, the meaning of aversion continued to be represented by the character "厌," while the meaning of oppression was written with the addition of the radical "土" as "壓 (压)." The meaning of satisfaction was expressed with the radical "食" as "餍," and the meaning of nightmares was conveyed with the radical "鬼" as "魇." Both "压," "餍," and "魇" are modern characters derived from the ancient character "厌."

It is worth mentioning that there is a certain connection between ancient and modern characters, borrowed characters, and cognate graphs (as shown in Figure 3.1). They are not strictly exclusive of each other.

However, the relationship between ancient and modern characters and allographs is much more complex.

At first glance, both ancient and modern characters and allographs use different character forms to represent the same word. Moreover, like ancient and modern characters, many allographs originated in different time periods, making their differentiation somewhat challenging.

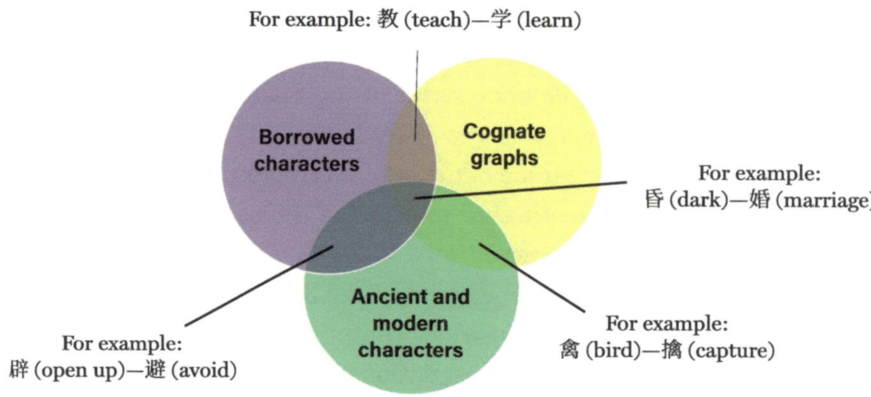

Figure 3.1 Relationship diagram of ancient and modern characters, borrowed characters, and cognate graphs

In most cases, the distinctions between them are relatively clear.

Firstly, ancient and modern characters can have different forms and different pronunciations, but allographs must have different forms with the same pronunciation.

Secondly, from the definition, the ancient and modern characters' ancient form and modern form cannot represent exactly the same meaning in the same era. For example, when using "鼻" to represent the nose, the ancient meaning represented by "自" for the nose cannot be used anymore. In contrast, allographs do not have this semantic restriction.

Take the common characters "韭" and "果" as examples. Both later adopted the addition of the "grass" radical in their writing forms, giving rise to the characters "韮" and "菓." As newly created characters, there doesn't seem to be a difference in the relationship between "韭—韮" and "果—菓." However, since "韭" and "韮" can be interchangeably used in any context, they are a pair of allographs. On the other hand, when representing the meaning of fruits, although "果" can be written as "菓," when expressing concepts like results or indeed, "果" cannot be written as "菓." Therefore, "果" and "菓" have different semantic functions and can only be considered ancient and modern characters.

5. Homographs

Homographs refer to Chinese characters with identical forms but differing pronunciations and meanings.

The nature of homographs is the opposite of allographs. While allographs may have different forms but serve the same function, homographs share the same form but represent distinct characters.

Homographs can be broadly or narrowly defined.

Broadly defined homographs arise when the same character is used to represent different words. This phenomenon also includes cases where one character is used to record multiple words due to semantic extension or borrowing relationships.

For example, the character "行" (háng) in "行列" is derived from the character "行" (xíng), which originally signifies actions or walking. These can be considered broadly defined homographs. Another example is the character "莫," originally meaning dusk, later borrowed as the negative adverb "莫." These can also be seen as broadly defined homographs.

Narrowly defined homographs specifically refer to characters with identical forms that lack semantic extension or borrowing relationships. In general discussions, homographs often refer to narrowly defined cases.

Common examples of narrowly defined homographs are listed in Table 3.6.

Table 3.6 Common examples of narrowly defined homographs

Homographs	Meaning
"吃" (chī) in "口吃" (speech impediment)	Picto-phonetic character Radical: 口 (mouth) Phonetic component: 乞 (ask)
"吃" (chī) in "吃饭" (eat a meal)	Picto-phonetic character Radical: 口 (mouth) Phonetic component: 契 Simplified form of "喫"
"体" (bèn) in "体夫" (laborer)	Picto-phonetic character Radical: 人 (person) Phonetic component: 本 (origin)
"体" (tǐ) in "身体" (body)	Picto-phonetic character Radical: 骨 (bone) Phonetic component: 豊 (abundant) Simplified form of "體"
"胄" (zhòu) in "贵胄" (noble lineage)	Picto-phonetic character Radical: 肉 (flesh) Phonetic component: 由 Indicates blood relations
"胄" (zhòu) in "甲胄" (armor)	Pictograph Represents the shape of a helmet, originally referring to headgear in the oracle bone script

"姥" (mǔ) in "天姥山" (Mount Tianmu)	Syssemantograph Combines "老" (old) and "女" (woman) Can be written as "姆," referring to an old woman
"姥" (lǎo) in "姥姥" (grandmother)	Picto-phonetic character Radical: 女 (woman) Phonetic component: 老 (old) Refers to a grandmother
"胜" (shèng) in "胜利" (victory)	Picto-phonetic character Radical: 力 (strength) Phonetic component: 朕 (a first-person pronoun by ancient Chinese emperors) Simplified form of "勝"
"胜" (xīng) in "胜味" (delicious)	Picto-phonetic character Radical: 肉 (meat) Phonetic component: 生 (raw) Original form of "腥"
"广" (yǎn) in "山广" (broad mountain)	Pictograph Represents the shape of a mountain slope in the oracle bone script
"广" (guǎng) in "广大" (vast)	Picto-phonetic character Radical: 广 (wide) Phonetic component: 黄 (yellow) Simplified form of "廣"

Homographs can easily lead to misunderstandings when reading classical texts, requiring careful attention.

For instance, when reciting Li Bai's poem 梦游天姥吟留别 (*Dreaming of Mount Tianmu and Bidding Farewell*), "姥" must not be pronounced as "lǎo," or even Grandma would burst into laughter.

6. Allographs

Allographs are characters that share identical pronunciation, meaning, and functional roles but differ in their graphical forms during a certain historical period.

The phenomenon of allographs has been present since the oracle bone inscriptions of the Shang Dynasty, as illustrated in Table 3.7.

Table 3.7 Allographs in oracle bone inscriptions of the Shang Dynasty

Regular Script	Oracle Bone Script	Explanation
牧	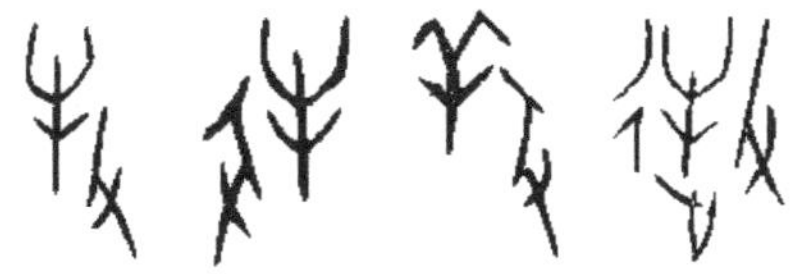	Depicts the shape of driving and herding cattle with a whip in hand, symbolizing the act of pasturing
牢	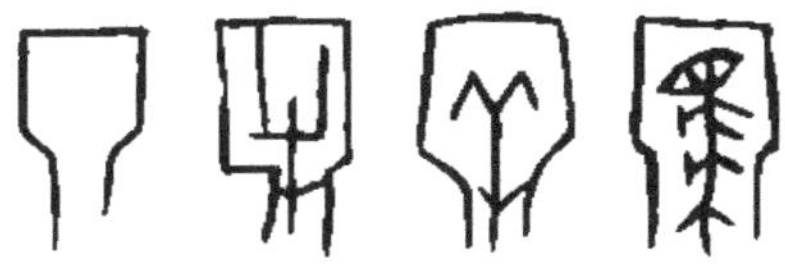	Depicts the form of an enclosure or an animal being confined in an enclosure, indicating the concept of an enclosure
陷	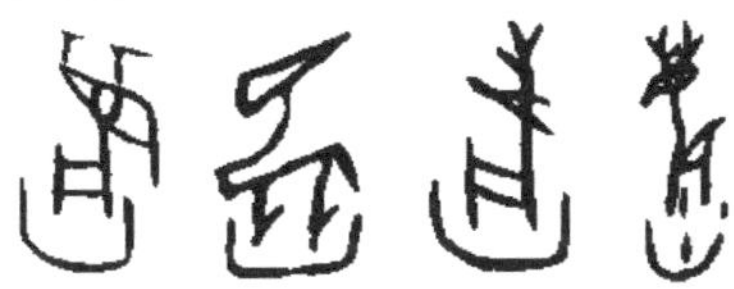	Depicts the shape of an animal falling into a trap, signifying the concept of a pitfall or trap
牡	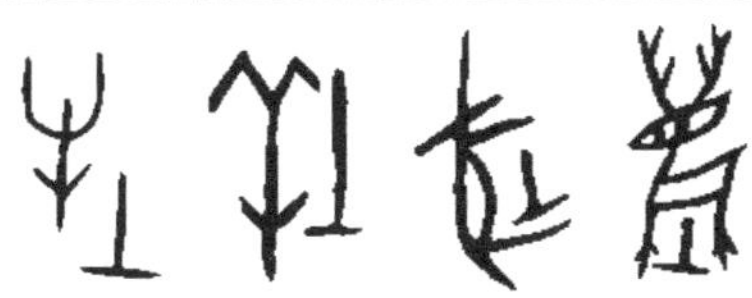	Combining the shape of an animal with symbols representing the male gender, indicating masculinity
牝	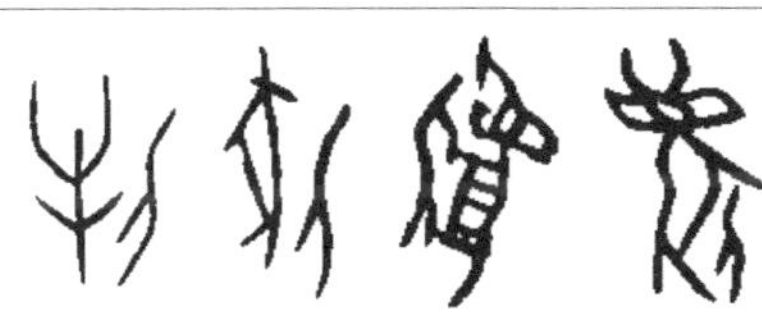	Combining the shape of an animal with symbols representing female gender, indicating femininity

After the Shang Dynasty, the phenomenon of allographs in Chinese characters increased rather than decreased. In different times, regions, and perspectives, people may choose different methods of character creation, select different components using the same method, or use the same components but arrange them differently to create characters for the same word, resulting in allographs.

(1) Allographs with different semantic components

In Chinese characters, similar radicals are sometimes interchangeable (as seen in the above examples of oracle bone inscriptions), resulting in numerous allographs, such as "磷—燐," "坑—阬," and "哲—悊."

(2) Allographs with different phonetic components

Chinese characters with the same pronunciation are numerous. And they can be distinguished by different phonetic components, like "裤—袴," "线—線," etc.

(3) Allographs with different positions of radicals

Throughout the development of Chinese characters, due to variations in writing materials and methods, a large number of allographs with flexible radical positions emerged, such as "翅—翄," "峰—峯," "群—羣," "略—畧," and "概—槩." Sometimes, a single character can have several allographs due to different radical positions, as seen in "鹅—鵞—䳘—鵝."

(4) Allographs with different methods of character creation

Different periods and distinct principles of character creation have led to a significant number of allographs, such as "哲—喆," "泪—淚," and "罪—辠."

Due to the overwhelming number of allographs, an effort was made to standardize the use of characters and simplify the number of Chinese characters for daily use. In 1955, the Ministry of Culture of the People's Republic of China and the Committee for Language Reform of China jointly issued the *First Batch of Allographs Sorting Table*, abolishing 1,055 commonly used allographs and significantly reducing the burden of character recognition. This move has made the application of Chinese characters more scientific and rational.

7. Characters in Popular Form

Characters in popular form, also known as colloquial characters, refer to a type of commonly used Chinese characters that differ from characters in standard form. The term "characters in standard form" generally implies characters that conform to the principles outlined in the *Analytical Dictionary of Characters*, have a certain structural basis, are officially recognized, and are used in formal situations as legitimate and standardized writing.

The concept of "characters in popular form" was first introduced during the Tang Dynasty. Yan Yuansun, in his work *Ganlu Zishu*, divided Chinese characters into three categories: popular, common, and standard. In his view, characters in popular form were considered as a form of simple writing that might not adhere strictly to the principles, unsuitable in formal contexts, but suitable for use by common people.

In other words, characters in popular form are non-standard allographs that were popular in various historical periods.

The Dunhuang manuscripts and many calligraphic works of the Tang Dynasty are filled with numerous popular characters. However, popular characters did not necessarily originate in the Tang Dynasty. A significant portion has been passed down from history. For instance, inscriptions on bronze mirrors of the Han Dynasty and inscriptions on stone tablets of the Six Dynasties contain many popular characters.

Throughout history, popular characters have demonstrated remarkable vitality. The eminent linguist Zhou Youguang once remarked, "The emergence of popular characters has never ceased in history. Popular characters are used not only in casual situations but also on solemn occasions. They are employed not only by ordinary writers but also by those who have undergone strict textual training. Popular characters can be found in various scripts, representing a form of simplified structure not constrained by formalities."

Table 3.8 Examples of Dunhuang popular characters

Character Radical	Character Form	Character Radical	Character Form	Character Radical	Character Form
各	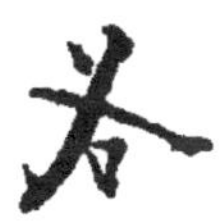	歌	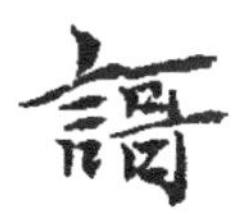	稿	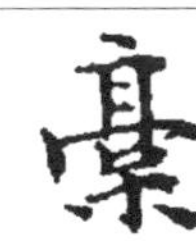
钢	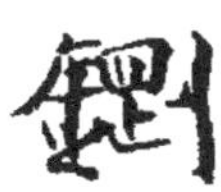	凫	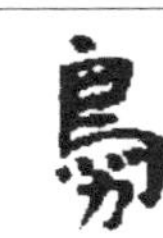	恩	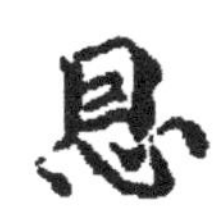
恶	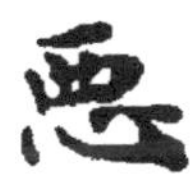	对	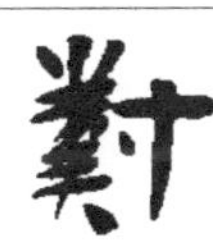	沟	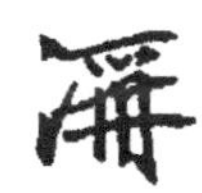
股	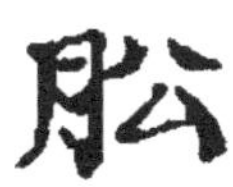	龟	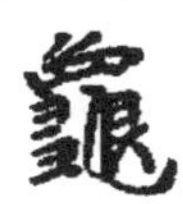	归	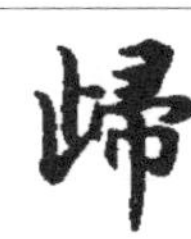
瓜	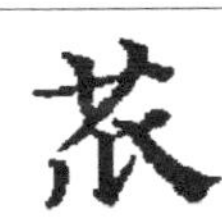	疆	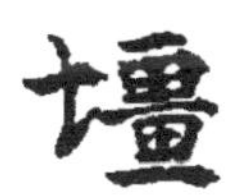	肉	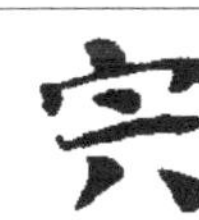

In a certain writing system, standard characters occupy a dominant position, while popular characters are in a subordinate position. However, it should be noted that the relationship between popular characters and standard characters is not fixed. When a popular character is widely used by the public and has a high frequency of usage, authorities may, through administrative means, replace the standard character with the popular one. For example, "儞" was replaced by "你," and "灋" was replaced by "法."

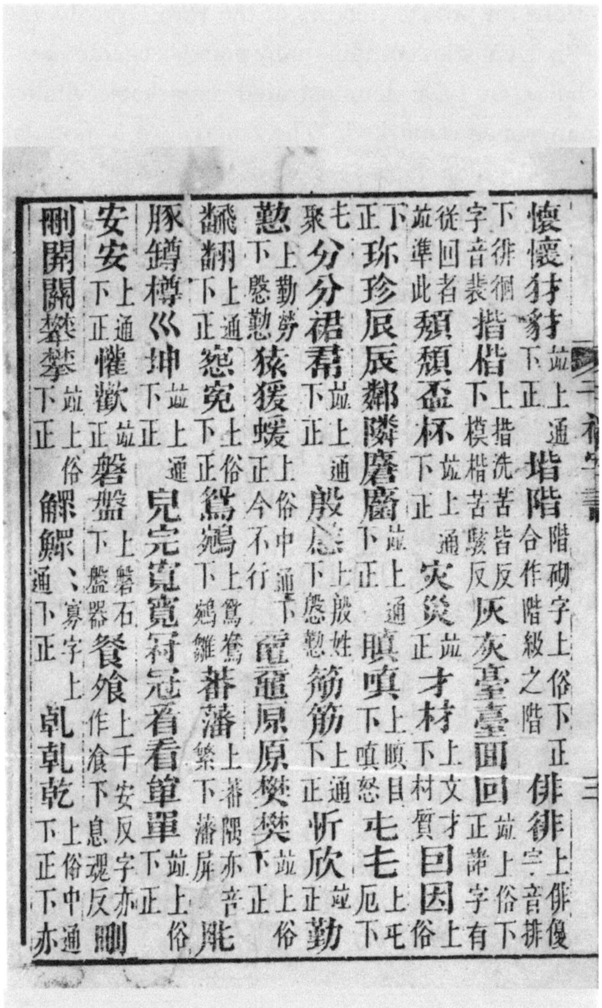

Figure 3.2 Photograph of *Ganlu Zishu*

But anyway, the extensive use of popular characters during a certain period will inevitably cause confusion and reading obstacles to varying degrees. Therefore, starting from the unification of characters during the Qin Dynasty, successive dynasties have consistently maintained efforts to standardize the characters used in formal settings. *The Scheme of Simplification of Chinese Characters*, established after the founding of the People's Republic of China, designated some popular characters as standard characters while abolishing many, playing a positive role in character standardization.

Nevertheless, it is not always easy to standardize popular characters.

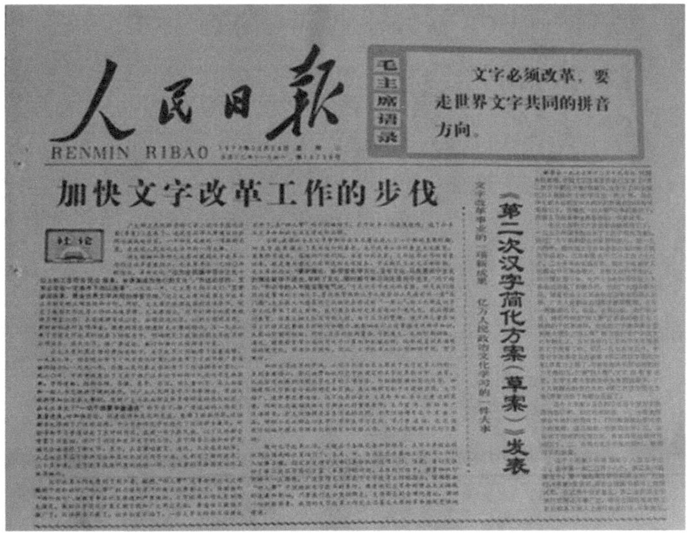
人民日报
RENMIN RIBAO
毛主席语录
文字必须改革，要走世界文字共同的拼音方向。
加快文字改革工作的步伐
社论
《第二次汉字简化方案（草案）》发表

Figure 3.3 December 1977, *People's Daily* published an editorial urging to "Accelerate the Pace of Characters Reform Work"

In 1977, the Committee for Language Reform of China issued *The Second Scheme for Simplification of Chinese Characters (Draft),* which included over 800 simplified characters, many of which were popular characters used by the public. Examples include "面—靣," "停—仃," "厅—庁," "餐—歺," and so on. Due to various issues, the Ministry of Education and the Publicity Department issued a notice to halt the trial use the following year. In 1986, the State Council forwarded a request from the National Language Commission titled *Regarding Abolishing the Second Scheme for Simplification of Chinese Characters (Draft) and Rectifying the Phenomenon of Chaotic Character Usage in Society,* officially discontinuing its use.

This not only reflects the difficulty in standardizing Chinese characters but also reflects the Party and the country's sincere and pragmatic attitude towards works on characters. It is precisely due to this pragmatic approach that, today, the age-old debate between the standard and popular characters has gradually come to an end. The occasions where popular characters appear in formal settings are becoming increasingly rare. Although they may occasionally be encountered in everyday life, they no longer pose significant challenges to people's daily routines.

8. Complex and Simplified Characters

In academia, simplified characters and their complex counterparts are collectively referred to as complex and simplified characters.

Why is the term "simplified characters" used instead of "simple-formed characters" in the definition?

This is because simplified characters and simple-formed characters are two related but distinct concepts.

Through research, linguists have discovered that the coexistence of complex and simplified characters dates back to oracle bone inscriptions and bronze inscriptions from the Shang Dynasty, as shown in Table 3.9.

Table 3.9 Examples of complex and simplified characters in ancient scripts

	Complex Character	Simplified Character	Explanation
莫	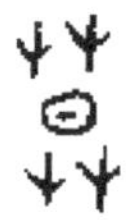	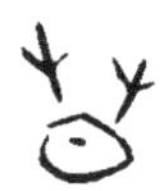	Resembles the sun setting in the midst of grass
箙	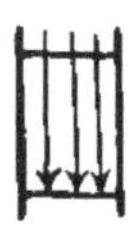	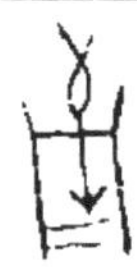	Resembles a container holding arrows
畀		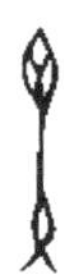	Resembles an arrow with a flat arrowhead
典	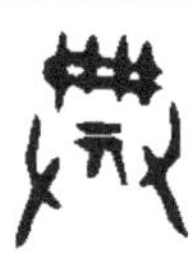	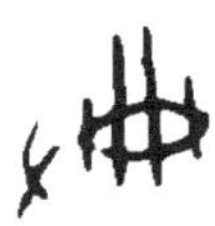	Resembles hands holding a written document
射	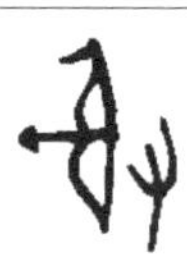	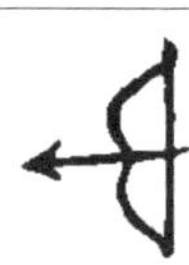	Resembles the action of shooting an arrow with a bowstring

As we move into the small seal script and clerical script, the phenomenon of simplification becomes more prevalent, as illustrated in Table 3.10.

Table 3.10 Examples of complex and simplified characters in ancient scripts

	Complex Character	Simplified Character	Explanation
尘	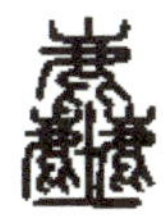 small seal script	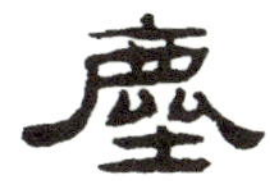 clerical script of the Han Dynasty	Represents the fine dust lifted when a herd of deer is running
袭	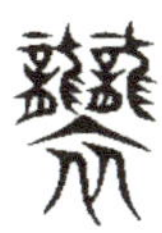 large seal script	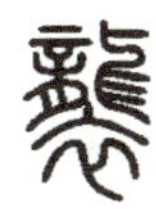 small seal script	Indicates two layers of clothing

After the Wei and Jin dynasties, there was a proliferation of popular characters on stone inscriptions, many of which were simple-formed characters. For example, the character "齐" was written as "亝," and the character "乱" was written as "亂." Such Chinese characters can be referred to as "simple-formed characters" or manifestations of "simplification." However, they cannot be termed "simplified characters" because the term we usually use has a specific meaning.

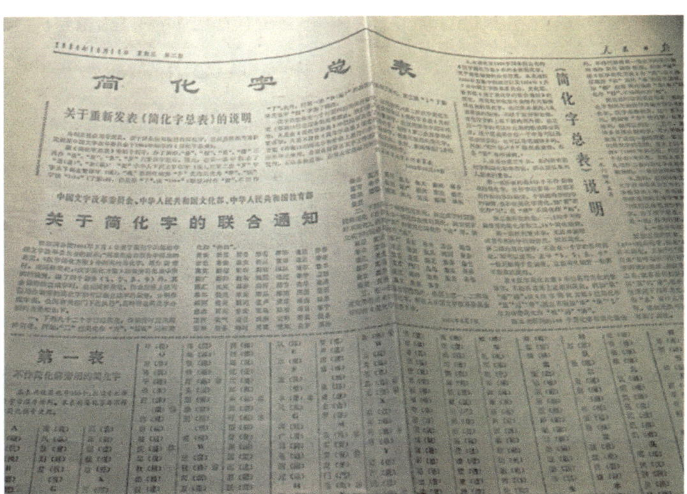
简化字总表
关于重新发表《简化字总表》的说明
关于简化字的联合通知
第一表
《简化字总表》说明

Figure 3.4 The *List of Simplified Characters*, published on October 15, 1986, in the *People's Daily*

In 1956, the State Council of the People's Republic of China promulgated the *Scheme of Simplified Chinese Characters*. In March 1964, the Ministry of Culture, the Ministry of Education, and the Committee for Language Reform of China jointly issued the *Joint Notice on Simplified Characters*. The *List of Simplified Characters* was officially released in May of the same year. In 1986, the *List of Simplified Characters* was reissued. The term "simplified characters" commonly refers to the characters specified in these documents. Simple-formed characters not included in these files are considered allographs or popular characters.

How many simplified characters are currently used in the Chinese mainland?

According to the *List of Simplified Characters* published in the *People's Daily* on October 15, 1986, there are 2,274 simplified characters and 14 simplified radicals recognized in the Chinese mainland. On June 5, 2013, the State Council issued the *General Standardized Chinese Character Table* (including the appendix *Comparison Table of Standard Characters with Complex and Allographs*). The simplified characters commonly used in society are based on this version.

It should be noted that, in practice, only a small portion of the simplified characters used today are newly created after the establishment of the People's Republic of China, such as "塵—尘," "隊—队," and "滅—灭." The majority of them are historical characters that have been used or slightly modified over time, as shown in Table 3.11.

Table 3.11 Partial source of simplified characters

Simplified Character	Complex Character	Source of Simplified Character
灾	災	From ancient characters
从	從	From ancient characters
气	氣	From ancient characters
回	迴	From ancient characters
弃	棄	From allographs used in ancient times
无	無	From allographs used in ancient times
唇	脣	From allographs used in ancient times
杰	傑	From allographs used in ancient times
礼	禮	From allographs used in ancient times
阴	陰	From popular characters used in ancient times
体	體	From popular characters used in ancient times

怜	憐	From popular characters used in ancient times
笔	筆	From popular characters used in ancient times
晋	晉	From popular characters used in ancient times
实	實	From the regularization of cursive script
车	車	From the regularization of cursive script
兴	興	From the regularization of cursive script
乐	樂	From the regularization of cursive script

Moreover, the promotion of simplified Chinese characters has not been an easy task. In 1935, the Ministry of Education of the National Government announced the first batch of simplified character lists, including 324 commonly used popular characters and ancient characters, but due to controversies, the list was withdrawn the following year. In 1977, the Committee for Language Reform of China proposed the *Second Scheme of Simplified Chinese Character (Draft)*. Still, due to numerous issues, the State Council officially halted its use in June 1986.

Therefore, the simplified characters used today have undergone repeated scrutiny and a long history of testing by linguists. Their adoption as standard characters in people's daily lives is truly a challenging achievement.

9. Composite Characters

Composite Characters, also known as combined writing, refers to the practice of combining two or more Chinese characters into a single unit in written text. In terms of structure, this involves the replacement, combination, or reuse of character components, while the pronunciation retains its original multi-syllabic form.

As early as the Shang Dynasty, oracle bone inscriptions began to extensively use composite characters. For example, "three oxen" was written as 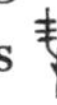, "November" was written as 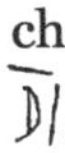, "nine hundred" was written as 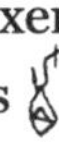, and "three thousand" was written as 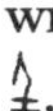.

After the Western Zhou Dynasty, the use of composite characters became even more widespread. For example, "ten friends" was written as , "riding in a chariot" was written as 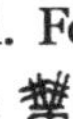, and sometimes a symbol of composite characters "=" was intentionally added as a reminder, such as "craftsman" written as 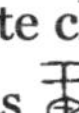, "grand master" written as 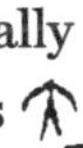, and "young lord" written as 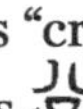.

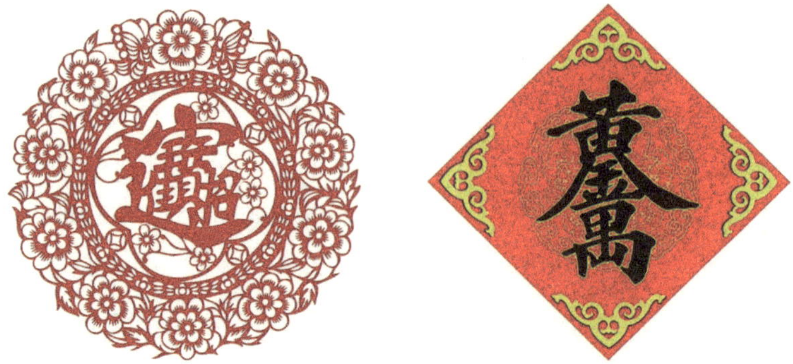

Figure 3.5 Composite auspicious characters

Since the Qin and Han dynasties, through multiple movements to standardize the written language, the use of composite characters gradually decreased. Starting from the Song Dynasty, it became popular to combine characters that carry auspicious meanings by replacing, combining, or reusing character components, forming what is known as "combining characters." These composite auspicious characters, like "招财进宝" (welcoming wealth and treasures) and "黄金万两" (ten thousand ounces of gold), as shown in Figure 3.5, are still beloved by people today.

However, this phenomenon of combining characters is mainly a form of wordplay and is not applicable to everyday writing.

Why did composite characters emerge in the development of Chinese characters?

Upon closer observation, it becomes apparent that composite characters are primarily used for official titles, surnames, place names, and some common words (see Table 3.12). Ultimately, the use of them stems from the need for convenient writing.

Interestingly, the creation of composite characters is not limited to ancient times. In 1924, librarian Du Dingyou created the character "圕" to represent the term "library," and it briefly gained popularity in the academic and cultural circles of China and Japan. In the early years of the People's Republic of China, some composite characters like "瓩" (kilowatt), "兛" (kilogram), "糎" (centimeter), and "嗧" (gallon) were created as units of measurement. However, due to various reasons, they were abolished after 1977.

Experts speculate that the decline of composite characters was driven by the need for standardization in Chinese characters. After all, one character per syllable is less prone to ambiguity.

Table 3.12 Common composite characters in ancient texts

上帝	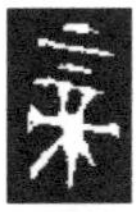	The Western Zhou Dynasty: Plate for Qiang, the Official Historian	上下	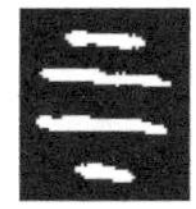	The Western Zhou Dynasty: Plate for Qiang, the Official Historian
寡人	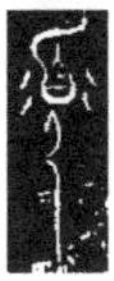	Warring States Period: cultural relics of King of Zhongshan	邯郸	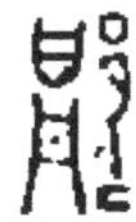	*Compilation of Seal Inscriptions* 4035
司马	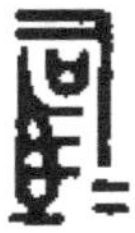	*Compilation of Seal Inscriptions* 0045	司工	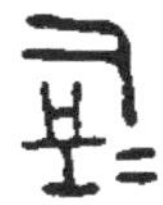	*Compilation of Seal Inscriptions* 5537
上官	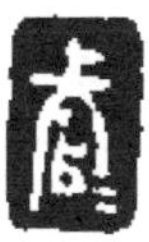	*Compilation of Seal Inscriptions* 3971	公孙	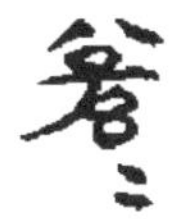	Warring States Period: Chinese Characters on Bamboo 145
鲜于	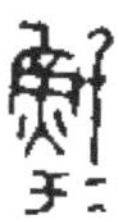	*Compilation of Seal Inscriptions* 4018	淳于	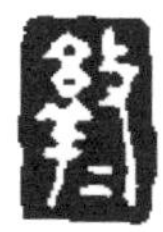	*Compilation of Seal Inscriptions* 4125
圣人	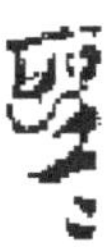	Warring States Period: Guodian Bamboo Slips *Respect Virtue Righteousness* Bamboo Slip 6	君子	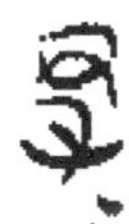	Warring States Period: Guodian Bamboo Slips *Chengzhi Wenzhi* Bamboo Slip 16
小人	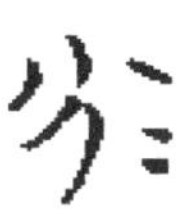	Warring States Period: Baoshan Bamboo Slips 144	小子	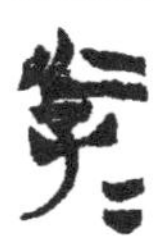	Warring States Period: Tsinghua Bamboo Slips *Cheng Wu* Bamboo Slip 1
相如	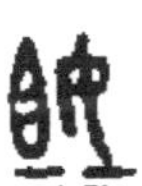	*Compilation of Seal Inscriptions* 0788	稽首	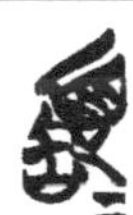	Warring States Period: Tsinghua Bamboo Slips *Speak of Commands* Bamboo Slip 4

CHAPTER IV

Chinese Character Culture

1. Knot Records and the Origin of Chinese Characters

There are legends and records of knotting records in some ethnic groups at home and abroad, and some still have the tradition of knotting records.

However, in terms of the effectiveness of recording, knotting can generally only help with recall, and it is difficult to independently and accurately record complete events. There are also significant deficiencies in representing pronunciation, making it challenging to express the phonetics of the language. Therefore, in the academic community, knotting is generally considered a primitive method of recording and cannot be regarded as a true form of writing.

In fact, in comparison to recording events, knotting for counting purposes might have been more effective. Remnants of the ancient practice of knotting for counting can still be found in Chinese characters today. For example, characters representing multiples of "ten" exhibit clear traces of knotting in the oracle bone inscriptions and bronze inscriptions of the Shang and Zhou dynasties (see Table 4.1).

Table 4.1 Partial list of characters from the Shang Dynasty with traces of knotting

	Character Form	Meaning	Modern Pronunciation	Original Pronunciation
廿	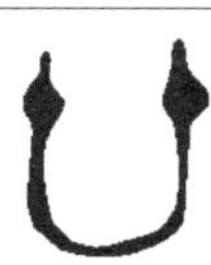	Represents twenty	niàn	èr shí
卅	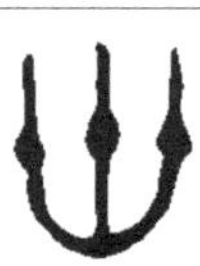	Represents thirty	sà	sān shí
卌	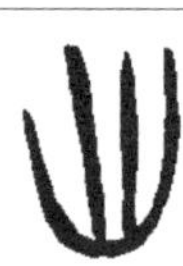	Represents forty	xì	sì shí

These characters, using the image of knots as component symbols, demonstrate that the method of knot-tying for record-keeping did indeed exist in history. Due to the predominantly pictographic nature of early Chinese characters, these knot images from daily life were recorded and preserved.

However, according to studies, many early Chinese characters, such as those in Table 4.1, can also be considered composite characters. They likely originally had two syllables, but their pronunciations changed during the development of Chinese characters.

Xu Shen mentioned in the *Preface to Analytical Dictionary of Characters* that "Shennong used knots for governance and to organize affairs." Although it could be a legend, knot-tying for record-keeping may have had some influence on the creation of Chinese characters.

2. *Wu Zetian's Creation of Characters*

In the year AD 689, Empress Wu Zetian issued an edict for the reform of writing.

To accomplish this feat, she convened contemporary scholars, using *Erya* and *Analytical Dictionary of Characters* as classics and promoting the spirit of character creation by Cang Jie. New characters were vigorously developed, and shortly afterward, the Tang government announced a batch of newly created characters, such as 日 (sun), 月 (moon), 星 (star), and 辰 (celestial bodies).

Today, many characters created by Empress Wu Zetian can no longer be found. Even the exact number of characters created at that time is a matter of debate.

According to the *Yiwenzhi of Tangshu*, there were one hundred scrolls of *Wushi Zihai*, but this book has long been lost. The *New History of the Tang Dynasty* records twelve newly created characters. Later, experts discovered some characters on relics from the period of Wu Zetian, and now people can see more than twenty characters created during her reign. To facilitate memorization, some people compiled the common nineteen characters into a character song: "Heaven, Earth, Sun, Moon, Stars, carrying the initial proofs of sanctity. Country ministers in proper years and months, ten thousand rulers illuminate human life" (see Figure 4.1).

Although few newly created characters from that time are visible today, experts can still explore some of the bases used during Wu Zetian's character creation based on these characters.

For example, some characters were derived from ancient characters. The character "天" (heaven) was directly adopted from the seal script in the *Analytical Dictionary of Characters*. The characters "地" (earth) and "国" (country) were already present in the *Yupian* written by Gu Yewang during the Southern Dynasties, where it mentioned: "埊, ancient character for 'earth.'" "圀, ancient character for 'country.'"

In addition to selecting ancient characters, the use of syssemantographs was also a common method, such as "曌" (bright) depicting the sun and moon overhead and "臣" (minister) representing loyalty and unity of heart.

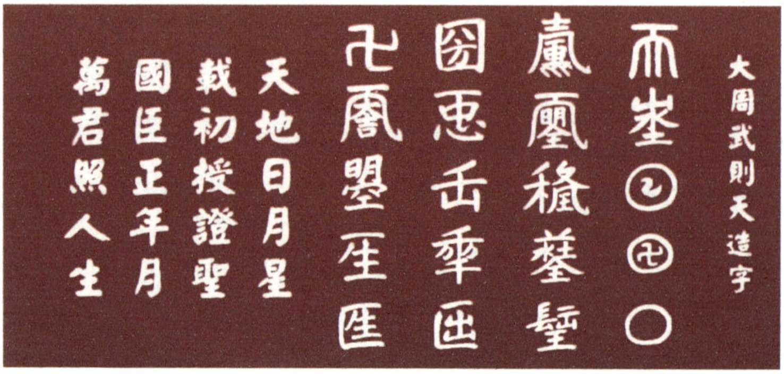

Figure 4.1 Newly created characters found in inscriptions from the period of Empress Wu Zetian

Some characters were derived from the modification of popular characters, incorporating hopes for a bright future for the Dazhou Dynasty, such as the auspicious character "君" (ruler) and the character "年" (year) repeated thousands of times.

Some characters even broke away from the square structure of Chinese characters and adopted a round structure, such as "日" (sun), "月" (moon), and "星" (star), which not only originated from ancient characters but also reflected people's simple understanding of celestial bodies. In oracle bone inscriptions, the characters "日" and "星" were originally composed of "○." Since the sun, moon, stars, and celestial bodies in general are often round (actually spherical), transforming them into a round shape is quite appropriate.

Therefore, the characters created during the period of Empress Wu Zetian were not arbitrarily invented but had some scholarly basis.

Moreover, these characters were highly practical, and Empress Wu Zetian made considerable efforts to promote them. During her fifteen-year reign, she used thirteen era names. Among them, four reign titles, "Tianshou," "Zhengsheng," "Shengli," and "Zaichu," before the era name "Dazhou," all employed newly created characters.

Empress Wu Zetian herself changed her name to "武曌" (Wǔ Zhào), leading by example in using the new characters. It's worth noting that the character "曌" (zhào) can be decomposed into "明" (míng) and "空" (kōng), exactly matching the Dharma name she received when she became a Buddhist monk at Ganye Temple, whether by coincidence or intention.

In 1982, a gold plaque from the Wu Zetian period was discovered at the Junji Peak of Mount Song in Henan Province (see Figure 4.2). The gold plaque, measuring 36.3 cm in length, 8.2 cm in width, and weighing 247 g with a gold purity of over 96%, featured 63 inscriptions in regular script on the front, "Urgent Report: Dazhou national leader Wuzhao, fond of true Dao, seeking longevity and immortality, reverently presents this gold plaque at the high gate of Mount Song to request the

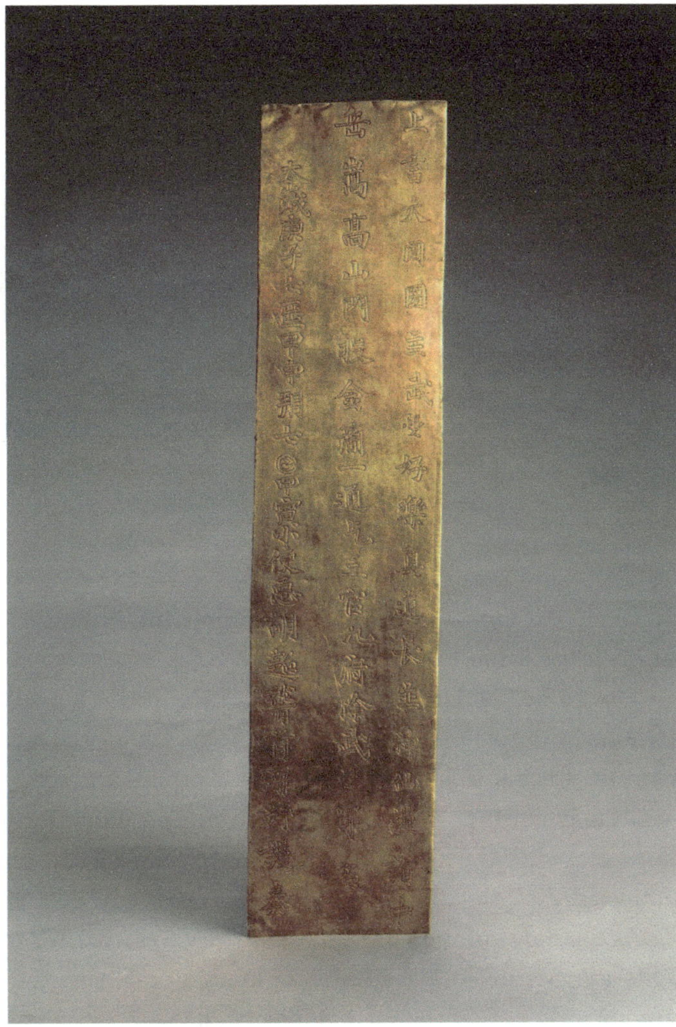

Figure 4.2 The Expiatory Gold Plaque discovered at the Junji Peak of Mount Song in Henan, Wu Zetian period

Three Officials and Nine Ministries to clear her crimes. On the seventh day of the seventh lunar month in the year of Gengzi, with utmost sincerity, the humble envoy Hu Chao respectfully reports once again."

According to the inscription, this gold plaque was an offering made by Wu Zetian on the seventh day of the seventh lunar month of the Jiushi year (AD 700) while praying at Mount Song to seek divine forgiveness. Five characters on it, "国" (country), "曌" (bright), "月" (moon), "日" (sun), and "臣" (minister), are all newly created characters.

In AD 705, Wu Zhao relinquished the throne to the Tang Dynasty and passed away shortly afterward. Her posthumous title became "Zetian Dasheng Huangtaihou,"

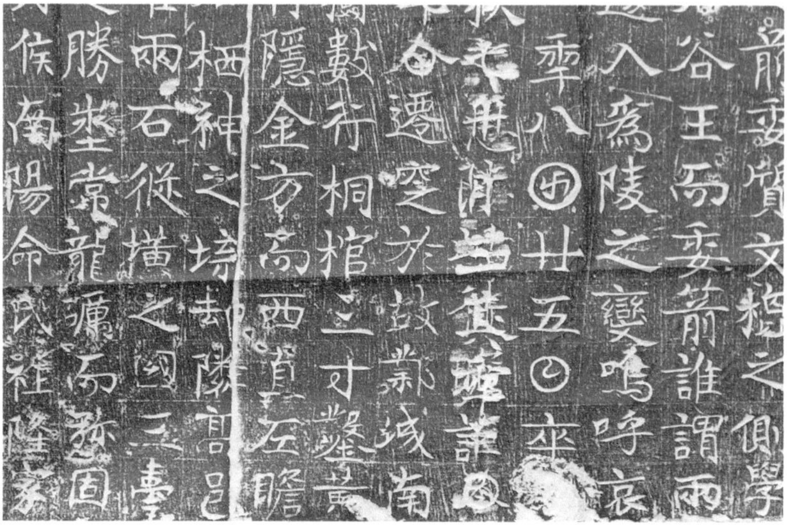

Figure 4.3 Partial rubbing of an epitaph from the reign of Wu Zetian (including characters created by Wu Zetian)

dropping the emperor title but retaining the honorific "Zetian Dasheng Hou" to signify her greatness.

The name "Zetian" was taken from Confucius's praise of Emperor Shun in the *Analects of Confucius*, "Confucius said: 'Great indeed was Yao as a sovereign! How majestic was he! It is only heaven that is grand, and only Yao corresponds to it. How vast was his virtue! The people could find no name for it. How majestic was he in the works which he accomplished! How glorious in the elegant regulations which he instituted!'"

As the only empress in Chinese history to formally ascend the throne, displaying achievements in both civil and military domains equal to male emperors, she is remembered fittingly by the name "Zetian."

After Emperor Zhongzong of the Tang Dynasty ascended the throne and ended the Dazhou regime, all the characters created during the Wu Zetian period were abolished, except for the character "曌." Only those characters inscribed on tomb epitaphs from the Wu Zetian era (Figure 4.3), enduring the tests of time, silently narrate the prosperity and glory of the era when the characters were created.

3. Character Divination and Word-Breaking Games

Character divination, also known as "literomancy," is a method of fortune-telling based on characters.

In the Shang and Zhou periods several thousand years ago, people used oracle bones and animal bones for divination, inscribing questions and results on the bones, forming what is known as "oracle bone inscriptions."

Even though the early divination was based on the burn marks on the oracle bones rather than written characters, it added a layer of mystery to the use of characters. In the minds of people at that time, characters themselves possessed a certain mystical power and even embodied the machinery of fate and the will of spirits.

In the development of Chinese characters, numerous geomancers interpreted characters' shapes to predict good or bad fortune, giving rise to the art of character divination.

There are various methods of character divination, with the most common one relying on the characters themselves. People analyze the shapes, split them apart, or recombine them, associating meanings to seek good or bad outcomes.

Many folk stories related to character divination have been passed down, including one about Emperor Chongzhen during the late Ming Dynasty.

> In the waning years of the Ming Dynasty, plagued by internal turmoil and external threats, the people were suffering. Emperor Chongzhen, amidst his governance, decided one day to disguise himself and privately visit the streets. There, he encountered a fortune teller and, seized by a sudden impulse, approached him to have his fortune told.
>
> At the fortune-telling booth, he wrote the character "友" (friend) at random, asking about the future prosperity of the Ming Dynasty.
>
> After examining the character, the fortune teller said, "The situation doesn't look good. The character '友' has the '反' (opposition) radical on top, indicating that rebellious individuals will rise. When rebels gain prominence, the country will be in danger!"
>
> Dissatisfied with the response, Emperor Chongzhen wrote the character "有" (have) and asked again about the fate of the Ming Dynasty.
>
> Unexpectedly, the fortune teller replied, "The situation is even worse. When the character '有' is split, the top part is '大' (big), missing a stroke, and the bottom part is '明' (bright) without the sun. '大明' (the Ming Dynasty) is missing half, indicating that the nation is going to fall apart!"
>
> Emperor Chongzhen, feeling resentful, wrote the character "酉" and inquired again.
>
> The fortune teller, looking terrified, exclaimed, "This character is extremely ominous. '酉' is '尊' (honorable) with the head and tail cut off. As the highest

authority, Your Majesty may face insult and disgrace. It could be an inauspicious omen!"

Emperor Chongzhen was sad and finally wrote the character "幽" (quiet).

After seeing it, the fortune teller sighed and said, "The character '幽' consists of two ropes in the mountains, a symbol of hanging. I'm afraid this character is not interpretable."

After that, the fortune teller hastily packed up and fled.

Emperor Chongzhen, filled with anxiety, broke into a cold sweat.

It is really surprising that the same or similar pronunciation of a few words, with different methods, the answer is surprisingly similar.

Of course, this is just a folk legend involving creative interpretations and should not be taken too seriously.

However, breaking down Chinese characters using specific methods and incorporating some life philosophy can indeed create an intriguing word game.

Renowned linguist Lin Yutang once provided an interesting breakdown of the characters "孤" (solitary) and "独" (alone) and composed a playful poem:

In the shade, a child holds a melon under the willow,
A small dog chases butterflies in the narrow lane.
Amidst the worldly hustle and bustle, full of laughter,
Only I remain, with two temples graying in the wind.

"孤" and "独," when separated, represent "子" (child) with "瓜" (melon) and "犬" (dog) with "虫" (butterfly), respectively. Lin Yutang's imaginative description transforms these few characters into a vivid painting: a child is playing happily under the cool willow tree, and a small dog is joyfully chasing butterflies in an ancient narrow lane. Looking around, every corner is filled with laughter, but "I" with two graying temples, facing the wind. Many people consider solitude to be unbearable, but in Lin Yutang's interpretation, solitude becomes full of humor and color, representing a high state of life even today.

Like "孤" and "独," many Chinese characters are composed of two or more individual characters, each with its own meaning. Through the playful technique of character dissection, people can express their philosophy of life and different understandings of existence. For example:

富

宀 + 畐

Half is “福” (fortune), and half is “灾” (misfortune). It means having a lot of money may not always be a good thing.

A noble person values wealth, acquires it with integrity, and uses it wisely. Unjustly gaining wealth and honor is like fleeting clouds to me.

停

人 + 亭

Life’s journey is long, requiring both the courage to move forward and the wisdom to pause. When reaching the end of a road, one can sit back and enjoy the rising clouds.

茶

艸 + 人 + 木

In a lifetime, there’s but one autumn for the grass and trees. Life is as fleeting as a dream, and existence is akin to tea. Only by getting close to nature and reconciling with one’s inner self can one experience bitterness before sweetness. Clarity of purpose comes from a tranquil heart, and only in serenity can one achieve far-reaching goals.

劣

少 + 力

One reaps what they sow. Without diligence in youth, one will regret it in old age.

怕

心 + 白

Fear is the emptiness within the heart. With aspirations and a purposeful path, one can overcome fear. Finding joy in self-contentment leads to peace, and when the mind is free from attachments, worries dissipate.

智

日 + 知

There are no born geniuses, only intelligent individuals who are adept at learning and reflection.

Confucius said, "I am not one who was born with knowledge, but one who is fond of antiquity and is diligent in seeking it."

4. Character Puzzles and Hidden Word Poetry

Character puzzles, a branch of riddles, are not only an interesting word game but also a unique linguistic and cultural phenomenon in Chinese characters. The principle behind them involves complex strokes, relatively independent radicals, and versatile structural combinations of Chinese characters. Various methods, such as disassembling, adding or subtracting strokes, and using imagery or ideographic meanings, are employed to create puzzles based on characters or words.

The history of Chinese character puzzles is ancient. During the Southern and Northern Dynasties, Bao Zhao wrote a poem titled *Character Puzzles*, "Two forms in one, four limbs and eight heads. Four eight plus one eight equals five eight. The flying spring splashes." Each line's answer is the character "井" (well). The character "井" has two horizontal and two vertical lines, representing "two forms in one," and it looks like four pillars with a total of eight heads, representing "four limbs and eight heads." The combination of "four eight" and "one eight" makes "five eight," and five multiplied by eight equals forty. Moreover, the character "井" (well) can also be deconstructed into four "十" (ten). The last phrase describes the splashing of well water when drawing it from the well.

In later years, poems specifically using characters as answers were called hidden word poetry. The answers mainly involve breaking down character forms and concealing within the poem. These poems often focus on the visual aspects of characters, and some also provide interpretations of their meanings. Some hidden word poems have the same answer throughout, like Bao Zhao's *Character Puzzles*. Others feature one answer per line, creating an overall hidden message. For example, a folk song known as *Breaking Love*:

> 下珠帘焚香去卜卦，问苍天，人儿落在谁家。恨玉郎，全无一点知心话。欲罢不能罢！吾把口来哑。
>
> 论交情不差，染成皂，难讲一句清白话。分明一对好鸳鸯，却被刀割下，抛的奴力尽才又乏。细思量，口与心俱是假。

Lowering the pearl curtains, burning incense to divine the oracle,
Questioning the heavens, asking whose home the lost child has fallen into.
Regretting the jade lover, devoid of a single heartfelt conversation.
Desiring to cease but unable to cease! My lips become mute.
In discussing intimacy, there's no deficiency.
Yet tainted as black, difficult to speak a single pure word.

Clearly, a pair of good mandarin ducks.
But they are severed by the knife's edge.
Discarding them, all strength depleted, yet still lacking.
Upon careful consideration, both heart and mouth are false.

It is said that this poem, attributed to Emperor Qianlong, appears to be a farewell poem but actually contains the numbers one through ten. It is indeed a marvelous character puzzles poem (下–卜=一, 天–人=二, 玉–丨–丶=三, 罢–去=四, 吾–口=五, 交–乂=六, 皂–白=七, 分–刀=八, 抛–扌–力=九, 思–口–心=十).

Additionally, some poems have each line's answer as a single stroke, forming a complete character throughout the entire poem. For example:

One dot and a horizontal line extended,
One slant reaching South Yang.
In South Yang, there's a person,
Who is merely one inch tall. (府 Mansion)

Aunt Wang and Aunt Bai,
Both sitting together on a stone. (碧 Jade)

These character riddles are not only brain exercises but also lively and entertaining, making them particularly suitable for use in festive settings, such as lantern riddle events during the Lantern Festival.

A story in *New Account of Tales of the World* narrates an episode where Cao Cao and Yang Xiu guessed a riddle.

One day, Cao Cao passed by Cao E's Stele (see Figure 4.4), where eight characters were inscribed: "黄绢幼妇, 外孙齑臼" (A young woman is dressed in a yellow silk garment. Her grandson is grinding sauce in a mortar). Puzzled by their meaning, Cao Cao turned to his chief secretary, Yang Xiu, and asked, "Do you know what this means?"

Yang Xiu replied, "I do."

Cao Cao hastily said, "Don't tell me the answer just yet. Let me think about it." After walking thirty miles, Cao Cao finally said, "I also know now." He asked Yang Xiu to write down his interpretation first.

This stele was erected during the Eastern Han Dynasty to praise the filial piety of Cao E. In the first year of the Yuanjia era (AD 151), the magistrate of Shangyu County intended to erect a stele in honor of Cao E. He initially ordered his subordinates to draft the text, but after a long time, they were unable to complete it. Therefore, he instructed his disciple Handan Chun to write the inscription. At that time, Handan Chun was very young, but he calmly seized the brush and completed the inscription effortlessly, leaving the onlookers in awe. After reading it, Cai Yong wrote, "A young woman is dressed in a yellow silk garment. Her grandson is grinding sauce in a mortar" on the side of the stele.

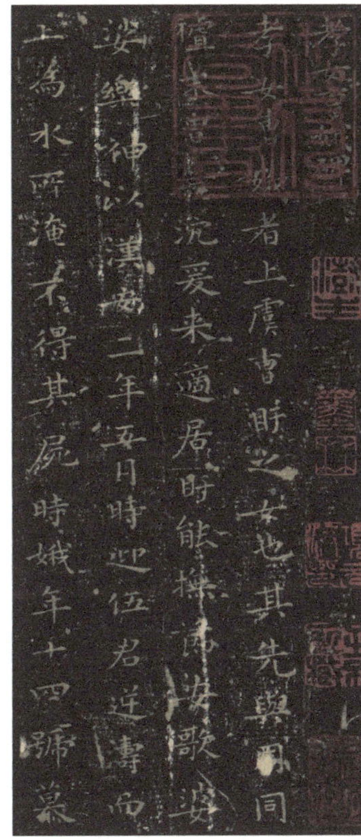

Figure 4.4 Partial rubbing of the "Cao E's Stele"

> Yang Xiu explained, "'黄绢' is colorful silk, interpreted as the character '绝' (extraordinary); '幼妇' means a young woman, interpreted as the character '妙' (exquisite); '外孙' refers to a daughter's son, interpreted as the character '好' (good); '齑臼' is a utensil used to contain and grind seasonings, and those seasonings are mainly spicy things like ginger and garlic, so it can be understood as '受辛' (enduring hardship), interpreted as the character '辤 (辞)' (speech). Taken together, it forms '绝妙好辞' (extraordinary and exquisite speech) (see Figure 4.5)."
>
> At this point, Cao Cao had also finished writing, and the content was exactly the same as Yang Xiu's. Cao Cao couldn't help but exclaim, "My talent is not as good as yours, a difference of thirty miles." Although he wore a smile, he couldn't hide his inner displeasure.

In the *Romance of the Three Kingdoms*, it is mentioned that Cao Cao built a new garden. After its completion, his subordinates invited him to see if there were any places that needed modifications.

Cao Cao was satisfied after inspecting the scenery inside the garden. However, when he reached the entrance, he stopped and frowned slightly. His companions were

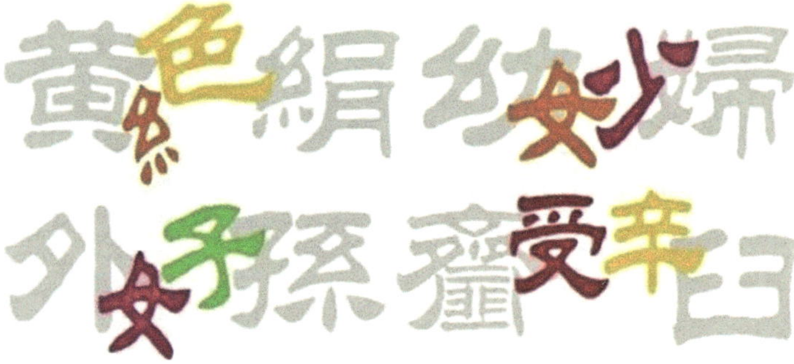

Figure 4.5 Extraordinary and exquisite speech

unsure of the reason. They only saw Cao Cao took a pen from an attendant, wrote the character "活" (alive) on the door, and left without saying a word.

The people present didn't know what it meant, so they went to ask Yang Xiu. Yang Xiu thought for a moment and said, "Adding '活' inside the door (门) makes it the character '阔.' The Prime Minister meant the door was too wide, and thus it should be made narrower." The craftsmen quickly narrowed the door according to Yang Xiu's suggestion. After seeing it, Cao Cao was very satisfied. Upon learning it was Yang Xiu's idea, he didn't say anything more and just laughed heartily.

Cao Cao presented a silent riddle; looking at the answer, it still falls into the category of a word puzzle. From these two stories, it can be seen that Cao Cao not only enjoyed solving riddles but also was skilled in creating them. Unfortunately, the Cao Cao portrayed in these stories is narrow-minded and lays the groundwork for Yang Xiu's death, which is somewhat lamentable.

5. Prophecies and Rumors

References to prophecies are often found in ancient texts.

For example, in the *Records of the Later Han · Annals of Emperor Guangwu*, it is stated, "There is a mention of Li Tong and others using an image to explain prophecies to Emperor Guangwu."

Similarly, in the *Records of the Grand Historian · Basic Annals of Qin Shi Huang*, it is stated, "The downfall of Qin was foretold by a prophecy."

So, what exactly is a prophecy?

In reality, a prophecy is a form of cryptic language created by ancient shamans or diviners using divination techniques. It is used to predict fortunes, foresee the future, and convey hidden messages. Prophecies primarily based on images are called "tu chen" (image-based prophecies), while those centered around language and writing are known as "zi chen," "chen yu," or simply "chen yan" (verbal prophecies).

For instance, the widely circulated *Tuibei Tu* belongs to the category of image-based prophecies, while the *Liu Bowen Pancake Song* falls under the category of verbal prophecies.

In ancient times, prophecies played a significant role in shaping public opinion.

According to the *Records of the Grand Historian*, before the uprising led by Chen Sheng and Wu Guang, they used cinnabar to write "Chen Sheng will be the king" on cloth and placed it in the belly of a captured fish. In the evening, they imitated the cry of a fox, shouting, "Great Chu will rise, and Chen Sheng will be the king!" This laid the groundwork for the success of their rebellion.

Similarly, Wang Mang reached the pinnacle of his life through prophecies.

According to the *Book of Han · Biography of Wang Mang*, in the third year of his regency, the Changxing Pavilion in Linzi County, Qi Province, had a caretaker named Xin Dang. One night, Xin Dang had several dreams in which a self-proclaimed envoy of the heavenly gods told him, "The provisional emperor will indeed be the true one." To prove the credibility of his words, the envoy claimed to have used divine power and left a new well in the pavilion. When Xin Dang woke up, he found a new well in the pavilion, reaching a depth of more than a hundred feet.

Soon after, a stone ox from the Ba-Shu region voluntarily ran to the Weiyang Palace in Chang'an, presenting a bronze token bearing the following words, "Heaven's proclamation to the emperor, the presenter is granted a noble title. Accept the heavenly mandate and use divine commands."

It was precisely with the impetus of these prophecies that Wang Mang finally transitioned from being a provisional emperor to a legitimate one, achieving a qualitative leap in his "official position and title."

Similarly, during times of dynastic change, Emperor Wen of Wei and his advisers also made extensive use of prophecies.

The *Prophecies in the Filial Piety Classic* states, "日载东, 绝火光, 不横一, 圣聪明。四百之外, 易姓而王。" (The sun travels to the east, extinguishing the firelight. The combination of "不" and "一" equals "丕." Holy and wise. Four hundred beyond, a change of surname results in kingship.)

The *Prophecies of the Changes in Fortunes* says, "言居东, 西有午, 两日并光日居下。其为主, 反为辅。五八四十, 黄气受, 真人出。" ("言" residing in the east, the west is "午," with two suns overlapping, residing below. The one as the master, the other as the assistant. Five multiplied by eight equals forty. The yellow energy is received, and a true person emerges.)

The *Changes in Fortunes* also states, "鬼在山, 禾女连, 王天下。" (Ghosts in the mountain, the lady and grains connected, ruling the world.)

"日载东" corresponds to "曹" (Cao), and "不横一" corresponds to "丕" (Pi), combining to form the name "曹丕" (Cao Pi). From the establishment of the Western Han Dynasty to the downfall of the Eastern Han Dynasty, it's approximately four hundred years. "鬼在山, 禾女连" combines to form the character "巍," which phonetically matches the "魏" in the title "魏王" (King of Wei). "言午" combined represents "许" (Xu), and the overlapping of two "日" characters forms "昌" (Chang), implying that the downfall of the Han Dynasty would occur in Xu (referring to Xu Province), while the rise of Wei would be centered in Xuchang.

These prophecies utilize the shapes of Chinese characters for their combination and separation. Why use the forms of Chinese characters?

Fundamentally, it stems from the ancient reverence for writing.

From the inception of Cang Jie's creation of characters, "Heaven raining grains, ghosts wailing at night," caused a shock to heaven and earth. From then on, in the minds of ancient people, writing became a mysterious force. People used writing for expression and communication, transmitting knowledge and experience. Compared with oral transmission, writing inadvertently broke the limitations of time and space.

As the functions of writing continued to develop, ancient people began to believe that writing could not only be used for communication among humans but also for communication with spirits, enabling divination.

For example, after Wang Mang established the Xin Dynasty, disliking the Han Dynasty's family name "刘" (Liu, which can be broken down into the characters for "卯," "金," and "刀"), he changed the character "钱" (money) to "泉" (spring), commonly known as "White Water Taoist." This change aimed to use water to counteract the fire element (Han represents the fire virtue and is wary of water.).

After the establishment of the Eastern Han Dynasty, it continued to be associated with the fire element. Due to concerns about avoiding water, the capital's name was changed from the three-water-pointed "洛阳" (Luoyang) to "雒阳" (Luoyang. According to legend, within the sun resides a three-legged crow, which is capable of carrying the sun and traveling through the skies. By altering it to incorporate the "隹" radical, it enhances the auspiciousness of the fire virtue). During the Cao Wei period, Wei emphasized the virtue of the earth. They revered water due to the characteristics of soil being "softened by water." As a result, the name was changed back to "洛阳."

The fact that ancient people were willing to repeatedly modify place names reflects their reverence for writing. Even in modern times, changes to place names have occurred.

For example, during Chiang Kai-shek's Nationalist government, Beijing was renamed "Beiping." This was done with the hope for peace in the north, and because Nanjing had become the capital, calling Beijing "Jing" was no longer suitable. In 1949, with the founding of the People's Republic of China, the name "Beiping" was reverted to "Beijing" according to convention.

Due to the vague and ambiguous nature of prophecies, misunderstandings and errors caused by prophecies have occurred throughout various dynasties.

For instance, in the *Records of the Grand Historian · Basic Annals of Qin Shi Huang*, it is mentioned that Lu Sheng from Yan once presented a book of prophecies that stated, "The downfall of Qin is caused by the Hu." Qin Shi Huang misunderstood "Hu" here to refer to the Hu people instead of his son Hu Hai. Consequently, he dispatched General Meng Tian with three hundred thousand soldiers to attack the Xiongnu and built the Great Wall to guard against the Hu people.

Another example from the *Comprehensive Mirror to Aid in Government* records during the reign of Emperor Taizong in the Tang Dynasty, the Left Military Guard General Li Junxian frequently observed the appearance of the planet Venus during the day, an unusual celestial phenomenon at the time. Emperor Taizong sought advice from Taishi, who interpreted it as "a woman in power." A prophecy book circulating among the people, called *Secret Records*, also stated, "After three generations of Tang, a woman surnamed Wu will rise to power, succeeding the martial king." Emperor Taizong was deeply worried upon learning this. One day, during a banquet in the palace, he played a drinking game where everyone had to reveal their childhood name. When he heard that Li Junxian's childhood name was "Wu Niang," Emperor Taizong was shocked. Since Li Junxian's official title, fief, and even his childhood name all contained the character "Wu," coupled with the presence of a female childhood name, it aligned with the prophecy. Soon after, Li Junxian was executed by Emperor Taizong, who was attempting to avoid the prophecy. However, he still couldn't escape the prophecy as Emperor Taizong failed to realize that the term "the king surnamed Wu" referred to his charming and talented concubine surnamed Wu by his side.

If prophecies are expressed in the form of songs, they become rhymes, with nursery rhymes being the most common form.

Nursery rhymes originally circulated among children, featuring simple language and a lively rhythm that could quickly spread to various corners of society. Due to the innocence of children, nursery rhymes, while superficial in content, are believed by many to convey the will of the heavens.

In the *Chronicles of the States in the Eastern Zhou Dynasty*, Grand Scribe Boyangfu spoke to King Xuan of Zhou, "Any speech without foundation on the streets is called a rumor. The heavens warn the rulers by transforming the Mars into the appearance of a child, creating rumors for children to learn, known as nursery rhymes. Whether small, implying the fortune or misfortune of an individual, or large, it may be related to the rise and fall of a nation. Mars, the fiery planet, is thus depicted in red."

In his view, when the heavens wanted to warn a ruler, they would make Mars appear in the form of a child to teach other children nursery rhymes. These rhymes, on a small scale, might contain the fortune or misfortune of an individual and, on a larger scale, could be related to the prosperity or decline of a nation.

Throughout history, there have been many nursery rhymes. Here are a few related to written characters. In the late Eastern Han Dynasty, when Dong Zhuo wielded power and committed numerous killings, ministers dared not speak out. At that time, a nursery rhyme circulated in the capital, Luoyang:

> 千里草，何青青。十日卜，不得生。
>
> A thousand miles of grass, yet why so green? For ten days, I have consulted, yet no growth has been seen. (*Records of the Later Han · Treatise on the Five Elements*)

"千" and "里" together form the character "重," and adding a "草" (grass) radical on top results in the character "董" (Dong). Reversing "十," "日," and "卜" gives the character "卓" (Zhuo). The nursery rhyme subtly predicts the imminent downfall of Dong Zhuo.

After the Western Jin Dynasty conquered the Wu Kingdom, there was a nursery rhyme in the south of the Yangtze River:

> 局缩肉，数横目，中国当败吴当复。
> 宫门柱，且当朽，吴当复，在三十年后。
> 鸡鸣不拊翼，吴复不用力。
>
> Tighten the flesh, reverse the "目" character. The dynasty will decline, and Wu will rise again.
>
> Palace door pillars, soon to decay. Wu will rise again, in thirty years.
>
> The rooster crows without flapping its wings, and Wu's resurgence won't require much effort." (*Book of Jin · Treatise on the Five Elements*)

"局缩肉" refers to the weak and inept Emperor Yuan of Jin. The reversed "目" character becomes "四," hinting that the time from the downfall of Wu to the establishment of Eastern Jin would be less than 40 years. According to historical records, from the fall of Eastern Wu in AD 280 to the establishment of Eastern Jin by Emperor Yuan in AD 317 in Jiangnan (mainly the former territory of Eastern Wu), it was indeed only 38 years, less than 40 years.

According to historical records, sometimes adults, in order to attack political opponents or seek self-preservation, would also fabricate rumors.

For example, during the Southern Song Dynasty in the reign of Emperor Ming, when the Crown Prince and other princes were very young, Emperor Ming feared that after his death, his relatives Wang Jingwen and General Zhang Yong might not be in control. Therefore, he fabricated the rumor "一士不可亲, 弓长射杀人" (One scholar is not trustworthy; a long bow can shoot and kill.) (*History of the Song · Biography of Wang Jingwen*), using it as a pretext to put Wang Jingwen to death. The combination of the characters "一" and "士" refers to "王" (Wang), and the combination of the characters "弓" and "长" refers to "张" (Zhang). The rumor directly targeted Wang Jingwen and Zhang Yong.

During the time of the Tang Dynasty, a man named Dong Chang declared himself emperor in Yuezhou. In response, an elderly person from Shanyin immediately composed a rhyme, "欲识圣人姓, 千里草青青;欲知圣人名, 日从曰上生。" (To know the surname of the sage, observe the green grass for a thousand miles; to know the name of the sage, look to the sun as it rises daily from the east.) (*Verification of Gods*). This rhyme subtly contains information about Dong Chang's name and implies a deeper meaning related to his actions.

Similarly, during the reign of Fu Jian in the Former Qin, the Xianbei people gradually gained strength. There was a popular rhyme that went, "鱼羊田斗当灭秦。" (Fish, sheep, fields, and a battle shall destroy Qin.) Combining the characters "鱼," "羊," "田," and "斗" forms the words "鲜卑." At that time, Fu Jian's state was named Qin, and this rhyme was likely spread by those who wanted to use Fu Jian to suppress the rising power of the Xianbei.

In the late Eastern Han Dynasty, when the Taiping Dao proclaimed, "The azure sky will perish, and the yellow sky will rise. In the year of Jiazi, there will be great fortune throughout the land." The intention behind this rhyme was quite clear, even specifying the time of the Yellow Turban Rebellion.

Although many prophecies and rhymes were artificially created, they easily formed powerful public opinion trends once they appeared. Therefore, individuals throughout Chinese history were adept at utilizing these means, often portraying themselves as the destined ones.

According to records in the *Taiping Imperial Encyclopedia*, one day during a gathering with his ministers, Emperor Wu of Han, Liu Che, unexpectedly said after drinking, "Han is currently facing troubles, and the law should be revived. Among the imperial clan's descendants, who should respond to this call? After forty-two emperors, one who could still lead the Han Dynasty must have been a formidable figure, Tu Gao, unafraid in the face of perilous circumstances."

Although many in ancient times manipulated prophecies to extend their mandate from heaven, it was rare, especially during a flourishing era, for someone like Liu Che to "self-deprecate" and use prophecies to argue that "the law should be revived." This statement essentially confirmed the legitimacy of replacing the Han Dynasty's mandate from heaven. The ministers present were genuinely startled by this unexpected proclamation.

In times of peace and prosperity, such statements might be seen as casual remarks made under the influence of alcohol. However, if turmoil arose, it would become a potent propaganda weapon for those aspiring to the throne.

For instance, during the later period of Wang Mang's rule, when the realm was in great chaos, those in control of significant military forces all harbored ambitions to proclaim themselves as emperors.

At that time, Liu Xiu, holding sway in the north, aspired to unify the entire realm, while Gongsun Shu sought to establish his dominance in the Shu region, leading to an imminent outbreak of war. Surprisingly, before engaging in warfare, the two leaders decided to have a "debate" concerning the attribution of divine mandate.

Liu Xiu referred to the records in prophecies and divinations that mentioned "卯金刀变青龙" (Metal knife transforming into a green dragon. With the combination of the characters "卯," "金," and "刀" forms the character "劉" representing Liu), claiming himself to be the legitimate emperor. On the other side, Gongsun Shu cited from the *Supporting Divine Contracts*, specifically "Western Provincial Governor, will sever the fate of Liu" (As Gongsun Shu had served as the governor of Shu, which is in the west, hence he has the title Western Provincial Governor), asserting that he would sever the fortunes of the Liu clan. Liu Xiu's faction invoked the widely circulated rumor of the time, stating, "The Liu clan will rise again, with the support of the Li clan," presenting himself as the people's choice. Gongsun Shu's side, in turn, utilized the established principle from ancient texts that "a single surname cannot receive the mandate again" to challenge Liu Xiu.

As the debate intensified, Gongsun Shu's faction, to prove the legitimacy of his self-proclaimed emperorship, went so far as to focus on the surname "Gongsun." They skillfully employed prophecies such as "Depose Emperor Chang, and enthrone Gongsun" from the *Record of Destiny Law* and "Emperor Xuanyuan receives the mandate, and Gongsun clan holds it" from the *Comprehensive Earthly Form* to illustrate that Gongsun Shu was the designated emperor appointed by the heavens.

In response, Liu Xiu directly wrote a letter to Gongsun Shu, emphasizing that he had misunderstood the references to "Gongsun" in those prophecies. The "Gongsun" mentioned in those prophecies refers to one's identity, not a surname. They were referring to Emperor Xuan of Han (whose grandfather was Crown Prince in the reign of Emperor Wu), not Gogsun Shu at all.

The climax of the debate returned to the prophecies presented by Emperor Wu of Han. Liu Xiu's faction questioned Gongsun Shu, "For the one who could still lead the Han Dynasty, would he be someone with the surname Gongsun?"

In the end, the debate did not yield a clear winner. Gongsun Shu persisted in declaring himself emperor, styling himself as the White Emperor (and the city derived its name from this, known as the White Emperor City, as referenced in Li Bai's verse "Leaving the White Emperor City, amidst colorful clouds" and the place where Liu Bei entrusted his son), while Liu Xiu achieved unification through the strength of his formidable military forces.

The development of history can be quite amusing at times. Despite Liu Xiu's earnest criticism of Gongsun Shu for not meeting the criteria as mentioned by Emperor Wu of Han, he could never have anticipated that his own actions would unexpectedly strengthen the legitimacy of using the prophecy to justify a change of dynasty.

In the late Eastern Han Dynasty, after the warlord Li Que seized control of Chang'an and dominated the political scene, there were courtiers who suggested, "Tu Gao is '阙' (que)." It was a veiled reference, indicating the lofty observatory on the palace gate—the Wei Que (Figure 4.6). According to the prophecies, someone with a name sounding like "que," such as Li Que, should soon inherit the imperial throne.

Unfortunately, he faced defeat before Li Que could contemplate whether this interpretation was correct.

Following his downfall, the stage was set for the privileged offspring of the "Four Generations and Three Dukes," with Yuan Shu stepping into the spotlight.

Yuan Shu's strategists suggested, "The 'Gao' in '涂高' (Tu Gao) refers to a high-ranking aristocrat, symbolizing status. 'Dang Tu' represents the name, and Yuan Shu's

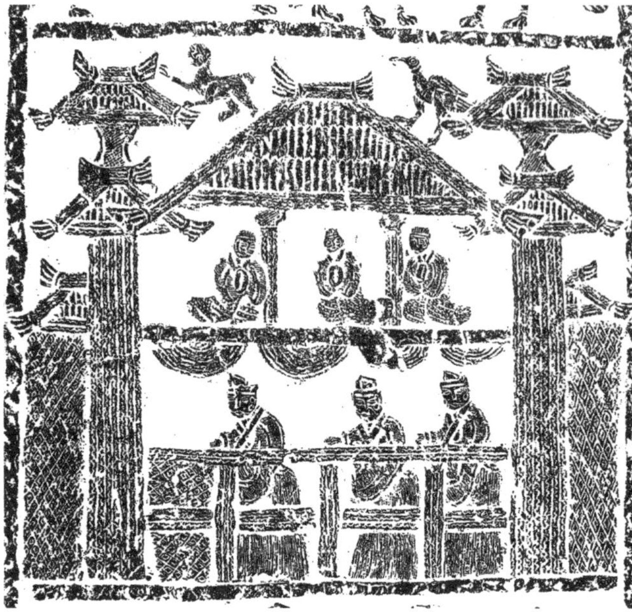

Figure 4.6 Twin Que in rubbings from stone portraits of the Eastern Han Dynasty

style name is 公路 (Gonglu), where '路' (lu) is synonymous with '途' (Tu) in Chinese. Moreover, "途" (Tu) has the same pronunciation as "涂" (Tu). Thus, the prophecy points to Yuan Shu." Yuan Shu suddenly realized that he was the true chosen one!

So, after obtaining the imperial seal and relying on the momentum created by the prophecy, Yuan Shu joyfully declared himself emperor. However, the result was that he was defeated in battle and became a laughingstock.

Decades later, when Cao Pi declared himself emperor, forcing Emperor Xian of the Han Dynasty to abdicate, Cao Pi's minister Xu Zhi once again brought up the prophecy and explained, "The one could still lead the Han Dynasty should be Wei, and the resemblance to Wei is the twin que. The road to greatness is Wei, and Wei will lead the Han."

At that time, there was Wei Que on the palace gates, high on the road, perfectly fulfilling the prophecy. This interpretation delighted Cao Pi, realizing the prophecy referred to him, dispelling all his anxieties.

A prophecy with several interpretations passed down through generations, inspiring heroes to come forward. Thus, Emperor Liu Che's influence lingered through time.

Is the prophecy truly so accurate?

In reality, the appeal of prophecies lies in their mystery and entertainment value. When a prophecy appears, people naturally contemplate its hidden meanings. When events or phenomena align with the prophecy, a sudden realization occurs, deepening the belief in its mystique.

From a modern perspective, the mystery of prophecies loses its allure. The "fulfillment" of prophecies is not so much due to the multiple meanings and interpretations of the text, but rather a form of linguistic play.

Words like "Gongsun" can be interpreted as both a royal grandson and the Gongsun family; "Hu" can mean both foreigners and Hu Hai. As long as associations can be made, people are inclined to believe.

Why are so many "fulfilled" prophecies passed down?

It's because only those that seem to have come true are recorded and circulated. Prophecies that did not come true may have been eliminated over time, making them appear absurd today.

Therefore, instead of exaggerating the accuracy of prophecies or dismissing them as mere superstition, it is wiser to approach this historical cultural phenomenon with reason. Understanding the social environment and cultural psychology of that time adds an element of fascination.

6. Xuanji Diagram *and Palindromic Poetry*

The first of the two poems, titled *Dream Recollections* by the great literary figure Su Dongpo in the Song Dynasty, is palindromic. If you read this poem backward, starting from the last character, it still forms a beautiful seven-character quatrain.

In ancient times, a literary style where the same text could be read forwards and backward was referred to as a palindrome.

In the *Dragon Carving and the Literary Mind · Ming Shi* section, it is mentioned, "The origin of palindromes lies in Dao Yuan," but the identity of Dao Yuan remains unknown. Today, the earliest work recognized as a true palindrome is Su Hui's *Xuanji Diagram*, which emerged during the Southern and Northern Dynasties period. Therefore, people commonly regard it as the ancestor of palindromes.

Su Hui, a woman from the former Qin period, is mentioned in the *Book of Jin · Biographies of Women*, "Dou Tao's wife, surnamed Su, was from Shi Ping, named Hui, styled Ruolan, skilled in composing prose. Tao, serving as the Inspector of Qin Prefecture during Fu Jian's reign, was later banished to the Desert of Sands. Su, missing him, wove a brocade, creating a *Xuanji Diagram* to present to Tao as a gift. When read cyclically, the verses were extremely poignant, totaling eight hundred and forty characters, with many lines not recorded."

Fu Jian was the unfortunate king of the Former Qin defeated by the Eastern Jin Dynasty in the famous Battle of Fei River, leaving behind the idiom "a fleeing army's suspicion of danger at the slightest sound." Su Hui's husband was a subordinate of Fu Jian. There are various versions of why Su Hui wove a palindromic poem on brocade.

Taiping Imperial Encyclopedia quotes *Records of the Former Qin* (a history of Former Qin compiled by the Northern Wei historian Cui Hong), stating that Su Hui "wove brocade and composed a palindromic poem to redeem her husband's sins." This implies that Su Hui created the palindrome to seek forgiveness for her husband, Dou Tao.

However, the *Selections of Refined Literature*, quoting the *Preface to the Palindromic Poem on Woven Brocade*, records that Dou Tao married a young and beautiful woman after being exiled to the border. Su Hui created the palindromic poem with the hope of winning her husband back.

Despite different versions, the stories converge at a happy ending: Dou Tao is pardoned, and the couple's love is rekindled. Thus, *Xuanji Diagram* fulfills its mission and becomes a lasting legacy.

In 1994, a mural featuring *The Brocade Weaving Palindrome Picture* was discovered in No. 2 Liao Tomb in Baoshan, Chifeng (Figure 4.7), vividly illustrating the intricate story behind Su Hui's creation of the palindromic poem.

However, there was no specific term for the *Xuanji Diagram* during Su Hui's time. It is speculated that the name may be related to Wu Zetian.

Wu Zetian, also a woman, highly praised the *Xuanji Diagram* to an extraordinary extent, even personally composing a preface for it.

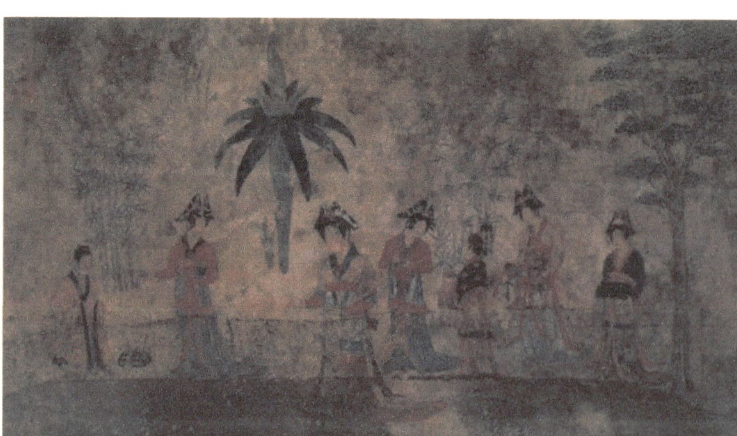

Figure 4.7 Mural *The Brocade Weaving Palindrome Picture* in the Liao tomb

In her preface, Wu Zetian lauded the palindromic poem as "colorful and expressive, dazzling the eyes," "running vertically and horizontally, all forming exquisite verses," and praised its "flawless strokes and dots, describing the brilliance of talent that transcends the present and surpasses the ancient, naming it the *Xuanji Diagram*."

Xuanji originally refers to an ancient instrument used for astronomical measurements, also indicating the stars of the Big Dipper. By naming the poem after Xuanji, she metaphorically describes the exquisite and diverse nature of crafting the palindromic poem.

This is indeed a very high praise. However, the *Xuanji Diagram* undoubtedly deserves such acclaim.

The creation is exceptionally intricate, comprising a total of 841 characters (with the addition of the character "心," which means "heart" in the middle during its transmission), woven with threads of five colors. It consists of 29 characters in both vertical and horizontal directions, and it can be read vertically, horizontally, diagonally, in various combinations, and in both normal and reverse order. One character removed or repeated can still form a poem, and it can form poetry ranging from three to seven characters.

For example, a poem with seven characters in one line expresses longing for the husband: "In sorrow and longing, my heart increases distress, yearning for the harmony of music. Concealing my grief, I sing a Qin song, and the zither resonates, flowing like a Qin."

Similarly, a poem with four characters to a line conveys concern for chaotic times, "Slanderous villains and wickedness harm my loyalty; disaster arises from reliance, thriving to the extreme of arrogance."

As Su Hui did not provide the method for reading the *Xuanji Diagram*, and historical records like the *Book of Jin* were not detailed in this aspect, the interpretation of the poem has relied on personal understanding and interpretation since the Tang Dynasty. Consequently, the understanding of the palindromic poem and the number of poems derived from it have varied over different times.

It is said that Wu Zetian initially deciphered over 200 poems from it. However, as time went on, the methods of interpretation became more diverse, and the number of poems deciphered continued to increase. As of now, approximately 7,958 poems have been statistically identified. The fact that over 800 characters can yield such a large number of poems is indeed surprising. The *Xuanji Diagram* naturally caused a sensation, astounding the world and making waves among people at that time.

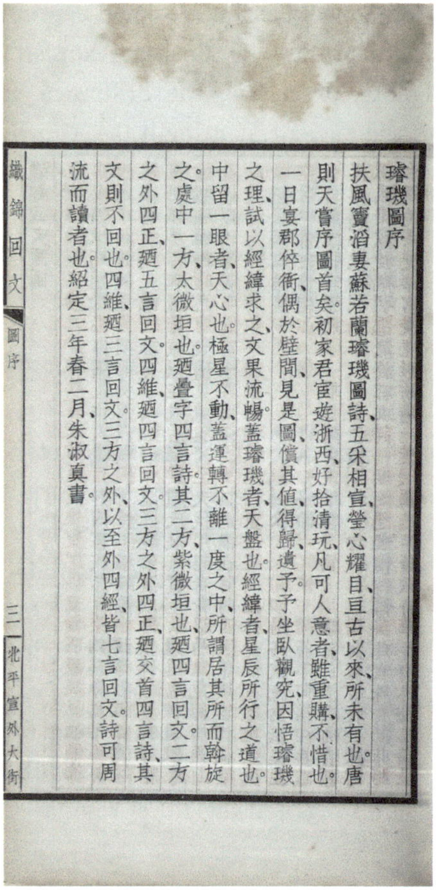

璿璣圖序

扶風竇滔妻蘇若蘭璿璣圖詩、五采相宣、瑩心耀目、亘古以來、所未有也。唐則天嘗序圖首矣。初家君宦遊浙西、好拾清玩、凡可人意者、雖重購、不惜也。一日宴郡倅衛、偶於壁間、見是圖、償其值、得歸遺予。予坐臥觀究、因悟璿璣之理、試以經緯求之、文果流暢、蓋璿璣者、天盤也、經緯者、星辰所行之道也。中留一眼者、天心也。極星不動、蓋運轉不離一度之中、所謂居其所而斡旋之處。中一方、太微垣也、迴疊字四言詩、其二方、紫微垣也、迴四言回文。二方之外四正、迴五言回文、四維、迴四言回文、三方之外四正、迴交首四言詩、其文則不回也。四維、迴三言回文、三方之外、以至外四經、皆七言回文。詩可周流而讀者也。紹定三年春二月、朱淑真書。

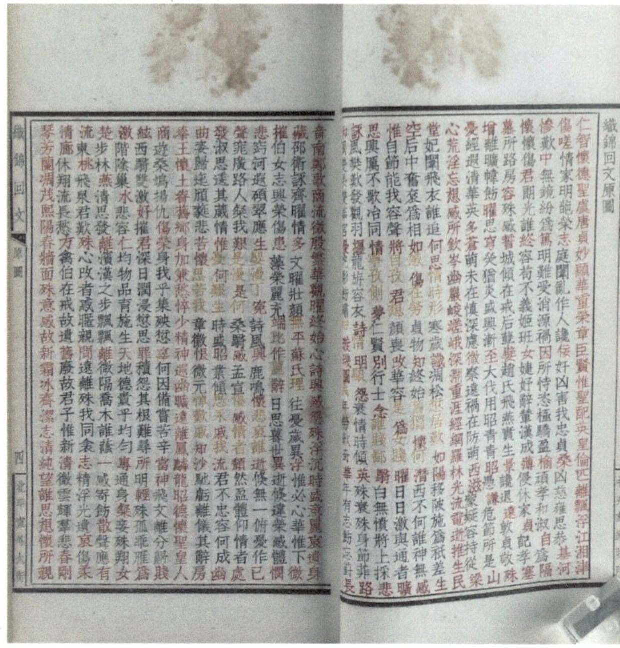

Figure 4.8 (LEFT) The record of Wu Zetian's preface to the *Xuanji Diagram* in *The Brocade Weaving Palindrome*

Figure 4.9 (ABOVE) *Xuanji Diagram* recorded in *The Brocade Weaving Palindrome*

However, among these over 7,000 poems, many verses are obscure and unintelligible, giving a sense of forced construction. Rather than displaying elegance and beauty typical of poetry, they resemble more of a linguistic game.

However, the impact of the *Xuanji Diagram* on literary creation is significant. Since the Southern and Northern Dynasties, there has been a continuous tradition of palindromic composition in various dynasties, including poets like Lu Guimeng and Pi Rixiu in the Tang Dynasty.

Pi Rixiu is also known as Xi Mei, and Lu Guimeng is also known as Lu Wang. They each made one palindromic poem as a poetic exchange between them. For ordinary people, crafting a palindromic poem is already a challenging task, but for Lu and Pi, it seems as effortless as writing an assigned composition. Moreover, they used

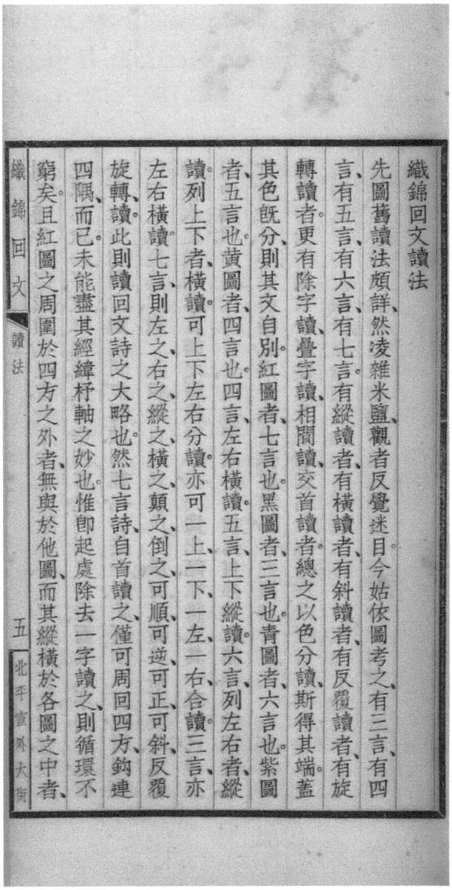

織錦回文讀法

先圖舊讀法頗詳、然淩雜米鹽、觀者反覺迷目。今姑依圖考之、有三言、有四言、有五言、有六言、有七言。有縱讀者、有橫讀者、有斜讀者、有反覆讀者、有旋轉讀者。更有除字讀、疊字讀、相間讀、交首讀者。總之以色分讀、斯得其端。蓋其色既分、則其文自別。紅圖者、七言也。黑圖者、三言也。青圖者、六言也。紫圖者、五言也。黃圖者、四言也。四言左右橫讀。五言上下縱讀。六言列左右者、縱讀。列上下者、橫讀。可上下左右分讀。亦可一上一下、一左一右、合讀。三言亦左右橫讀。七言則左之右之、縱之橫之、顛之倒之、可順、可逆、可正、可斜、反覆旋轉讀。此則讀回文詩之大略也。然七言詩、自首讀之、僅可周回四方、鈎連四隅而已。未能盡其經緯杼軸之妙也。惟即起處除去一字讀之、則循環不窮矣。且紅圖之周圍於四方之外者、無與於他圖、而其縱橫於各圖之中者、

織錦回文　讀法　五

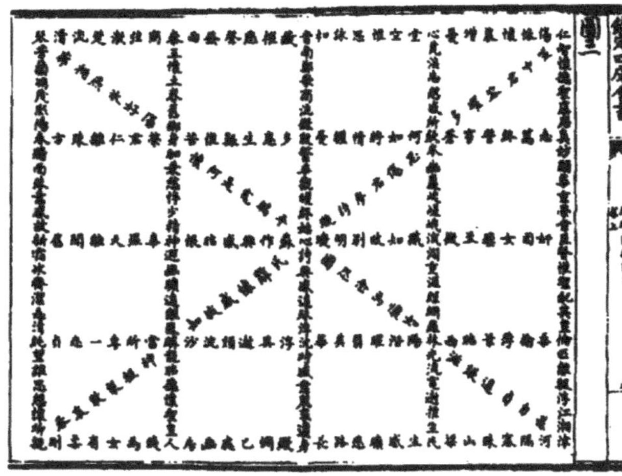

Figure 4.10 (LEFT) The reading method of the *Xuanji Diagram* in *The Brocade Weaving Palindrome*

Figure 4.11 (ABOVE) The *Reading Method of Poems in the Xuanji Diagram* recorded in the *Complete Library in the Four Branches of Literature*

palindromic poems as gifts, elevating the art of palindromic composition to a new level.

In the Song Dynasty, the popularity of palindromic poems soared, with many renowned literary figures, such as Wang Anshi, Su Shi, and Qin Guan, writing such poems. Building on the tradition of palindromic poems, palindromic ci-poem works emerged, with Su Shi, Huang Tingjian, Zhu Xi, and others contributing numerous works, many of which are preserved in the *Complete Ci-Poem Works of Song Dynasty*.

In the third year of the Yuanfeng era (1080), during the reign of Emperor Shen Zong of the Song Dynasty, Su Shi, due to the "Wutai Poetry Case," was exiled to Huangzhou, facing solitude and hardship. He composed palindromic ci-poem works as a means of release.

"Guiyuan" originally served as a medium for women to express loneliness or the longing in separation. When written by others, it typically came as a singular piece. Su Shi, however, penned four *Bodhisattva's Lament* at once, reflecting the depth of his emotional turmoil during that period. Despite being a "mass production" of sorts, these four ci-poem works collectively convey a poignant and unified sentiment, showcasing the profound talent of the poet.

7. Taoist Talismans

Fulu (talismans), also known as "danshu" or "fuzi," are a combination of symbols and written characters in Taoism. "Fu" refers to symbol books drawn with vermilion or ink,

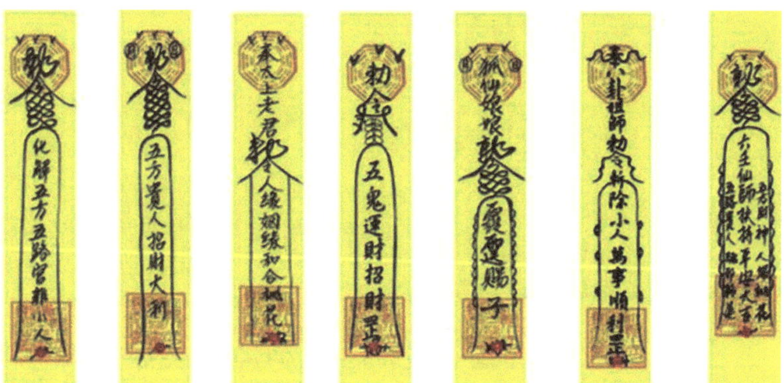

Figure 4.12 Taoist talismans

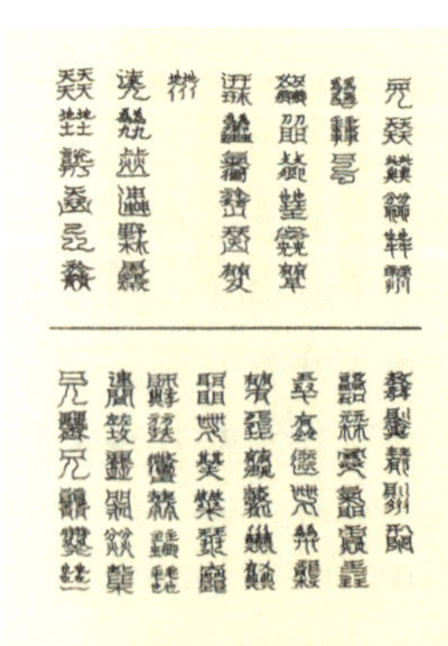

Figure 4.13 Taoist composite characters

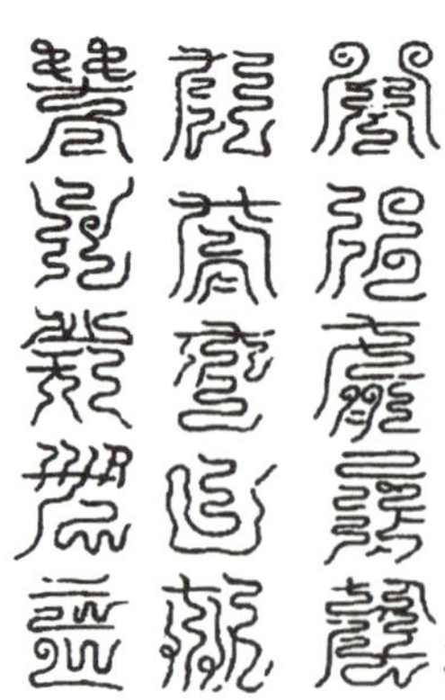

Figure 4.14 Tianshu cloud seal script

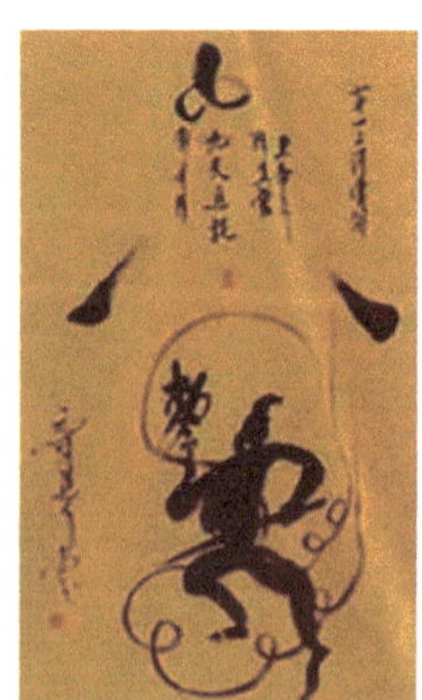

Figure 4.15 Taoist symbolic drawings

combining dots and lines with characters, characterized by mainly winding strokes. "Lu" records the names, forms, and related information of Taoist deities.

The content of Taoist talismans is profoundly esoteric. There are several types closely related to written characters:

(1) Fuwen (Composite Characters). Resembling auspicious characters seen during festivals, Taoist composite characters are formed by combining two or more characters. Some are composed of complex strokes and twists. Early examples can be found in the Eastern Han Dynasty's *Scripture of Great Peace*, with over 2,000 characters, many of which remain undeciphered.

(2) Yunzhuan (Cloud Seal Script). Also known as Tianshu Yunzhuan, this is a unique Taoist script that resembles the seal script. Characterized by intricate and overlapping strokes, it creates a visually impactful and mysterious effect, earning it the name "Heavenly Script."

(3) Futu (Symbolic Drawings). There are two main types. One involves printing celestial images around the edges of the talisman paper, accompanied by symbolic characters. The other consists of highly intricate patterns formed by circles, dots, and lines.

Sometimes, to enhance the effect, symbolic drawings, composite characters, and others are combined for use, as seen in the Taoist eight trigrams talismans and astrological signs on a Tang Dynasty bronze mirror (Figure 4.16, Figure 4.17).

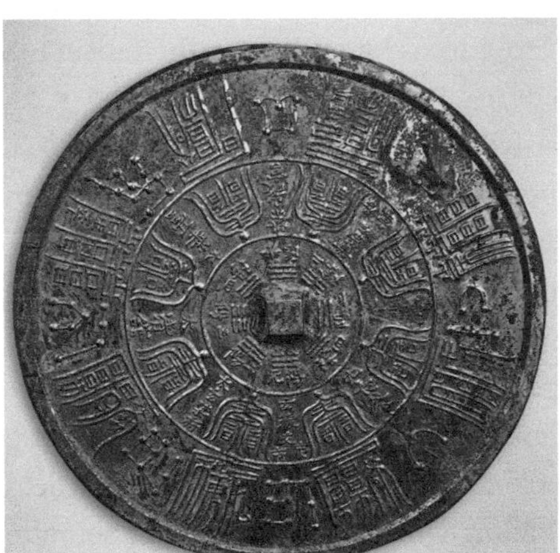

Figure 4.16 Tang Dynasty eight trigrams talisman astrological signs mirror unearthed in Mengzhou, Henan (currently stored in the Luoyang Museum)

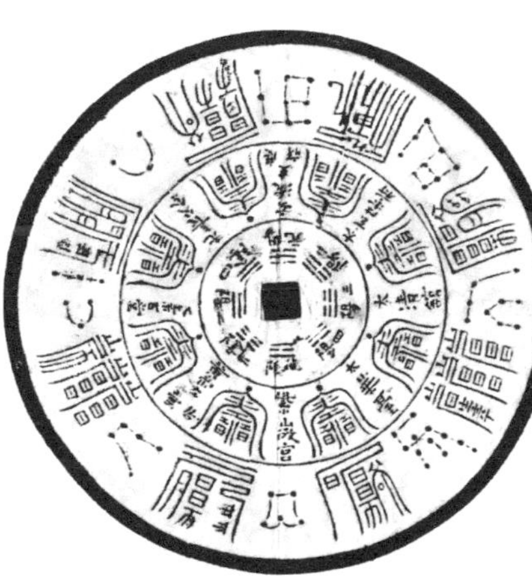

Figure 4.17 Rubbing of the Tang Dynasty eight trigrams talisman astrological signs Mirror unearthed in Mengzhou, Henan

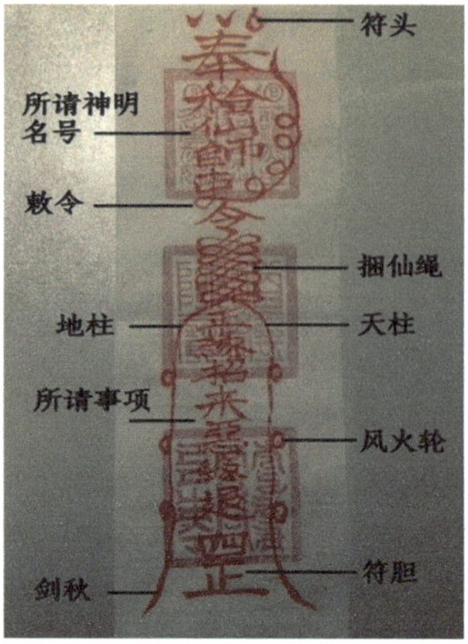

Figure 4.18 Main content of Taoist talismans

Common talismans generally include the talisman head, body, and foot, along with the names of the invited deities, instructions, and the requested matters (Figure 4.18).

The talisman head is like the eyes of a talisman, often represented by three hooks, symbolizing the Taoist Three Pure Ones, or City God, Earth God, and Ancestral Master. The talisman body is where the soul of the talisman resides, determining whether the talisman is effective. It often contains secret characters, such as "正" (zhèng), "罡" (gāng), and "井" (jǐng). In Taoism, drawing a talisman is essentially inviting divine spirits to guard within the talisman. Without a proper talisman body to guard within, the talisman cannot fully exert its effects. The variation in the talisman foot depends on its purpose.

Additionally, there was a close relationship between writing talismans and calligraphy in the early days. Those proficient in writing talismans within Taoism were often accomplished in calligraphy. Likewise, many renowned calligraphers throughout history were skilled in writing talismans.

To ensure the effectiveness of a talisman, it was common practice to silently recite an incantation while writing it. Starting from the talisman's head, if the strokes seamlessly aligned with the incantation, it was referred to as "stepping on the talisman's head."

During the Eastern Jin period, Ge Hong recorded a secret incantation called "Liu Jia" in his work *Inner Chapters of Master Embracing Simplicity · Ascending in River*. It goes, "When entering the mountains, one should know the secret invocation of the Liu Jia. The incantation goes, 'Those facing the battlefield should advance to the front of the formation.' It consists of nine characters, and one should frequently recite it secretly. It wards off all dangers without fail and is the essential path to tranquility."

In the concept of Ge Hong and many Taoist practitioners of that time, when entering the mountains, silently reciting the incantation "Those facing the battlefield should advance to the front of the formation" along with specific steps can serve to protect oneself and ward off evil.

After completing a talisman, it often required the application of Taoist-specific seals to enhance its efficacy. While some believed that talismans didn't necessarily need seals, the vast majority of talismans observed typically featured these seals.

In addition to seals, Taoist talismans sometimes incorporated spells, steps, ritual tools, and other elements. The intricate process of creating a talisman highlights the systematic and mysterious nature of Taoist culture.

Taoist talismans come in various types, and their usage methods are strictly differentiated. Sometimes, to fulfill the needs of ordinary people seeking wealth, home protection, relationship enhancement, and evil warding, talismans are crafted for purchase and intended for people to carry with them for good fortune.

The money charms depicted in Figures 4.19 to 4.22 are all cast with Taoist talismans or incantations, which can be read fluently when recited. In addition, there are many money charms in people's lives that feature only symbols or immortal figures without any written words. As these are not directly related to the discussion of Chinese characters in this book, I will refrain from providing further details on them.

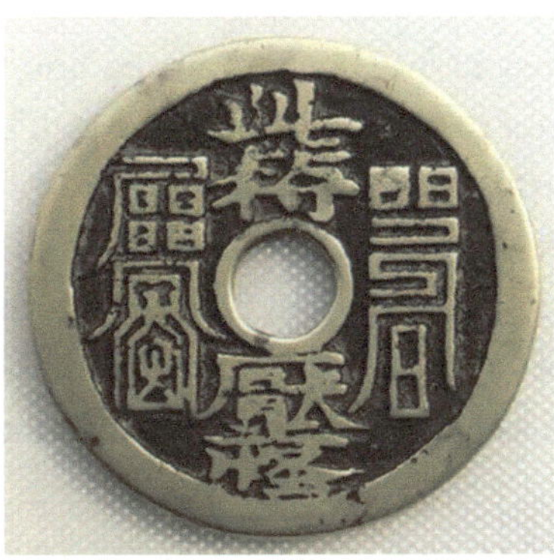

Figure 4.19 Money charm

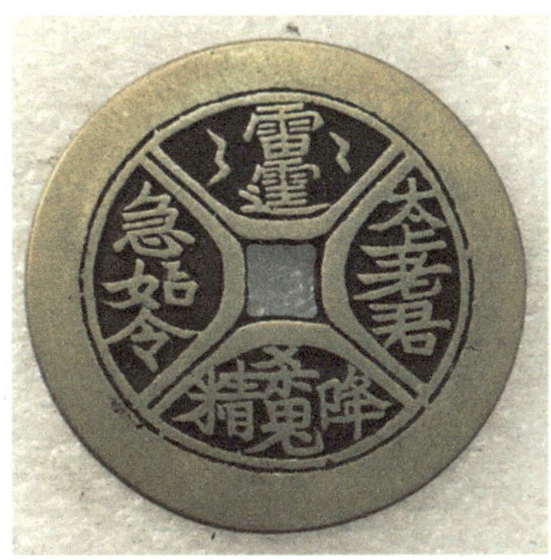

Figure 4.20 Money charm

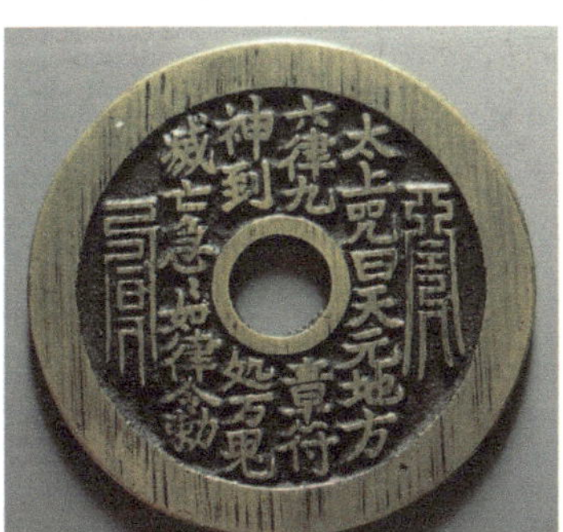

Figure 4.21 Money charm

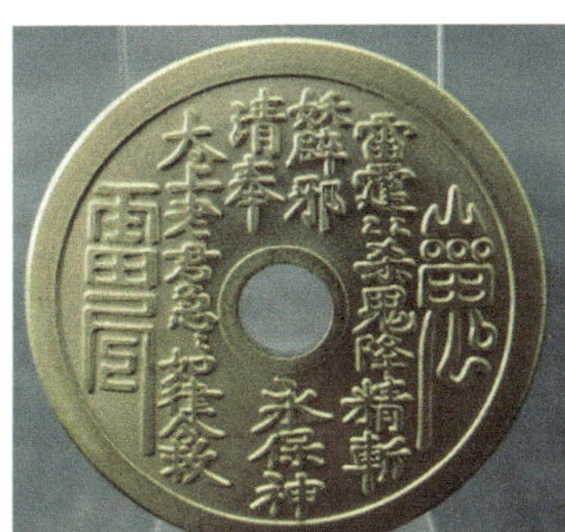

Figure 4.22 Money charm

8. Idioms Least Like Idioms

Idioms are fixed phrases composed of several Chinese characters, often refined through long-term usage. According to incomplete statistics, over 50,000 idioms have been used by people throughout history, most of which are four-character phrases and often have literary sources.

Examples include "狐假虎威" (Fox Borrowing the Tiger's Ferocity) from *Intrigues of the Warring States*, "刻舟求剑" (Carving a Boat to Seek a Sword) from *Master Lü's Spring and Autumn Annals*, "自相矛盾" (Self-Contradictory) from *Han Feizi*, and "完璧归赵" (Returning a Jade Intact to Zhao) from *Records of the Grand Historian*. These idioms either originate from fables or historical stories, often with precise structures and profound meanings.

However, there are also some idioms with distinctive personalities, emphasizing beauty, such as "岸芷汀兰" (Fragrance by the Shore) and "梨花带雨" (describing the delicate and beautiful appearance of a woman), or appearing somewhat silly, like "博士买驴" (describing writing or speaking that is overly complicated and verbose, lacking in capturing the essence or core points of the issue.) and "冬日可爱" (Like the sun in winter, it brings warmth and comfort to people); or being refreshing, such as "莼羹鲈脍" (referring to the delicious dishes from one's hometown) and "早韭晚菘" (referring to seasonal vegetables); or being extremely tongue-twisting, like "蹑蹻担簦" (describing a person wearing grass shoes and carrying a bamboo hat on their back, suggesting a long journey or arduous trek) and "滂渤怫郁" (describing a scene of turbulent waves or surging waters).

There are also some idioms that, at first glance, don't look like idioms, such as:

"蛤蟆夜哭" (Frog Weeping at Night. It's usually used to describe baseless accusations made against innocent people), from *Miscellaneous Notes by Ai Zi*, attributed to Su Dongpo.

Legend has it that a person named Ai Zi sailed in the sea, anchored on an island at night, and heard someone crying underwater. It sounded like someone was talking.

One voice said, "Yesterday, the Dragon King issued an order that all aquatic creatures with tails should be beheaded. I am a toad, and I am very afraid of being killed, so I am crying. But you are a frog without a tail; why are you crying non-stop?"

Then another voice said, "I currently don't have a tail, but I'm afraid the Dragon King will investigate that I used to be a tadpole!"

A frog doesn't have a tail, but tadpoles, just born, do have tails. This idiom illustrates that you can always find a reason if you want to find fault with someone. Later, it came to mean groundless accusations against innocent people.

For instance, "破马张飞" is said to originate from an argument between Zhang Fei and Ma Chao. It is now often used to describe a person dancing with excitement, showing a lively and vigorous appearance.

"汝成人耶" (Are you a true person?) is also an idiom. It questions whether someone can truly be considered a person. Indeed, this is an idiom.

In fact, there are quite a few idioms with unexpected meanings. Some interesting examples include:

"惨绿少年": It's from Zhang Gu's *Youxian Guchui* in the Tang Dynasty, "Upon arrival, the lady looked at him through the curtain and, after the meeting, happily said, 'All your peers are here; there is nothing to worry about. But who is that miserable green youth in the last seat?'" Originally referred to a young man wearing light green clothes, it later extended to describe a handsome young man. Under no circumstances should this person be understood as being "miserable to the point of turning green."

"女生外向": It's from Ban Gu's *The Confucian Classics Discussions in Bai Hu Hall Meeting* in the Han Dynasty, "With males being introverted, there is a sense of staying at home; with females being outgoing, there is a sense of following their husbands." Legend has it that when a girl is born, her face is turned outward, suggesting that a daughter's thoughts are oriented towards her future husband. Here, "外向" means "facing outward" rather than having an extroverted personality.

"灾梨祸枣": Also written as "祸枣灾梨." From Ji Xiaolan's *Notes of the Thatched Abode of Close Observations* in the Qing Dynasty, "Calamity follows calamity, disasters pass on to each other." In ancient woodblock printing, pear or jujube wood was often used for carving printing blocks. If someone's work is of poor quality, it is considered harmful to the trees cut down to make the printing blocks, describing poorly engraved or useless books. Here, one can't help but exclaim that the literati of the past were sharp-tongued enough; they could scold people without using profanity.

"鲁鱼亥豕": "鲁鱼" is from Ge Hong' s *Master Embracing Simplicity*, "There is a saying that goes like after writing for three times, the character '鱼' will become '鲁,' and the character '虚' will become '虎.'" "亥豕" is from *Master Lü's Spring and Autumn Annals*, "There are readers of the *Records of the Grand Historian* who say, 'The Jin army crossed the river with three pigs (三豕).' Zixia said, 'No, it's 己亥 instead of 三豕. Because the character 己 looks similar to 三, and 亥 looks similar to 豕.'" This originally referred to textual errors in the writing or printing process of books, but now often refers to writing errors or inadvertent mistakes made in general.

"加减乘除": It's from Wang Jiusi's *Admiring the Goodness · Following Rhymes, Dedicated to Shao Jinfu on His Retirement*, "What is truly a peaceful figure, who would have thought, in the calculations of fate, addition, subtraction, multiplication, and division." Originally referred to as the four arithmetic operations, it was extended to indicate changes and fluctuations. It shows that addition, subtraction, multiplication, and division were not terms invented by modern people; ancient people used them too.

"博士买驴": It's from Yan Zhitui's *Yan Family's Instructions*, "There is a saying that goes like 'A doctor buys a donkey. Three deeds are written, but the character for the donkey is not written.'" It sarcastically criticizes verbose and tedious writing without getting to the point. It seems Kong Yiji was not the only scholar who suffered from such ridicule.

"又弱一个": It's from *Zuo Qiuming's Commentary on Spring and Autumn Annals*, "Both brothers were exemplary, but then one died. How regrettable it is!" In this context, "弱" refers to the loss or decrease, mourning for someone's death. Without a good understanding of ancient Chinese, it's hard to imagine that this is its actual meaning.

"令人喷饭": It's from Su Shi's prose *Record of Huayun Daigu Yanzhu with Wen Yuke*, "Yuke went with his wife to wander in the valley during the day, and they cooked bamboo shoots for dinner. When he received a letter with a poem, he burst into laughter and sprayed food all over the table." It is often used to describe something or someone extremely amusing. Su Dongpo was indeed a magical master of idiom creation.

Chinese is vast and profound, and many words are indeed "surprising in expression and ceaselessly impressive." If you don't know the specific origin and usage, you might think they have infiltrated the ranks of idioms. Therefore, only continuous learning and accumulation can accurately use idioms, avoiding misinterpretations.

9. Easily Confused Complex and Simplified Characters

In today's usage of Chinese characters, there are often differences between complex and simplified characters. However, not all characters have complex forms. When creating calligraphy works, if one cannot distinguish between complex and simplified characters, it can lead to embarrassing mistakes.

For example, the character "后," meaning "behind," can be written as "後," but when used to mean "queen," it must be written as "后." In oracle bone inscriptions, they are two completely different characters with distinct forms.

Similar characters that are prone to confusion include:

(1) 丑: When expressing ugliness, it can be written as "醜," but when used in the context of the Chinese zodiac, it must be written as "丑," as in "子丑寅卯."

(2) 范: When indicating a model, it can be written as "範," but as a surname, it should only be written as "范," as in "范仲淹" (Fan Zhongyan).

(3) 姜: When referring to ginger as a vegetable, it can be written as "薑," but as a surname, it must be written as "姜," as in "姜子牙" (Jiang Ziya).

(4) 卜: When representing radishes, it can be written as "蔔," but in other contexts, it should only be written as "卜," as in "占卜" (divination).

(5) 干: When expressing dryness or firmness, it can be written as "乾"; when used in the sense of the trunk of the body or in administrative terms, it can be written as "幹"; but when indicating interference, it should only be written as "干."

(6) 发: When describing hair on the head or fur, it can be written as "髮," but when referring to wealth or development, it must be written as "發."

(7) 困: When conveying weariness, it can be written as "睏," but when indicating difficulties, it should only be written as "困."

(8) 余: When expressing spare time or surplus, it can be written as "餘," but when used as the first person pronoun, it should only be written as "余."

(9) 云: When representing clouds, it can be written as "雲," but when used to convey speech, it must be written as "云," as in "子曰诗云" (Confucius said, as the poem goes...).

(10) 里: When indicating the interior or inside, it can be written as "裏," but when measuring distance, it should only be written as "里."

(11) 斗: When expressing battle or struggle, it can be written as "鬥," but when referring to the Big Dipper or a funnel, it must be written as "斗."

(12) 谷: When representing rice grains, it can be written as "穀," but when indicating a mountain valley, it should only be written as "谷."

(13) 咸: When describing a salty taste, it can be written as "鹹," but when conveying all or universally, it should only be written as "咸," as in "老少咸宜" (suitable for the young and the old alike).

(14) 据: When used to represent vouchers or based on certain evidence, it can be written as "據," but when conveying financial difficulties, it should only be written as "据."

(15) 胡: When indicating facial hair like a beard, it can be written as "鬍," but when expressing unruly behavior, it must be written as "胡."

(16) 舍: When expressing abandonment or charity, it can be written as "捨," but when indicating dormitories or buildings, it should only be written as "舍."

10. Old Characters Gaining New Meanings on the Internet

In the development of Chinese characters, many characters, after disappearing for a certain period, often find their way back to the stage of Chinese characters in unique ways, becoming part of people's lives again, either borrowing their form or meaning. This is precisely the unique charm of Chinese characters.

For example, the original meaning of "囧" is brightness. Due to its resemblance to a face with eyes, eyebrows, and mouth, it has become one of the most frequently used characters in online chatting and forums. It has been imbued with a sense of depression, sadness, and helplessness, even earning the title of the "most popular Chinese character of the 21st century."

Another example is the character "槑," originally an allograph of "梅" (plum blossom). Only because this character consists of two "呆" characters, it is used in online language to describe someone as silly and naive, not only foolish but extremely so.

Similar examples include characters like "巭," "烎," "兲," "曼," "嫑," "孬," "甭," and "靐," which share the ingenious concept with the character "囧."

Additionally, there are emojis created by slightly modifying oracle bone inscriptions and pairing them with modern popular internet phrases, appearing adorable and making people want to use and share them with friends immediately, as shown in Figure 4.23.

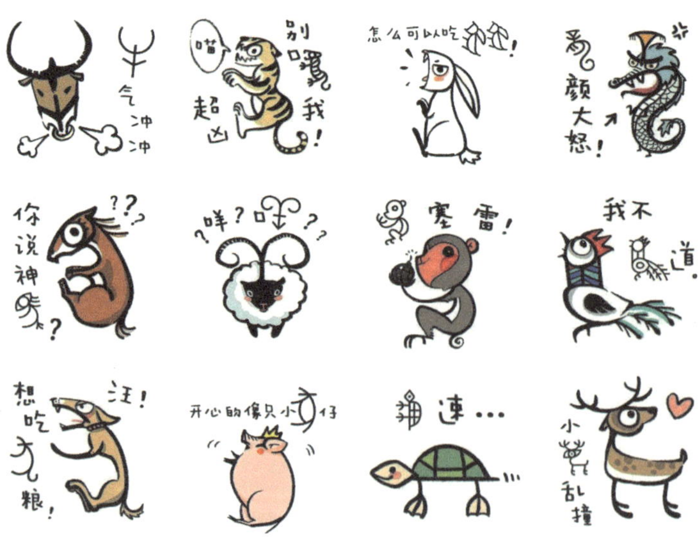

Figure 4.23 Image emoticons

CHAPTER V

Chinese Character Challenges

1. Recognizing Characters from Pictures

Oracle bone script is one of the most commonly used divinatory scripts during the Shang and Zhou dynasties, containing numerous pictographs. Can you identify the ancient representations of animals based on the Oracle bone script in the table below?

Table 5.1 Oracle bone scripts

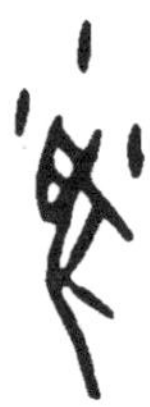	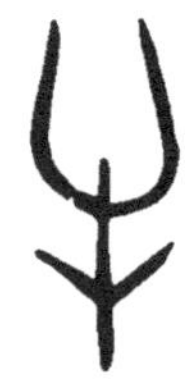	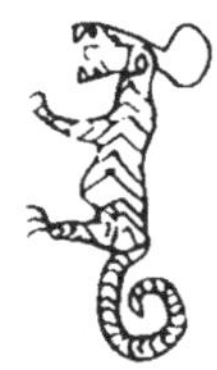	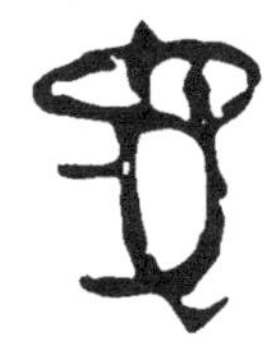
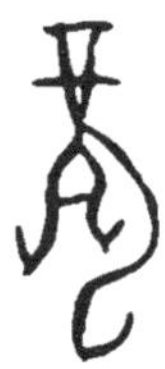	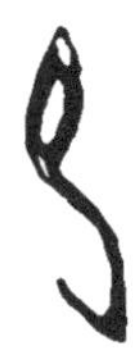	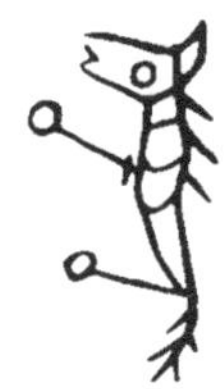	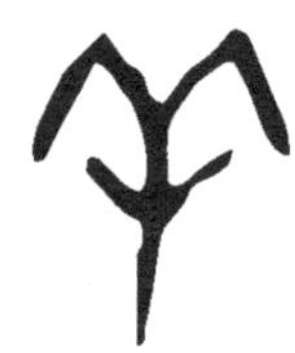
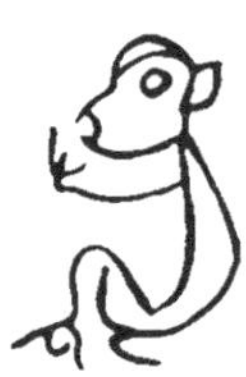	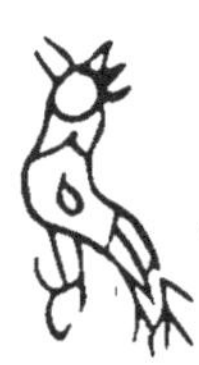	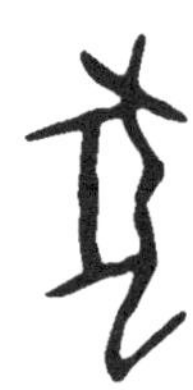	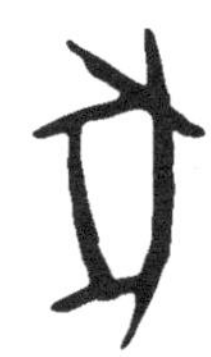

2. Chinese Calligraphy

Chinese calligraphy is an artistic form centered around Chinese characters, encompassing brushstrokes, character structure, composition, arrangement, ink application, and brush techniques.

With a long history, Chinese calligraphy has evolved through various styles, from oracle bone script and bronze inscriptions in the Shang and Zhou dynasties to regular script and cursive script in the Wei and Jin dynasties. Numerous outstanding works have achieved remarkable success.

Please identify the calligraphy content in Figures 5.1 to 5.5, along with their script styles (oracle bone script, small seal script, semi-cursive script, cursive script, slender gold style).

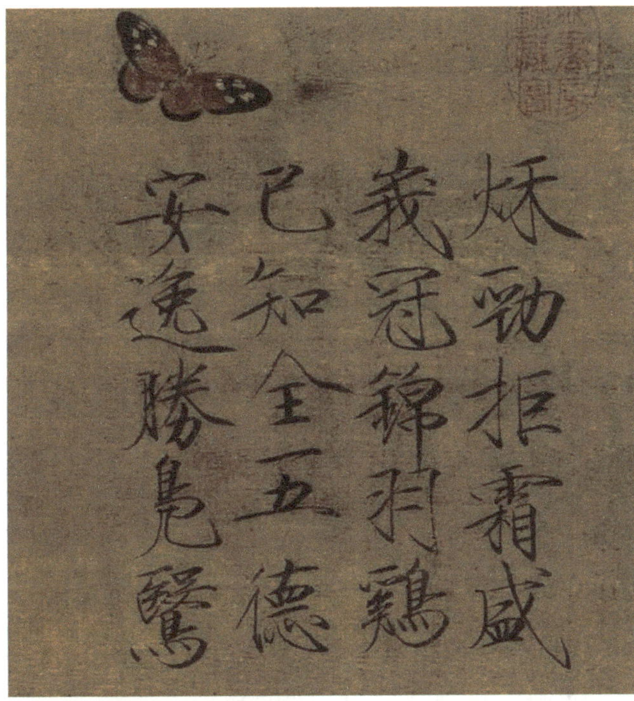

Figure 5.1 (RIGHT) Difficulty level for identification: ★☆☆☆☆

Figure 5.2 (BOTTOM) Difficulty level for identification: ★★☆☆☆

Figure 5.3 (BOTTOM RIGHT) Difficulty level for identification: ★★★☆☆

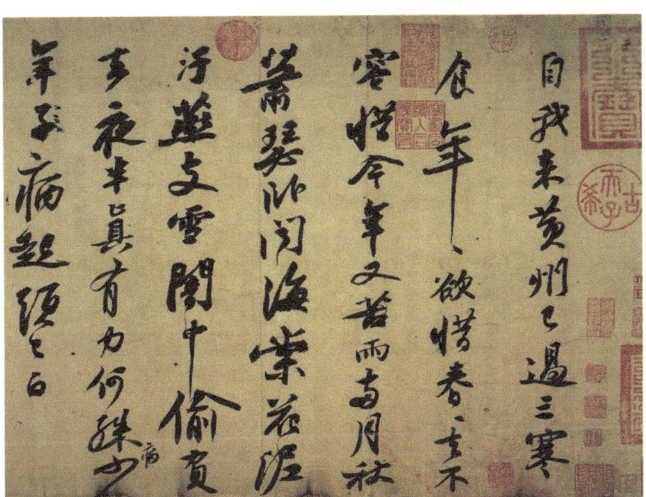

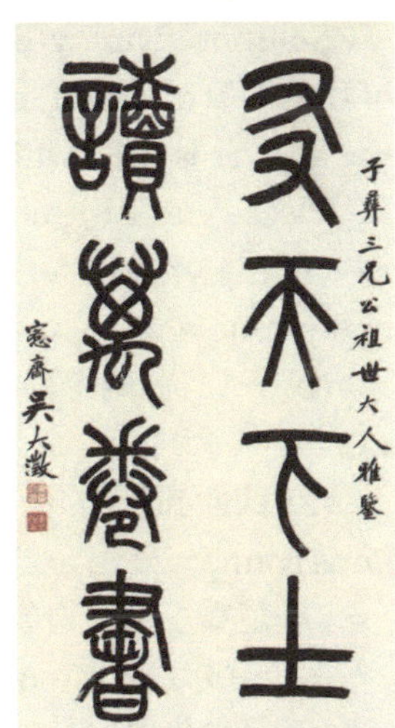

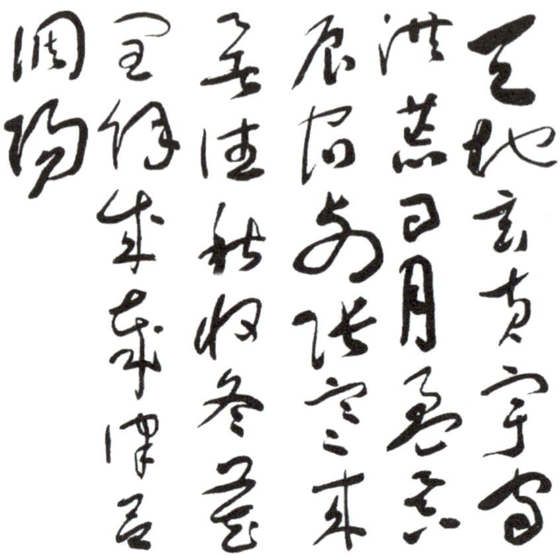

Figure 5.4 Difficulty level for identification: ★★★★☆

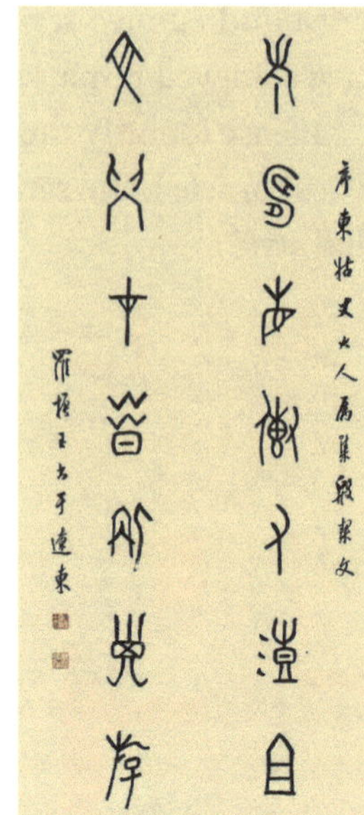

Figure 5.5 Difficulty level for identification: ★★★★★

3. Chinese Character Detective

Word puzzles are a branch of riddles, an interesting game that has been popular for thousands of years. For example:

Ninety-nine (Guess the character)

Solution: Ninety-nine is one less than one hundred. Remove the "一" (one) on top of the "百" (hundred) character, and it becomes the character "白" (white). Therefore, the answer is "白" (white).

Please guess the characters based on the riddles.

(1) 存心不让出大门, 你说烦人不犯人 (Keep the heart from leaving the gate. It's really annoying.)

(2) 一只狗, 两个口, 谁遇它谁发愁 (A dog with two mouths, whoever meets it will worry.)

(3) 四面都是山, 山山都相连 (Surrounded by mountains on all sides, and mountains connected to each other.)

(4) 楚霸王乌江自刎 (The King of Chu self-immolated in the Wu River.)

(5) 云破月来 (Clouds break, and the moon appears.)

(6) 算命先生 (Fortune-telling master)

(7) 一千零一夜 (One thousand and one nights)
(8) 上下难分 (Difficult to distinguish between top and bottom)
(9) 八十八 (Eighty-eight)
(10) 银川 (Silver River)

4. Word Match

In the current territory of China, alongside Chinese characters, there were other ethnic languages and scripts in historical circulation, such as the Khitan script of the Liao Dynasty, the Tangut script of the Western Xia Dynasty, and the Phags-pa script during the Yuan Dynasty.

In contemporary China, except for the Manchu and Hui ethnicities, who no longer use their own scripts and instead directly use Chinese characters, 29 ethnicities, including the Mongolian and Tibetan ethnicities, have scripts consistent with their languages. Moreover, some ethnic groups use more than one script, such as the Naxi people, who use four scripts, and the Jingpo people, who use two scripts.

After the establishment of the People's Republic of China, to preserve and develop ethnic cultures, the government specifically assisted ethnic groups without scripts for their languages. In the 1950s, linguistic experts and intellectuals from ethnic minorities conducted investigations and research. Latin alphabet-based writing systems were developed for 14 ethnic groups, including the Zhuang, Yi, Miao, Hani, and Lisu. Among them, four writing systems were devised for different dialects of the Miao language, and two writing systems were devised for different dialects of the Hani language. In the 1980s, in response to the requests of some ethnic minorities, phonetic writing systems were designed for the Bai, Dulong, Tujia, and Qiang ethnicities.

Some of the scripts of ethnic minorities, like Tibetan and Yi scripts, have a history of over a thousand years. Others, like Miao and Zhuang scripts, although relatively recent, have a significant impact due to their widespread usage.

The following are some scripts used by ancient people from ethnic minorities. Try to match the scripts with the corresponding figures.

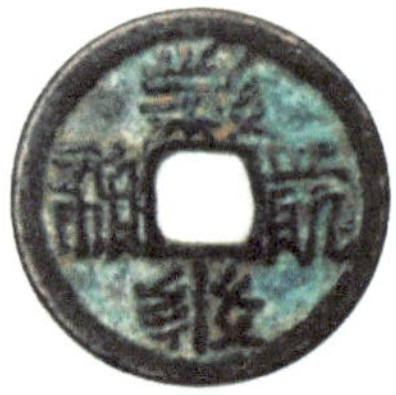

Figure 5.6

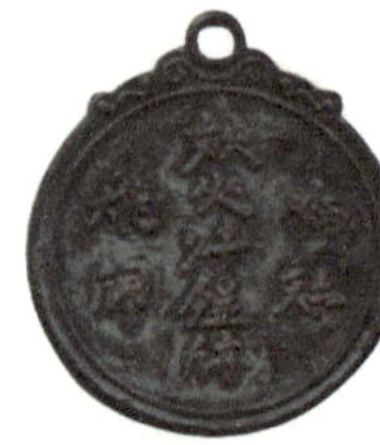

Figure 5.9

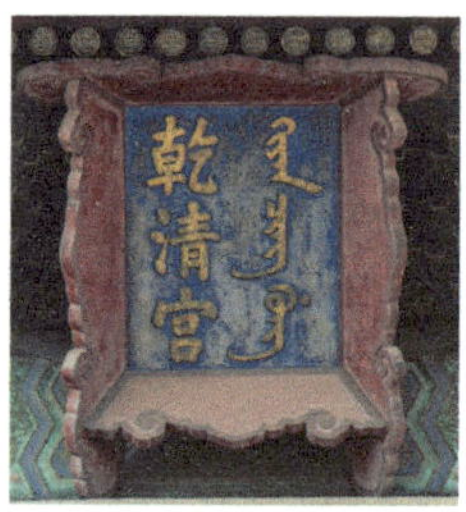

Figure 5.7

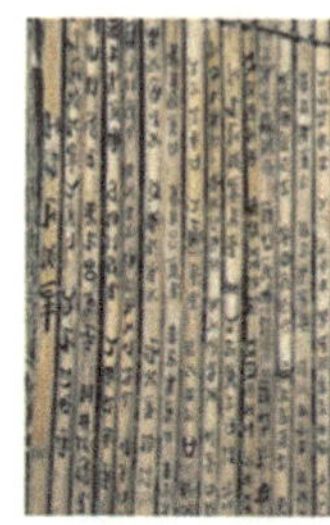

Figure 5.10

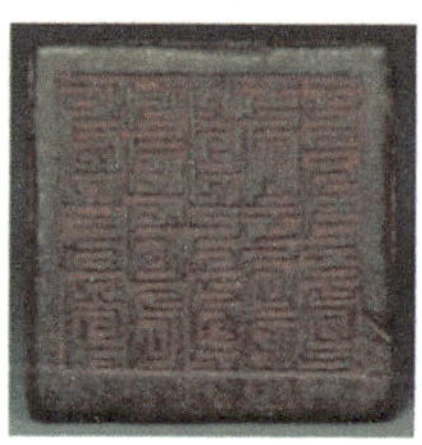

Figure 5.8

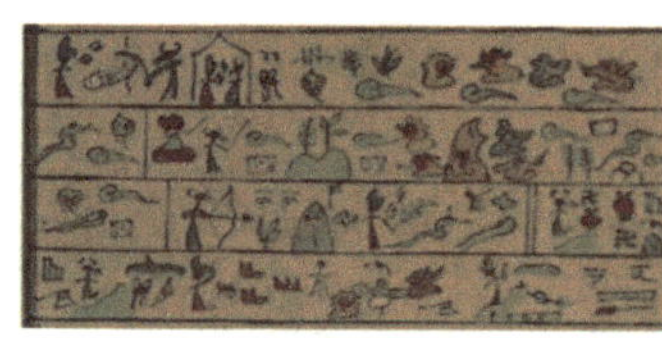

Figure 5.11

Yi script

Tangut script

Dongba script

Phags-pa script

Khitan script

Manchu script

5. Emperor's Seals

Emperor Qianlong of the Qing Dynasty is probably the emperor with the most seals in the world.

It is said that when Emperor Qianlong was a child, he and his younger brother Hongzhou both liked seals, but Qianlong could never win against his brother when it came to good seals. Whether influenced by this childhood trauma or not, Emperor Qianlong developed a special fondness for collecting various seals as he grew older.

In the Qing Dynasty, each emperor's seals had a catalog called "Baosou," and Emperor Qianlong's *Baosou* included more than 1,000 imperial seals. Additionally, more than 700 seals went missing, indicating the vast number of seals he possessed.

Emperor Qianlong not only enjoyed collecting seals but also loved using them. The more he admired a piece of calligraphy or painting, the more seals he would impress upon it. For instance, the revered *Timely Clearing after Snowfall* is considered the foremost of the "Three Rarities" by Emperor Qianlong, which originally contained just 28 characters. However, every time Emperor Qianlong appreciated it, he couldn't help but praise it, resulting in over 70 inscriptions, with the total character count exceeding tens of thousands. The seals alone were pressed more than 170 times, expanding the original 14.8-centimeter-wide scroll to a whopping 5.5 meters (see Figure 5.12).

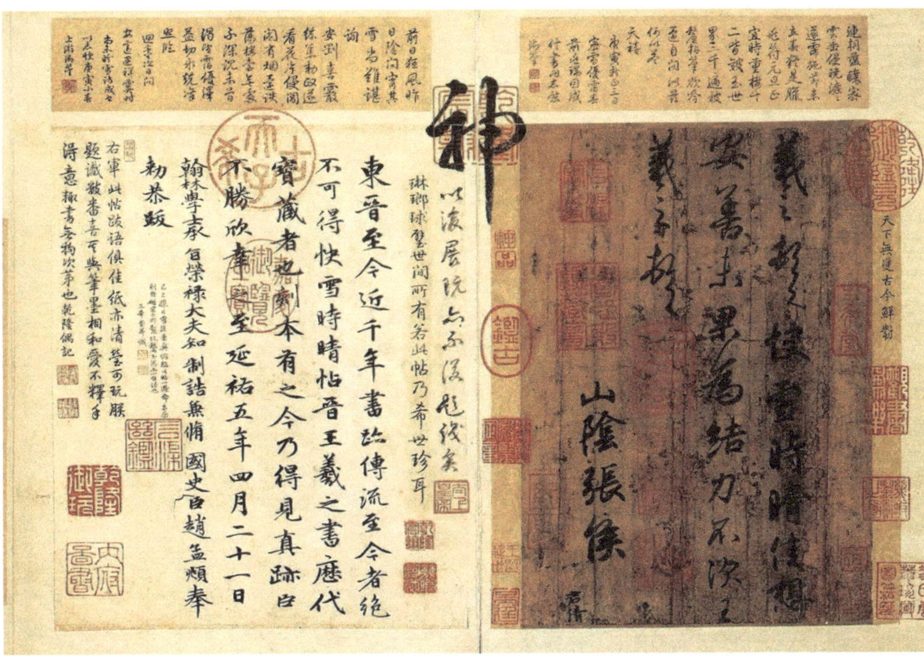

Figure 5.12 Partial view of Wang Xizhi's *Timely Clearing after Snowfall* (currently housed in the National Palace Museum in Taipei)

However, one should not assume that these seals were applied haphazardly. It is essential to note that Emperor Qianlong was one of the most meticulous emperors in Chinese history when it came to using seals. He personally supervised the work, compiling a set of "Twenty-Five Treasures" seal catalogs based on the occasion for using each seal. Emperor Qianlong established a rule that any item included in *The Precious Collection of the Stone Canal Pavilion* must bear five unified seals: "Qianlong's Imperial Appraisal," "Qianlong's Imperial Inspection," "Precious Works in Stone Canal Pavilion," "Precious Selection from the Three Rarities Halls," and "Suitable for Future Generations." Moreover, depending on the palace where the item was housed, he would add the palace's seal (see Figure 5.13).

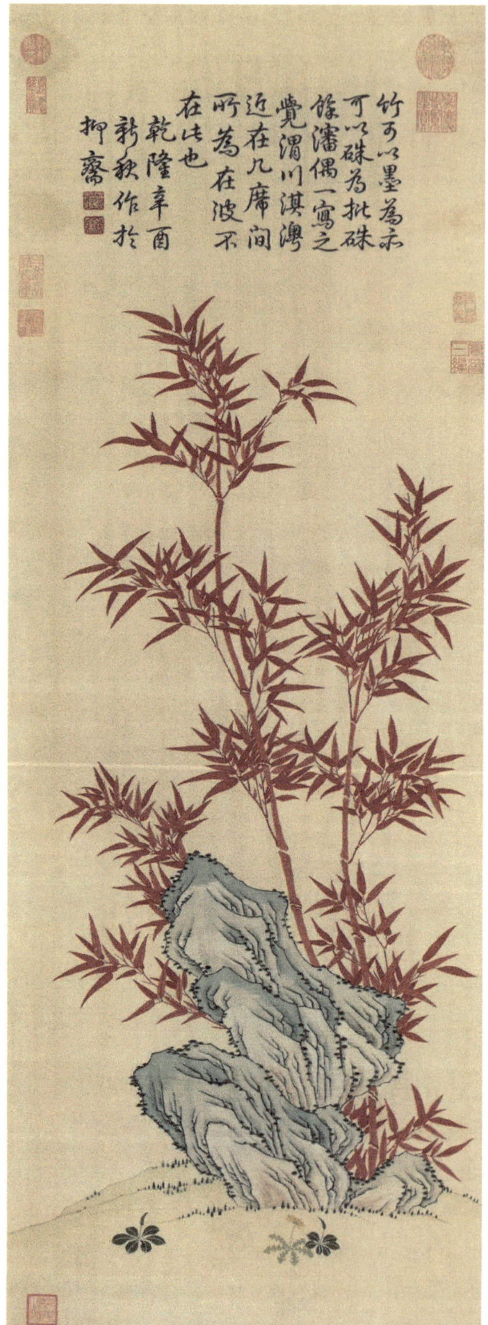

Figure 5.13 Silk-woven and vermilion bamboo painting scroll from *The Precious Collection of the Stone Canal Pavilion* (currently housed in the Palace Museum)

Now, the question arises: since Emperor Qianlong loved to "stamp" on calligraphy and paintings so much, do you know the content engraved on the seals in Figures 5.14 to 5.28?

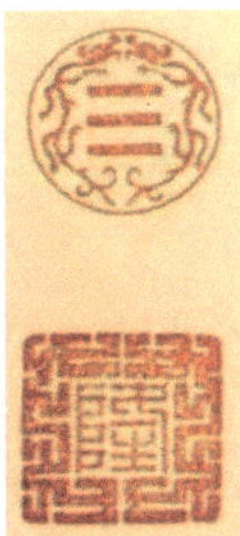
Figure 5.14

Figure 5.15

Figure 5.16

Figure 5.17

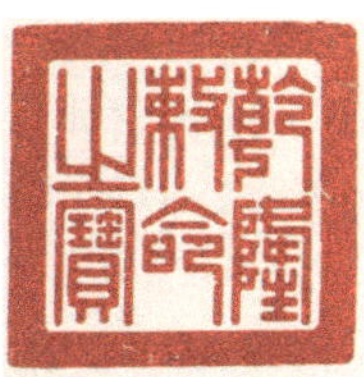
Figure 5.18

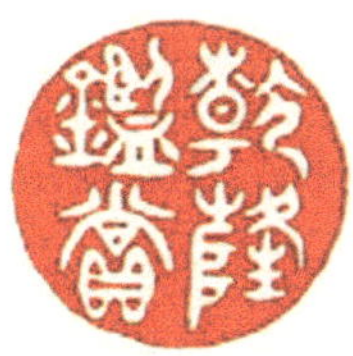
Figure 5.19

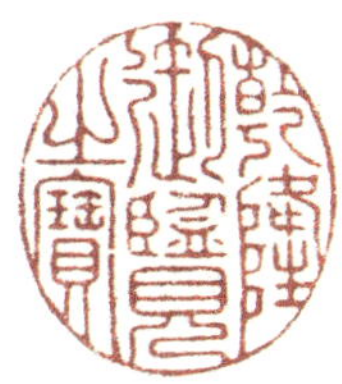
Figure 5.20

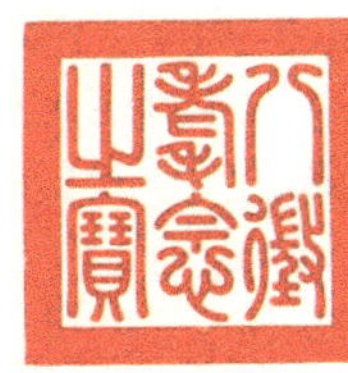
Figure 5.21

Figure 5.22

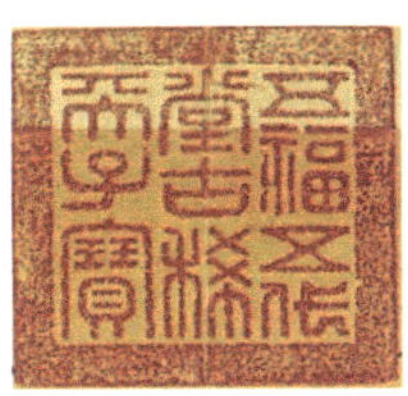
Figure 5.23

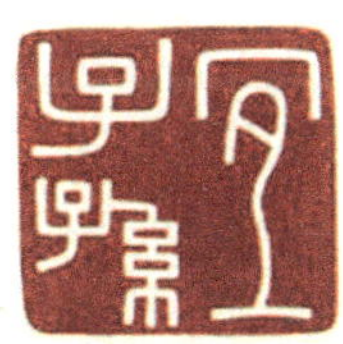
Figure 5.24

Figure 5.25

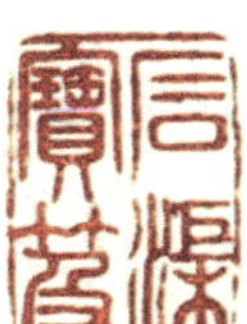
Figure 5.26

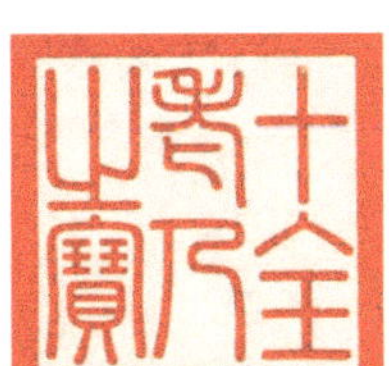
Figure 5.27

Figure 5.28

6. Rotating Chinese Characters

As is well known, the sequence of Chinese characters has changed over the ages, with ancient Chinese characters often being read from right to left. In today's context, however, Chinese characters are typically read from left to right (except in calligraphy). But did you know that in ancient times, there were occasions when Chinese characters could also be read in a rotating manner? For instance, in 1982, cultural relics workers discovered the "Panjian Picture" on a Southern Song Dynasty bronze mirror in Shunyi, Beijing (Figures 5.29 and 5.30). The characters are intertwined, continuously winding from start to finish, and the content is the lyrics of the *Full River Red.*

> Snow shares the plum blossoms, thinking that the movements are like parting for many years. Meeting again, the jade-like true demeanor, is marked with a similar elegance. Who would say that there is no envy without emotion? The hidden fragrance is buried, teaching no one to recognize it. Following the wind, stealthily entering the nearby dressing table, lingering on the curtain edges.
>
> Surprised, drunk eyes, red turns into green. With temperature changes, it divides into blue and white. Sighing, the red strings freeze and break, and the high mountain melody fades. Gazing at the passes and rivers with no courier, the river's enthusiasm exhausts into historical traces. It appears like a branch but delights in facing the willow flowers; we should remember each other.

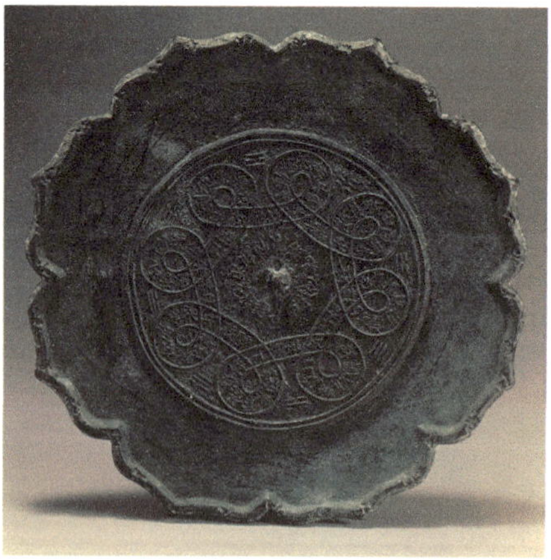

Figure 5.29 "Panjian Picture" on a Southern Song Dynasty bronze mirror

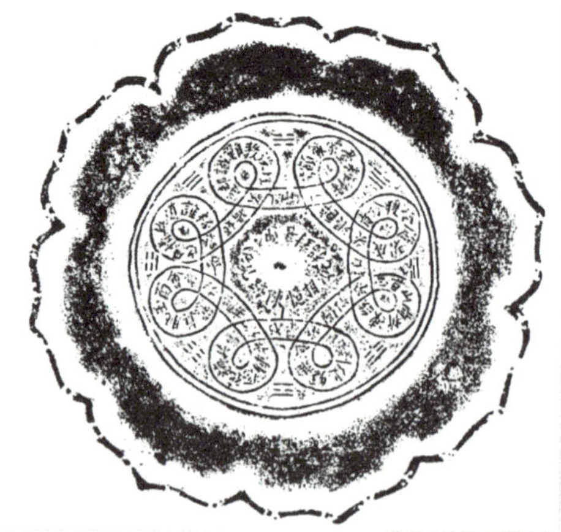

Figure 5.30 Rubbing of the "Panjian Picture" on a Southern Song Dynasty bronze mirror

This poem was also included in the *Complete Ci-Poem Works of Song Dynasty*.

Sometimes, such rotating text can also outline images, such as the "Difficulty in Old Age" (Figure 5.31), which was quite popular among the people during the Republic of China period.

"Difficulty in Old Age" is an image of an elderly person composed of text, with only the head, hands, feet, and cane represented by actual illustrations. Please try to decipher its content through these texts.

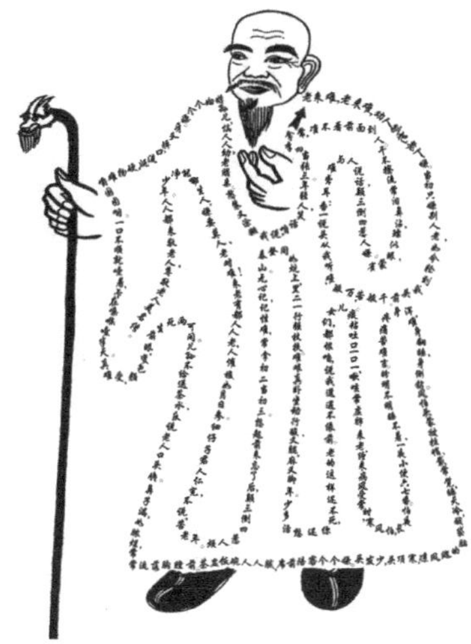

Figure 5.31 A folk depiction of "Difficulty in Old Age"

7. Difficult to Utter

In Chinese characters, there are many words composed of identical component characters, as shown in Table 5.2.

Table 5.2 Words composed of identical component characters

Character	Pronunciation	Character Form	Explanation
吅	xuān	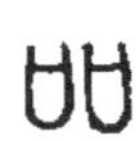	Represented by two open mouths, indicating a noisy or bustling atmosphere
从	cóng	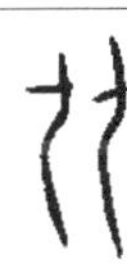	Depicted by two people facing the same direction, symbolizing the concept of following or imitating
友	yǒu	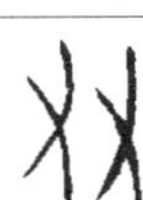	Illustrated with two hands facing the same direction, representing the idea of friendship
多	duō	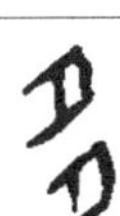	Shown with two pieces of meat together, symbolizing the abundance or possession of many

步	bù	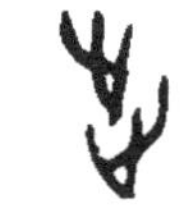	Depicted with left and right feet moving forward, indicating the concept of walking
雔	chóu	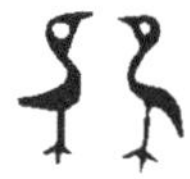	Represented by two birds facing each other, indicating the concept of being opposite or companionship
豩	bīn	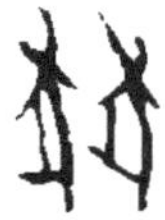	Depicted with two pigs chasing each other, symbolizing the playfulness
聑	zhé	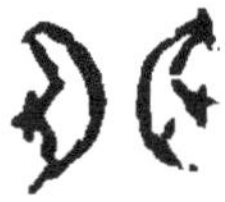	Illustrated with the merging of left and right ears, signifying focused and attentive listening
品	pǐn	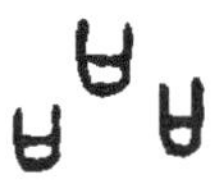	Using the mouth to represent a person, with three mouths indicating a large population.
歮	sè	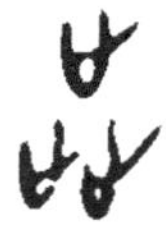	Depicted with numerous feet, suggesting the difficulty of coordinating steps in unison
雥	zá	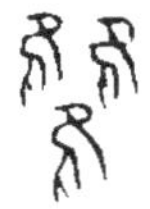	Formed by three overlapping birds, representing a flock of birds
焱	yàn	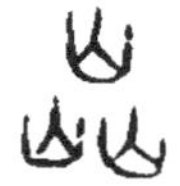	Depicted with numerous fires together, symbolizing the brilliance of flames
㗊	jí	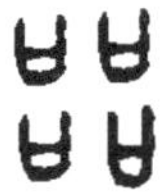	Represented by numerous mouths, symbolizing a noisy or bustling atmosphere

These characters, some commonly used and some rare, generally have clear principles of character composition.

Although Chinese characters combine sound, form, and meaning, there are times when one may encounter characters and recognize the form but not know the pronunciation or meaning. If you don't believe it, try pronouncing the following Chinese characters.

Table 5.3 Pronunciation of words composed of identical component characters

Character	Pronunciation	Character	Pronunciation
珏		沝	
秝		竝	
斦		棘	
舛		騳	
㹜		虤	
轟		飝	
淼		鑫	
垚		犇	
猋		羴	
骉		麤	
鱻		赑	
惢		畾	
掱		劦	
姦		众	
嚞		皛	
譶		矗	
馫		毳	
靐		龘	
叒		燚	
朤		𣡕	

8. *Skillful Reading of Jade Serial Ring*

The jade serial ring is a type of palindrome poem named for its eight characters, forming a circular shape like a jade ring when connected from the beginning to the end. The content often includes inscriptions and maxims. The reading of it involves starting from any character and rotating either to the left or right. Forming a sentence of four characters can create coherent text. An example is the Inscription on a Wine Plate (Figure 5.32), composed by Yin Zhongkan, a prominent military commander and Inspector of Jingzhou during the Eastern Jin Dynasty.

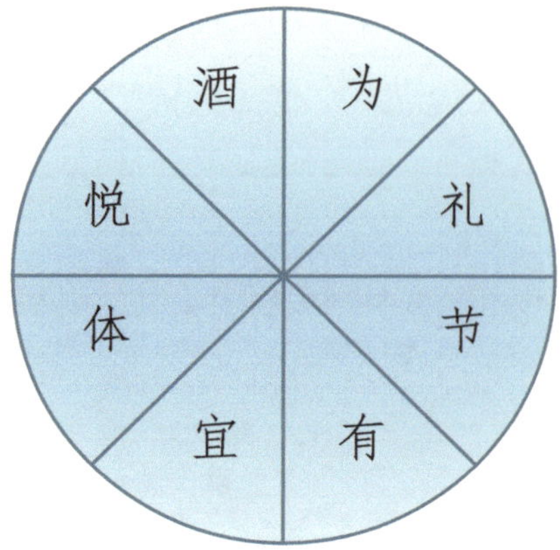

Figure 5.32 Inscription on a Wine Plate

Reading Method: “酒为礼节，有宜体悦。酒悦体宜，有节礼为。为礼节有，宜体悦酒。为酒悦体，宜有节礼。”

Try to interpret the various jade serial rings in Figures 5.33 to 5.35 and see how many reading methods can be identified.

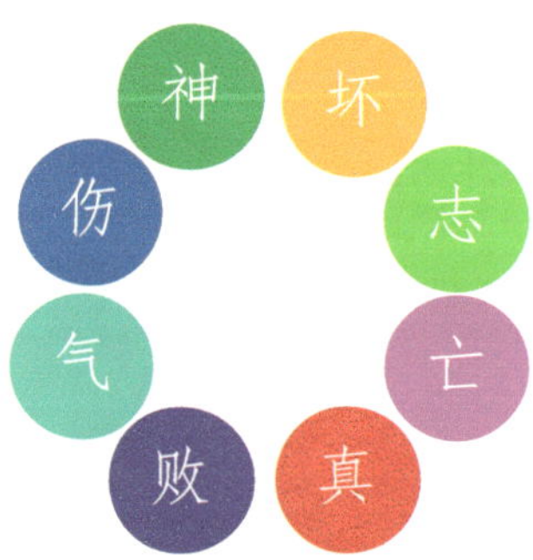

Figure 5.33 Color inscription

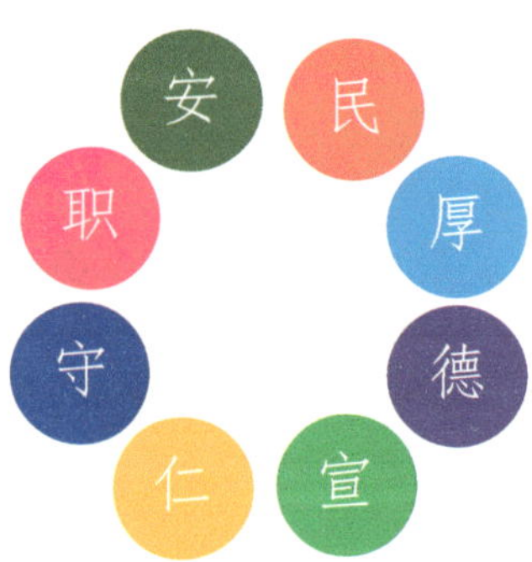

Figure 5.34 Seal inscription

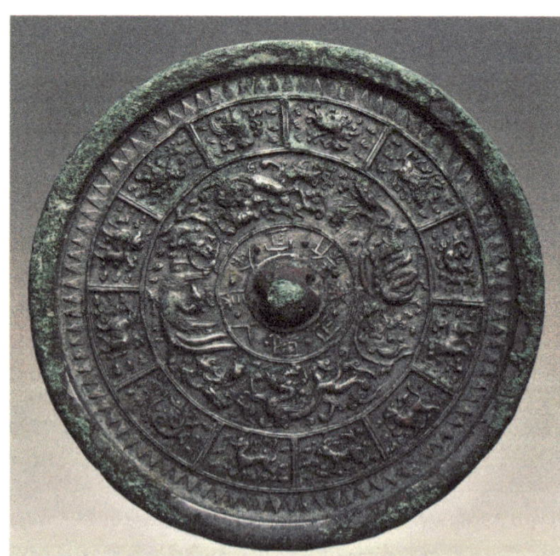

Figure 5.35 Mirror inscription (“光正随人长命宜新”)

9. Hear Words and Distinguish Sounds

The picto-phonetic method is one of the commonly used methods in Chinese character construction. Most of the picto-phonetic characters have a structure where the left part indicates the meaning and the right part indicates the sound. However, there are also many exceptions.

Please state the sound components of the picto-phonetic characters listed in Table 5.4.

Table 5.4 Sound components of picto-phonetic characters

Character	Phonetic Component	Character	Phonetic Component
鸠		和	
筑		旗	
徒		辨	
问		街	
孟		在	
到		布	
冯		贼	
视		阁	
颖		截	
空		寺	

10. Striking a Balance between Complex and Simplified Characters

Today, the simplified characters used by people have more than one source, and they correspond to more than one ancient character form. For example:

历: 曆/歷　复: 複/復　苏: 蘇/甦　钟: 鐘/鍾　汇: 匯/彙
须: 鬚/須　台: 臺/颱　发: 發/髮　系: 係/繫　只: 衹/隻

Try to write the corresponding complex characters for the following simplified characters.

历 < 历（ ）史 / 历（ ）法

复 < 复（ ）杂 / 复（ ）习

苏 < 苏（ ）醒 / 苏（ ）州

钟 < 钟（ ）表 / 钟（ ）情

汇 < 汇（ ）款 / 词汇（ ）

须 < 必须（ ） / 胡须（ ）

台 < 台（ ）风 / 舞台（ ）

发 < 发（ ）展 / 毛发（ ）

系 < 关系（ ） / 联系（ ）

只 < 只（ ）言片语 / 只（ ）进不出

11. The Skillful Butcher Dissecting an Ox

During the prevalence of Taoism in the Han Dynasty, Taoist priests often combined words such as "兴善除害" (promoting goodness, eliminating harm), "令尊者无忧" (bringing peace to the ancestors), and "急急如律令" (urgent as if following orders) on talismans to summon spirits and ward off evil. Influenced by this practice, starting around the Song Dynasty, there was a gradual rise in the folk tradition of combining auspicious words to form characters. Ligatured characters, initially used by Taoist priests in drawing talismans, transformed into a means for the common people to express wishes for avoiding misfortune and seeking good fortune. Even today, many ligatured characters are still in use.

Please decipher the phrases or sentences in the ligatured characters in Figures 5.36 to 5.40, like a butcher skillfully cutting up an ox.

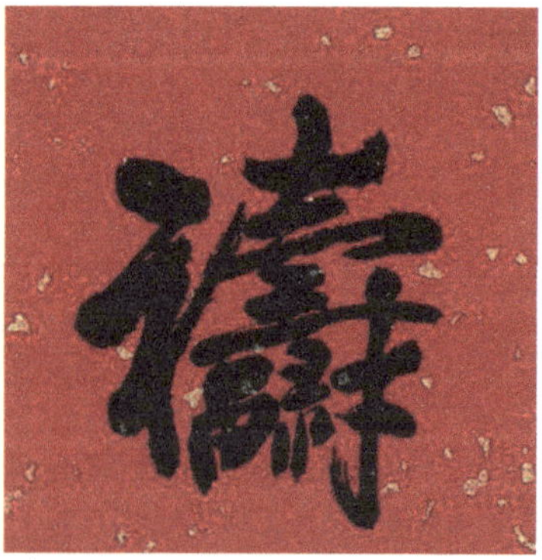

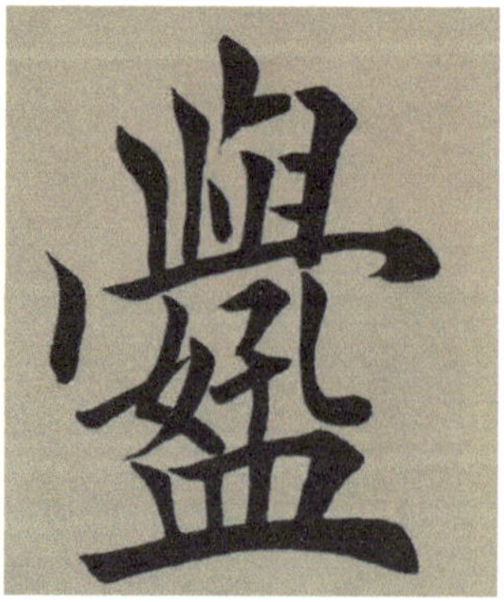

Figure 5.36 (FAR RIGHT)

Figure 5.37 (FAR RIGHT)

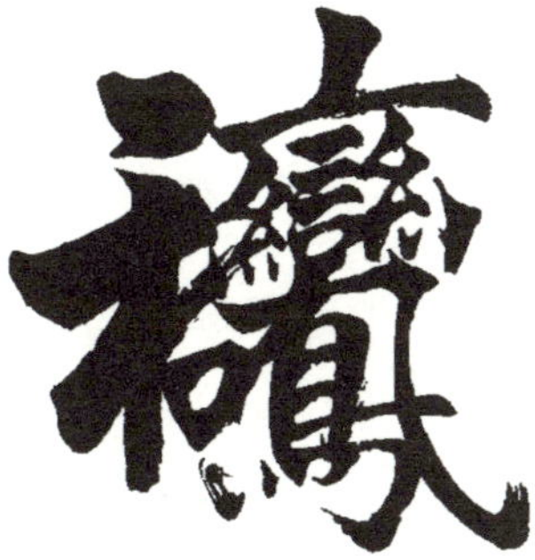

Figure 5.38

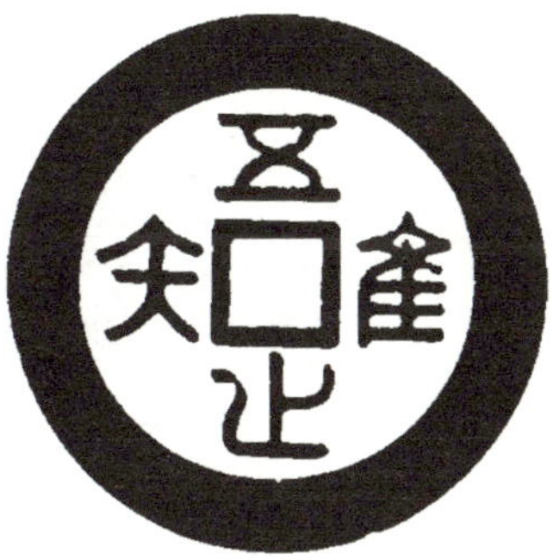

Figure 5.39

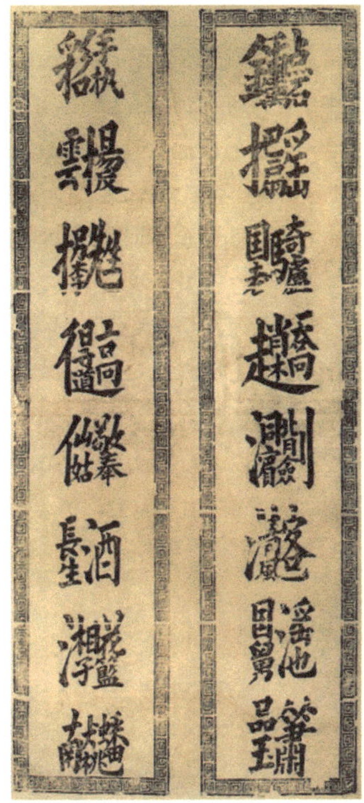

Figure 5.40

12. Photographic Memory

In the 1980s and 1990s, there was a popular children's rhyme called *Uncle Ding* in China. The specific gameplay involved simultaneously reciting and drawing, and by the time you finished reciting the rhyme, you would have drawn an image of an old man. Although there were various versions and regional dialects of the rhyme across the country, the resulting drawings were mostly similar.

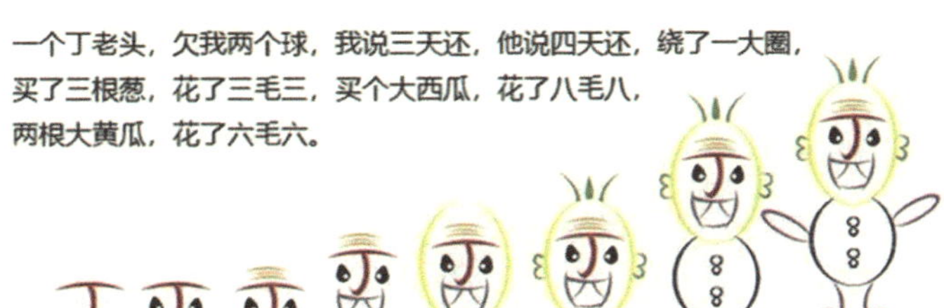

There was an old man named Ding,
Who owed me two balls, I said three days to repay,
He said four days, took a big detour,
Bought three green onions for three cents,
Bought a large watermelon for eighty-eight cents,
Two large cucumbers for sixty-six cents.

In reality, rhymes are surprisingly effective for aiding the memorization of Chinese characters with numerous strokes.

According to the following rhyme, try to memorize and correctly write the uncommon character in Figure 5.41 within one minute.

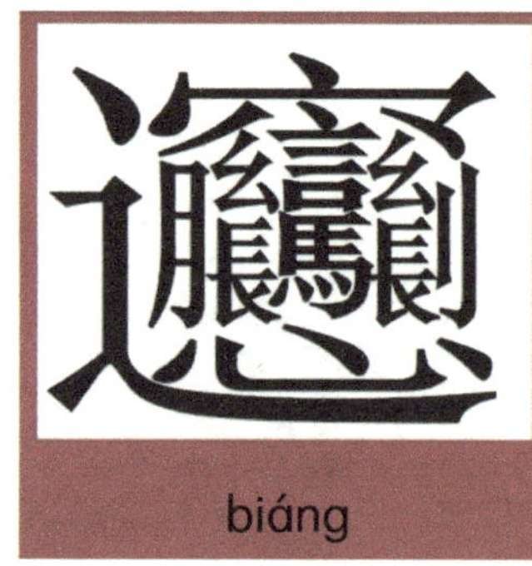

Figure 5.41

A dot flies up to the sky,
and the Yellow River bends on both sides;
The character "八" opens its big mouth,
and the character "言" goes inside;
Twist to the left, and twist to the right;
A long stroke to the west, and a long stroke to the east,
In the middle, there's a character "马";
At the bottom, there is the character "心," with a radical "月" on the left,
Leave a hook to hang a piece of maltose;
Push a cart to stroll around Xianyang.

ANSWERS TO CHINESE CHARACTER CHALLENGES

1. Recognizing Characters from Pictures

Rat, Ox, Tiger, Rabbit, Dragon, Snake, Horse, Goat, Monkey, Rooster, Dog, Pig

2. Chinese Calligraphy

Figure 5.1: Slender gold style. Poem from Emperor Huizong of the Song Dynasty on *Cottomrose Hibiscus and Golden Pheasant*
Figure 5.2: Semi-cursive script. Poem from Su Shi's *Cold Food Scroll.*
Figure 5.3: Small seal script
Figure 5.4: Cursive script. Poem from Yu Youren's *Thousand-Character Classic*
Figure 5.5: Oracle bone script

3. Chinese Character Detective

(1) 闷 (2) 哭 (3) 田 (4) 翠 (5) 育 (6) 仆 (7) 歼 (8) 卡 (9) 米 (10) 泉

4. Word Match

Figure 5.6: Tangut script
Figure 5.7: Manchu script
Figure 5.8: Phags-pa script
Figure 5.9: Khitan script
Figure 5.10: Yi script
Figure 5.11: Dongba script

5. Emperor's Seals

Figure 5.14: Qianlong
Figure 5.15: Qianlong's Imperial Reward
Figure 5.16: Qianlong's Imperial Penmanship
Figure 5.17: Qianlong's Imperial Brush
Figure 5.18: Qianlong's Imperial Edict
Figure 5.19: Qianlong's Imperial Appraisal
Figure 5.20: Qianlong's Imperial Inspection
Figure 5.21: Eightieth Birthday Imperial Treasure
Figure 5.22: Supreme Emperor's Imperial Treasure
Figure 5.23: Five Generations Imperial Treasure
Figure 5.24: Suitable for Future Generations
Figure 5.25: Precious Selection from the Three Rarities Halls
Figure 5.26: Precious Works in Stone Canal Pavilion
Figure 5.27: Imperial Treasure of a Perfect Old Man
Figure 5.28: Returning to Politics and Teaching Politics

6. Rotating Chinese Characters

老来难, 老来难, 劝人别把老人嫌。当初只嫌别人老, 如今轮到我头前。
(Life is difficult when getting old. Advising others not to despise the elderly. Back then, only despised others for being old. Now it's my turn, the story unfolds.)

千般苦, 万般难, 听我从头说一番:耳聋难与人说话, 颠三倒四惹人嫌。
(A thousand hardships, ten thousand difficulties. Let me tell you from the start, with no indemnities. Deafness makes it hard to talk with ease. Confusion and trouble, making people displease.)

雀蒙眼, 似鳔沾, 鼻泪常流擦不干。人到面前看不准, 常拿李四当张三。
(Blind as a sparrow, with a fishy smell. Nasal fluids often flow, never dries well. Can't see people clearly when facing me. Often mistake Li Si for Zhang San, you see.)

年轻人, 笑话咱, 说我糊涂又装憨。亲朋老幼人人恼, 儿孙媳妇个个嫌。

(Young people mock me, finding me amusing. Calling me confused and pretending, accusing. Relatives and friends, everyone gets annoyed. Children, grandchildren, and in-laws, all avoid.)

牙又掉, 口流涎, 硬物难嚼囫囵咽。一口不顺就噎着, 卡在嗓喉噎半天。
(Teeth are falling, drooling mouth. Hard to chew solid food, swallow south. Choking easily, stuck in my throat. Gasping for air, a half-day bloat.)

真难受, 颜色变, 眼前生死两可间。儿孙不给送茶水, 反说老人口头馋。
(Very uncomfortable, colors fade. Between life and death, a perilous trade. Children won't bring me tea or water. Instead, they say I'm orally greedy, their laughter.)

鼻子漏, 如脓烂, 常常流落胸膛前。茶盅饭碗人人腻, 席前陪客个个嫌。
(Nose leaks, like a festering sore. Constantly flowing down to my chest core. Teacups and rice bowls, everyone's tired. Guests in front of me, all uninspired.)

头发少, 头顶寒, 凉风飕的脑袋酸。冷天睡觉常戴帽, 拉被蒙头怕风钻。
(Hair is thin, head feels cold. Cold wind makes my head ache, I'm told. Sleeping in cold weather, always wear a cap. Covering my head, afraid the wind will trap me.)

侧身睡, 翻身难, 浑身疼痛苦难言。盼明不明睡不着, 一夜小便六七番。
(Sleep on the side, turning is hard. Whole body aches, words can't discard. Longing for daylight, yet sleepless at night. Urinating six or seven times, quite a sight.)

怕夜长, 怕风寒, 时常受风病来缠。老来肺虚常咳嗽, 一口一口吐粘痰。
(Fearful of the long night, afraid of the cold wind. Frequently afflicted by colds, tangled within. Weak lungs in old age, constant cough. Spitting sticky phlegm, each time enough.)

儿女们, 都恨咱, 说我邋遢不像前。老的这样还不死, 你还想活多少年。
(Children and grandchildren, all resent me. Saying I'm sloppy, not like before, can't you see? In such an old state, why not just die? How many more years do you want to try?)

脚又麻, 腿又酸, 行动坐卧真艰难。扶杖强行一二里, 上炕如同登泰山。
(Feet are numb, and legs are sore. Moving, sitting, and lying are a chore. With a cane, it's a struggle for a mile. Climbing the bed, like ascending a peak, meanwhile.)

无心记, 记性难, 常拿初二当初三。想起前来忘了后, 颠三倒四惹人烦。
(Forgetful mind, memory is frail. Often mistaking the second for the third tale. Thinking of the past, forgetting the latter. Confusion and trouble, a constant cater.)

年老苦, 说不完, 仁人君子仔细参。日月如梭催人老, 人人都有老来难!
(Old age is bitter, can't say it all. Kind-hearted people, please take a close call. Time flies like a shuttle, rushing old age near. Everyone will face the difficulty of getting old, that's clear!)

对老人, 莫要嫌, 人生哪能净少年。人人都来敬老人, 尊敬老人美名传。
(For the elderly, don't disdain. Life can't always be young and gain. Everyone should respect the elderly's name. Honor and respect for the old, a tradition to proclaim.)

7. Difficult to Utter

玨 (jué) 沝 (zhuǐ) 秝 (lì) 竝 (bìng) 斦 (zhì) 棘 (jí) 舛 (chuǎn) 騳 (dú) 炏 (yín) 虤 (yán) 轟 (hōng) 飝 (fēi) 淼 (miǎo) 鑫 (xīn) 垚 (yáo) 犇 (bēn) 猋 (biāo) 羴 (shān) 骉 (biāo) 麤 (cū) 鱻 (xiān) 赑 (bì) 惢 (suǒ) 畾 (léi) 掱 (pá) 劦 (xié) 姦 (jiān) 尛 (mó) 嚞 (zhé) 皛 (xiǎo) 譶 (tà) 矗 (chù) 馫 (xīn) 毳 (cuì) 靐 (bìng) 龘 (dá) 叒 (ruò) 燚 (yì) 朤 (lǎng) 𣡕 (màn)

9. Hear Words and Distinguish Sounds (Phonetic Components in Parentheses)

鸠 (九 jiǔ) 和 (禾 hé) 筑 (竹 zhú) 旗 (其 qí) 徒 (土 tǔ) 辨 (辡 biàn) 问 (门 mén) 街 (圭 guī) 孟 (皿 mǐn) 在 (才 cái) 到 (刀 dāo) 布 (父 fù) 冯 (冫 bīng) 贼 (则 zé) 视 (示 shì) 阁 (各 gè) 颖 (顷 qǐng) 截 (雀 què) 空 (工 gōng) 寺 (之 zhī)

10. Striking a Balance between Complex and Simplified Characters

历(歷)史　历(曆)法　复(複)杂　复(復)习　苏(甦)醒　苏(蘇)州　钟(鐘)表
钟(鍾)情　汇(匯)款　词汇(彙)　必须(須)　胡须(鬚)　台(颱)风　舞台(臺)
发(發)展　毛发(髮)　关系(係)　联系(繫)　只(隻)言片语　只(祇)进不出

11. The Skillful Butcher Dissecting an Ox

Figure 5.36: 福禄寿 (Prosperity, Status, and Longevity)
Figure 5.37: 好学孔孟 (Diligent in Learning, Following Confucius and Mencius)
Figure 5.38: 鸾凤和鸣 (Phoenixes Singing Together)
Figure 5.39: 唯吾知足 (Only I Know Contentment)
Figure 5.40: 钟离点石把扇摇, 果老骑驴走赵桥, 洞宾背剑清风客, 国舅瑶池品玉箫, 彩和手执云杨板, 拐李先生得道高, 仙姑敬奉长生酒, 湘子花篮献蟠桃。(A poetic passage describing various legendary figures and their attributes.)

Afterword

This is a popular book centered on the basic knowledge of Chinese characters.

In terms of the theory of characters and other aspects, this book mainly refers to Mr. Qiu Xigui's *Summary of Philology*, Mr. Zhan Yinxin's *Chinese Characters*, Mr. Lu Xixing's *Folklore History of Chinese Characters*, and other books. On the one hand, the author deeply agrees with these views. On the other hand, most of them have become the consensus of the academic community, so there is no need to propose a new one.

In addition, in the process of writing this book, Mr. Hua Jueming of the Chinese Academy of Sciences, Mr. Feng Lisheng of Tsinghua University, and Mr. Wang Xueying have provided a lot of help. Thus, I would like to express my gratitude to them all.

Due to space constraints, it is inevitable that something will be missed. Although I have been very hardworking, limited by knowledge, mistakes or inappropriacies may occur. And I'm willing to accept advice from experts or people with the same hobby.

I hope you will enjoy this little book.

ABOUT THE EDITORS

HUA JUEMING, a researcher and former associate director of the Institute for the History of Natural Sciences at the Chinese Academy of Sciences, is a renowned expert in the history of science and technology in China. His main research areas include ancient bronze metallurgy, steel technology, the history of machinery, and the philosophy of technology. In recent years, he has been devoted to the research and preservation of traditional crafts. He is the author of several works, including *Essays on the History of Chinese Metallurgy, Ancient Chinese Metal Technology, Five Thousand Years of Chinese Science and Technology*, and *Ancient Chinese Metal Technology.*

FENG LISHENG, a researcher and director of the Institute for the History of Science and Ancient Documents at Tsinghua University, is mainly engaged in research on the history of mathematics in China and abroad, the history of Chinese machinery, the history of metrology, the history of physics, and the history of science and technology among Chinese ethnic minorities. He is the author of works such as *The History of Ancient Chinese Surveying* and *The History of Sino-Japanese Mathematical Relations.*

ABOUT THE AUTHOR

PENG YU is a lecturer at the School of History and Culture at Southwest University. His main research areas are unearthed documents, ancient characters, and ancient Chinese bronzes. He participated in multiple major national social science projects and independently presided over one project of the National Social Science Fund for Young Scholars.

ABOUT THE TRANSLATORS

CHEN WEI: PhD, English professor of Jiangnan University, Wuxi, Jiangsu Province, PRC.

CHEN ZHIJIA: MA candidate of Jiangnan University, Wuxi, Jiangsu Province, PRC.